Lucy's LAW

THE STORY OF A
LITTLE DOG WHO
CHANGED THE WORLD

MARC ABRAHAM

MIRROR BOOKS

First published by Mirror Books in 2020

Mirror Books is part of Reach plc
10 Lower Thames Street
London EC3R 6EN

www.mirrorbooks.co.uk

ISBN 978-1-912624-98-0

Typeset by Danny Lyle

Printed and bound in Great Britain by
CPI Group (UK) Ltd, Croydon, CR0 4YY

A CIP catalogue record for this book is available from the British Library.

Every effort has been made to fulfil requirements with regard to
reproducing copyright material. The author and publisher will be
glad to rectify any omissions at the earliest opportunity.

1 3 5 7 9 10 8 6 4 2

Cover images: Pete Chatterton, iStockphoto, Guy Lockwood

To Lucy, Dad,
and all the other two- and four-legged legends
we lost along the way

Foreword

If you are reading this foreword, you have either purchased this remarkable book or are thinking about doing so. If the latter is the case, then think no further. Buy it. And prepare yourself for a rollercoaster of a read.

I met Marc Abraham about 10 years ago. It must have been at one of the many animal events I attend regularly. I am a devoted animal-lover and my commitment to the welfare of all species on this wonderful planet of ours is the most abiding passion of my life.

When I first met Marc and heard him speak, I was intrigued to hear that he was not only a vet, but also a passionate man, deeply committed to the ending of a trade I'd never heard of: the puppy farm trade.

First impressions can be misleading, and the first impression I had of Marc was that he looked like he'd stepped out of central casting as an action hero. Shaved head, dark brooding looks, a hugely impressive presence in the Vin Diesel mould. Certainly not the geek he describes himself as.

You will be deeply moved by this book. You will be exhilarated and you will be educated at the same time. You will also be shocked at how the Goliaths of the pet industry in our country tried to suppress the most exciting piece of animal legislation of the century: the ending of third-party sales of puppies and kittens. Or, as we've come to know it, Lucy's Law.

You will learn all about campaigning, lobbying, and commitment.

You will come away understanding how wrong it is to dedicate your time and attention to replacing your mobile or servicing your car when you could be introducing a new member into your family – be it a dog or a cat!

Most importantly, though, you will come away knowing that an animal is not a commodity, but a beautiful sentient creature that will enhance and enrich your life forever.

You will meet an extraordinary team who supported, inspired and helped Marc fight his battles and find his way to the seat of government in our country, Number 10 Downing Street.

It is a compelling story full of love, commitment, compassion and kindness.

I know also that you will come away from this book loving little Lucy, and Marc and his team, as much as I do.

So get reading. You're in for a treat.

Peter Egan, March 2020

Chapter 1

❧

She was staring into space in a dark corner of a lone barn in deepest Wales when they came to grab her. A small Cavalier King Charles Spaniel who, just like thousands of other Cavaliers in this part of the world, has never been given a name. Let's face it, why would she? It's not as if someone is going to tell her that her dinner's ready, or call her back for a recall reward while out walking, or even surprise her with a brand new squeaky toy. Occasionally a thick plastic sheep tag forced through an ear will help identify these dogs for their farmer, to help them plan their breeding program more efficiently, but more often than not these are the insignificant dogs, the invisible dogs. There's really no need to give them names. This particular Cavalier is a tricolour: black, tan, and white with some brown spots around her nose to vaguely distinguish her from the others. She's smaller than most Cavaliers of her age.

This breeding facility has very few, if any, significant windows to let in any light, so almost pitch darkness is the norm, as is the smell. The stench of ammonia from decomposing straw mixed with the thick, tar-like sludge of faeces and urine is overpowering, and such an irritant that the dogs' eyes stream constantly. A dog's sense of smell has been estimated to be tens of thousands of times more acute than ours, and this smell is all she's known her whole life. Even though it's not uncommon for there to be another 200 female dogs in a building like this one, all confined to tiny pens literally yards from one another, there's a deathly silence. They can't see out or engage with each other. The only noise they hear is the rustling of straw, the occasional litter of puppies crying out for their mother's milk, and perhaps a random bark from a dog that thinks they've heard a human coming. Other breeding establishments, where dogs can see each other, are the opposite, with constant barking and higher stress levels often proving even more detrimental to adult and newborn ears alike, especially when this deafening frenzy is further amplified by four surrounding corrugated iron walls and a metal roof.

But why on earth, in this twenty-first century, are all these dogs being kept in what is technically a giant shed, on bedding more suited to housing cows or sheep, and without even the dignity of a name? Just as humans have been responsible for domestication of the dog and all the species' various breed and mixed-breed forms, it's humans that are responsible for these intensive breeding conditions; and just like most forms of factory farming nowadays, the fate of most animals is determined by their sex. For example, in the dairy industry female calves re-enter the herd and at the first available opportunity begin a life of repeat impregnation to produce more calves and more milk. Male calves on the other hand are often surplus to requirements, so unless they're genetically worth allowing to reach adult age for breeding purposes, it's not uncommon for them to be destroyed at one day old, or to spend a few miserable weeks in a veal crate before being shot for their anaemic meat instead. Laying hens have a similar fate, with one-day-old female chicks permitted to live to produce more eggs, but once again, the technically useless male chicks are often killed by gassing or maceration as soon as they've hatched and had their sex identified, or frozen and sent to pet shops to be bought by reptile enthusiasts and fed to pet snakes.

This barn is quite simply a factory farm for dogs, with the same aim as most factory farms, whatever the animal kept imprisoned inside: to produce as many units of that animal as possible for the smallest amount of financial outlay or investment. Factory farming commodifies sentient beings, turning them into nothing more than crops. In this particular industry (and an industry is exactly what it is), male dogs aren't killed off like male calves or chicks, but the often isolated stud dogs' lives can actually be worse than the bitches' because of their extreme sensory deprivation. Unlike the females, they have no interaction with the pups and can literally lose their minds. On the plus side, unlike their cattle or chicken counterparts, if they aren't chosen for stud, they are rarely killed at birth, but are sold off as puppies.

Normal dogs sharing normal households with normal families would usually be housetrained. They'd enjoy healthy food, clean water, and daily walks. There would be games to stimulate their minds, and toys to play with. And of course they would be showered with praise and affection until finally, at the end of their day, they would fall fast asleep curled up in a warm, cosy bed. They are called domestic companion animals for a reason. Yet for these factory farmed dogs, they must endure being incarcerated in places that are, frankly, nothing short of hell on earth. Why? Two reasons spring immediately to mind: firstly, because there's money to be made, and secondly, because they are invisible – no one sees their suffering. Worse still, this whole set-up (the hundreds of dogs, the smell, solitary confinement for a very social animal, the utter despair in their sore, weepy eyes) is completely legal, and is signed off inspection after inspection, time after time, by local authority officials. In other words, these types of premises are fully licensed. A completely legal puppy farm: it sounds like the ultimate oxymoron. And there are dogs kept in these shameful conditions, not just in this dark corner of Wales, but in England, Scotland, Northern and Southern Ireland, across Eastern Europe, the United States and elsewhere across the globe. Millions and millions of them.

Almost too weak to stand on her wet, straw bed and without enough room to give herself one of those long

4

relaxing stretches that even us humans need from time to time, this Cavalier has no toys or blankets, no decent food or treats, no access to clean water, and no option to go outside to the toilet, or for exercise, or even to play with another adult dog – let alone a human being. Occasionally they'll be kept in small groups, then separated as soon as they have their pups, removing any chance of maintaining longer-term canine friendships. But sometimes when a dog dies in a group, a new dog will be shoved in to replace her, and often be mauled to death immediately. It's impossible for this Cavalier to be even a fraction of the dog she could be, as it is for most dogs kept in these types of breeding establishments. In the high-walled pens that surround her, rows and rows of female dogs are all in various stages of pregnancy, or 'in whelp' to use the technical term. A dog's gestation period is nine weeks, and they usually come into heat on average every six months. Some under this roof will have only just been mated, some have slightly swollen abdomens containing developing embryos, some are at full term and about to give birth, and some will even be quietly nursing their newborns. But not our Cavalier. It's unlikely that she's nursed a litter for over six months now so, for whatever reason, she isn't likely to nurse another.

The possible causes of her infertility are numerous and unsurprisingly often related to overall health and genetics. Perhaps it's hormonal or maybe there's a serious womb infection festering. Or it could just be due to poor diet and breeding management. In our Cavalier's case it's probably all of them. But this will never be investigated. No veterinary treatment will be sorted, or treatment given, to even try and attempt to cure her.

From the moment she was born here five years ago, her fate was sealed within these four cold metal walls. As soon as she was old enough, roughly six months of age, her life will have been forced to fit into a continual cycle of mating, pregnancy, and whelping. It's likely that in these five bleak years she's already given birth to nine or ten litters. She has never known life outside these four walls. The only interactions she has had with other dogs will have been when she endured brief, savage matings with equally stressed male dogs, or in the weeks when she was caring for the results of those matings: her tiny, vulnerable pups. Her offspring would normally have been removed before they were fully weaned, leaving lifelong emotional and physical scars for both mother and children.

Our Cavalier won't ever have felt the wind in her coat, the sun on her back, or even the grass beneath her filthy, urine-scalded paws. The same would have been true for her mother, and for her mother before her. It's been scientifically proven that it's not uncommon for stressed breeding dogs to give birth to damaged offspring, so you can imagine the state of this particular Cavalier's genetic make-up, cruelly predetermined years before even being born into this place.

The brutal irony of the location of this factory farm for dogs cannot be ignored either. This part of Wales, with its abundant green fields, plentiful forests, shallow streams, and unrestricted terrain, couldn't be more attractive to dogs, whatever their age or breed. Separated from this countryside paradise by just one wall, our Cavalier is forced to suffer zero enrichment, severely limited human or canine interaction, and apart from her various stages of reproduction, day in, day out, nothing ever changes. It might seem a wonder that these dogs don't go mad from sensory deprivation. But they already have: their madness stage has gone unnoticed for years. Such is the level of psychological torture that they tend to stare blankly into space, totally broken, emotionally shut down. It's no wonder she hasn't appeared to be able to get into pup for another season: sadly this Cavalier now seems to be infertile. In strictly economic, factory farming terms, it doesn't take much calculation to understand that, by taking up space that a healthy, fertile dog could technically be paying her way for, our Cavalier is now costing her farmer more than she's worth. Her outlook is grim, and that's exactly why they're on their way to grab her. Her infertility has rendered her worthless.

But why a Cavalier in the first place? When we look at the breed's history it's clear they were once held in very high regard and had friends in very high places indeed. So how on earth have we got to this point? Where Cavaliers are so disrespected that it's now perfectly legal to treat them worse than farm animals and breed them to death in cold dark sheds? It's thought that this type of 'toy' spaniel was first brought back to Europe from China by Italian traders in the 12th and 13th centuries, and as with many other so-called toy breeds, it's likely they were bred down from sporting breeds adept at flushing game. Queen Elizabeth I had a 'spaniel gentle' as a comforter, a dog extremely popular with noble ladies, often used as playthings and bed-warmers. Mary Queen of Scots' spaniel was even found hidden in her petticoat after she was beheaded! However, it was in the courts of Charles I, and his son Charles II, that the toy spaniels became well-established and their popularity spread, particularly amongst the nobility. Sharing its origin with the not too dissimilar, albeit smaller, King Charles Spaniel, the longer-muzzled Cavalier was also named after a seventeenth-century British king; so how can these special dogs, with an incredible breed backstory and very royal connections, be factory farmed in these disgusting conditions 400 years later?

There's even an urban legend claiming that Charles II issued a special decree granting King Charles Spaniels permission to enter any establishment in the UK, therefore overriding its 'no dog except service dogs' rules. A variant of this myth relates specifically to the Houses of Parliament, and is sometimes instead applied to the Cavalier King Charles Spaniel. However the UK Parliament website states: 'Contrary to popular rumour, there is no Act of Parliament referring to King Charles spaniels being allowed anywhere in the Palace of Westminster. We are often asked this question and have thoroughly researched it.' Hold that thought, folks.

Cavaliers have always been one of the world's most popular breeds of dog, and to anyone fortunate enough to have spent any

Chapter 1

time with one, it's not difficult to understand why. This gentle breed is almost always super-friendly, affectionate, playful, and good with both children and other animals. Whether in a warm home surrounded by love, or kept confined in a cruel puppy farm, Cavaliers always yearn for human interaction, and just like any dog, it's recommended to not leave one alone for long periods at a time. Sadly one of the most prominent characteristics of the Cavalier acts as both a blessing and a curse. One of the breed's pioneers in the 1940s, Mrs Amice Pitt, once described them as having a 'lovely expression and huge dark round eyes'; decades before the internet it was these features that caught peoples' eyes, and made them crave one of these adorable pups for themselves, often resulting in a higher demand for some breeds over others.

Of course, it's not just Cavaliers that are found languishing on puppy farms like this. Any dog that shares a higher level of attractiveness to prospective purchasers, especially as a puppy, will be greatly sought after, and therefore exploited for money. From Pugs to French Bulldogs, Westies to Labradors, a pair of huge dark eyes staring at you from a pet shop cage or from your internet browser is a trigger for many a human to release oxytocin and feel that 'need' to have that puppy. It's also thought that 'brachycephalic', or flat-faced, breeds resemble the characteristics of a human baby's face, activating even more nurturing instincts for many: powerful stuff and understandably hard for some of us well-meaning humans to resist. But the one constant that always stands true, whatever the breed, and in whatever corner of the world the puppy farm is located, you can bet that only the bare minimum in welfare standards is ever being met; and by welfare I don't mean just their mental wellbeing. We know dogs locked up in these places suffer terribly from lack of socialisation and communication, just like our shut down, broken-spirited Cavalier; but their physical welfare is compromised on a number of levels too. For example a closed population of Cavaliers, inbred to produce as many pups as possible, will have had not one thought spent considering their genetics or family history. This is especially relevant in this breed, because Cavaliers are terribly prone to life-threatening mitral valve disease (MVD). It leads to heart failure in many Cavaliers at some point in their lives, and is one of the most common causes of death in this sweet, vulnerable breed.

Other serious and often painful genetic health problems commonly suffered by poorly bred Cavaliers include syringomyelia (a heartbreaking condition that affects the brain and spine), hip dysplasia, luxating patellas (slipping kneecaps), blood disorders, episodic falling (ranging from mild, occasional falling, to freezing, to seizure-like episodes lasting hours), hearing problems, and eye-related problems such as keratoconjunctivitis sicca (dry eye) and cataracts. Today's population of Cavaliers descended from only six dogs, meaning any inheritable disease present in at least one of the original founding dogs can easily be passed onto a significant proportion of future generations. And that's just the main genetic diseases. On legal, licensed puppy farms like this one there are even simpler, more common infectious diseases too. For example, most dogs on puppy farms will also, at some point, most likely encounter parasites such as fleas, lice, and worms.

With limited veterinary care such as preventative vaccination, highly contagious diseases are also extremely common such as parvovirus, a particularly nasty virus which attacks the intestines and can affect both dogs and puppies, causing severe diarrhoea and vomiting, and which is usually fatal if left untreated. With poor ventilation comes debilitating pneumonia and painful conjunctivitis, not to mention extremes of hot and cold temperatures. Newborn pups are at an even higher risk from infection, as immunity from their stressed mother's first milk, or 'colostrum' to give it its proper name, often lacks sufficient antibody protection compared to healthy mums of the same age and breed. Worse still, puppies are often removed from their mothers far too young just so they can be sold before losing their cuteness. This gives them the worst possible start in life, as their poorly developed immune systems are one of the main reasons for pups becoming sick and dying from infectious diseases so soon after purchase. Early removal of pups from their mothers is also thought to be one of the main contributing factors to separation anxiety in the pup's new home, an extremely serious behavioural trait that can be difficult to treat and may never go away during the dog's life, along with other puppy farm-related mental health issues like soiling indoors, excessive barking, noise phobias, and nervous aggression. Little wonder many of these dogs are abandoned to rescue shelters.

Knowing the background and squalid conditions in which they're kept, it's easy to understand why such puppies are born so utterly loaded with all these potential medical, surgical, and behavioural problems. They are basically just cute and fluffy ticking time-bombs of pain, misery, and suffering, not to mention the resulting financial and emotional stress on their unsuspecting new owners.

What is staggering is that puppy farming isn't a new problem. It's been around for decades. There are millions of dogs across the world, confined in cages, sheds, barns and any number of other inappropriate dwellings, producing puppies of all shapes and sizes. It's a multi-billion pound global industry based on greed, cruelty, and profiteering. We've domesticated and trained these poor dogs over thousands of years to do exactly what we want them to do: look cute, be our eyes, be our ears, detect an explosive threat, sniff out our cancer; and how do we repay these incredible animals – our best friends? We betray them by allowing the legal exploitation of their bodies and the thoughtless torment of their fragile minds for money.

All breeds and mixed breeds are special, of course they are, but there's something even more disturbing about abusing the most vulnerable-looking tiny breeds, bred purely for companionship, like the Cavalier, a breed so patient and eager to please, which wants nothing more than to play, or simply cuddle up on a comfy cushion or warm lap. Cavaliers are active and sporting, obedient and agile, and it's no surprise that due to their sweet, gentle natures, they make some of the most successful therapy dogs around too. Cavaliers also possess a strong instinct to chase most things that move, and because they tend to regard all strangers as friends, they make the worst guard dogs! Yet puppy farmers deny them any opportunity to exercise this normal behaviour. Our Cavalier, a tiny tricolour stuck in her filthy pen, staring into space, waiting to be grabbed, is no different from all the others.

On puppy farms like this one, there are usually three reasons she'd be grabbed by the puppy farmer. Firstly, to be mated with one of the resident stud dogs. Secondly, when breeding dogs, male or female, are physically worn out and therefore no longer productive, they're technically useless so need to be disposed of. It's not uncommon, or illegal, even today, for a bolt gun to be used to kill dogs in puppy farms – and their bodies are tossed into an incinerator with the rest of the farm waste.

The third reason is also related to their lack of fertility. Instead of destroying them, some puppy farmers find it in their hearts to hand these ex-breeders into a local rescue shelter. That's where, for the first time in their awful lives, they are given a name, often experience their first-ever veterinary treatment, and are rehabilitated so they have the chance to start a new life, away from pain and cruelty. Thankfully, for our exhausted, nameless little Cavalier, this is the reason she's being grabbed today. She's being spared the cold steel of the farmer's gun, or a rope around her neck until she can no longer breathe, or a bucket of water to be drowned in. Instead she's being given a lifeline. She's one of the lucky ones. Poorly treated, devoid of any interaction with humans or other dogs, institutionalised her entire life, it's hardly surprising that she leaves the puppy farm totally ill-equipped to even know how to be a dog.

Fortunately for her, this is all about to change.

Chapter 2

✤

On Wednesday 30 January 2013 our nameless little Cavalier was set free from the walls that had confined her for the last five years. But she was far from free from her physical and emotional scars. Tiny, emaciated, and terrified of everything, she now had the daunting matter of the outside world to deal with for the first time in her life. Her rescuer, who has requested to remain anonymous, immediately saw how thin and frightened she looked, but named her 'Halo' because her initial impression was that she 'was a little angel.' In fact, Halo was so skinny and broken emotionally that her rescuer, who was very experienced in the health conditions of ex-breeding dogs, didn't think she'd live more than a couple more months.

That particular winter's day, Halo was rescued with another ex-breeding dog, a Bichon Frise. They were driven back to the rescue centre together and immediately given a warm medicated bath, as most dogs rescued by this shelter are. It's never right that the first act of kindness shown to one of 'man's best friends' such as Halo should be in her middle age. This warm bath is the first positive human interaction these dogs have ever experienced; occasionally puppy farm dogs are hosed down and left dripping wet even in winter, or given freezing cold baths in toxic sheep dip which are meant to remove external parasites like lice and fleas, but which also expose them to dangerous chemicals – detrimental to their eyes, noses, ears, and other sensitive membranes.

On the flipside, breeding dogs owned by high welfare breeders are, on the whole, much-loved and named pets that have the occasional litter. Usually they're microchipped, kept inside homes, fed highly nutritious food and treats, taken to the vet for regular health checks and vaccinations, and have toys to play with as well as a nice comfy bed to sleep in every night. They'll experience the odd health problem related to their reproductive system, like a phantom pregnancy, a fascinating and relatively common condition in non-pregnant female dogs that show symptoms of pregnancy, lactation, and nursing, without actually producing puppies, thought of as a clever survival instinct to feed orphaned pups in the wild should their mother in the same group be killed. But any problems affecting owned breeding dogs are treated by the vet as soon as they arise, like any condition suffered by any loved pet, anywhere in the world.

For our unnamed and previously unloved breeding dogs, however, the list of commonly observed health conditions is vast, and can be simplified by dividing their most common diseases into three main categories.

Firstly, medical issues include parasites such as severe mange, as well as fleas, lice, and ticks; life-threatening cases of kennel cough and pneumonia; painfully sore eyes from conjunctivitis and corneal ulcers; heart murmurs (unusual sounds in the heart caused by blood passing through a problem heart valve); cases of the highly contagious and usually lethal parvovirus; and nasty bacterial gastrointestinal infections.

Secondly, surgical problems seen and treated by these dedicated puppy farm rescue organisations include blindness; nasty tumours (especially mammary growths on tired, exhausted, and enlarged teats); serious hernias (umbilical and inguinal, the latter sometimes even containing the dog's bladder or even a dead puppy); entropion (a painful condition in which the eyelid is rolled inward against the eyeball causing serious damage and often ulceration of the cornea); 'cherry-eye' (prolapse of the gland of the third eyelid); cruciate disease (ligaments inside the knee joint); and pyometra (womb infection), one of the most common reasons for infertility and therefore being of no further use to the puppy famer. It is most likely because of this last scenario that little Halo has been released.

Thirdly, when it comes to behavioural matters, dedicated rescuers of puppy farm breeding dogs who've been extracted after years in solitary confinement commonly refer to these dogs as resembling 'zombies' when they come out, appearing 'shut down' and with no social skills whatsoever with humans or other dogs. They literally have no idea how to be dogs.

Once safe in rescue, as well as bathing and weighing enough (usually over two kilograms) to be neutered (spaying if female or castrating if a stud dog), dental procedures are usually carried out too: often removing all rotten teeth, then cleaning and polishing the remainder, if of course there are any left. It's not uncommon to discover odd abdominal structures and weird growths when spaying a rescued ex-breeding dog, such as adhesions and scarring from botched caesarian sections, or strangely formed and often deceased puppies, along with the usual pyometras and reproductive tumours from years of excessive hormonal influence.

Most males on puppy farms are either kept back for stud duties, or sold on to dealers as puppies, so shelters dedicated to rescuing these puppy farm dogs mostly deal with ex-breeding females like Halo, and occasionally puppies with obvious external problems who are unlikely to be sold, and whose precious little lives have been given a rare chance by the puppy farmer. After dogs have been examined, bathed, neutered, and received their dental treatment, they are vaccinated, wormed, deflead, have their nails trimmed, and lastly are checked for a microchip. As well as not having names it isn't uncommon for dogs to not have microchips either. Limiting their identification means traceability is often virtually impossible, which suits a lot of puppy farmers just fine. These poor souls have just been breeding machines, discarded when their machinery stops working.

As Halo and her Bichon friend were first bathed by the soft, caring hands of their rescuers, the warm soapy water immediately turned a dark reddish brown, as it often does when washing dogs extracted from an intensive breeding establishment. On discovering flea dirts, those shiny black specs in the pet's coat that are actually flea faeces comprising dried blood, one of the tests we use as vets in the consulting room to diagnose flea infestation is to carefully place these dark particles on some damp cotton wool and watch the surrounding area turn a dirty dark red colour. It's a quick, easy, cheap, and very reliable diagnostic tool which owners, although often embarrassed, can see for themselves before applying appropriate flea treatment. You can imagine how many fleas and flea dirts would have been present on Halo and her friend, two untreated, scrawny dogs. But, on the positive side, how clean they must've felt after their first rejuvenating bath. As with all ex-breeding dogs entering the rescue system, it's important that they are spayed as soon as they are considered, in the vet's opinion, healthy enough to survive a general anaesthetic. With the state of some of these dogs it's no surprise that to even achieve this basic level of health it can take weeks, even months, of expert help and specialised treatments. Believe it or not, some dogs rescued from puppy farms are in even worse condition than poor little Halo.

When Halo was examined by the shelter vet, a few obvious issues were noted right from the start. As well as being extremely frightened of everything, a trait displayed by the majority of rescued breeding dogs, Halo also had extensive and clearly desperately itchy skin due to her mange, caused by a microscopic burrowing mite called *Sarcoptes scabiei* that can prove extremely challenging to treat. In addition she was severely malnourished and underweight, another common symptom. Dogs like Halo often have to scrabble around, or even fight with other dogs, for food that's not only poor nutritionally, but often ends up mixed with contaminants like faeces and urine on concrete floors, or combined with soiled sawdust or dirty straw.

The rescue centre's vet also diagnosed a condition called 'dry-eye', a relatively common disease in Cavaliers and other dogs resulting from a number of potential factors, including inadequate or insufficient production of the watery portion of the dog's tears produced by the lacrimal gland and/ or gland of the third eyelid that helps with lubrication of the external surfaces of the eye. Left untreated, dry-eye, as the name suggests, classically leads to dry corneas and conjunctivae, increasing the likelihood of serious ulcers and painful conjunctivitis. It's unlikely Halo would've ever received treatment for dry-eye in the puppy farm, even more relevant considering her constant exposure to the dirty ammonia-smelling bedding that would've proven such an irritant to her eyes. The vet immediately started her on two types of medication in the form of eye-drops, both to be administered two to three times daily, and Halo instantly began to feel much better.

Halo's hunched appearance and bent-over stance were characteristic of how fearful she was, but also spoke of the cramped conditions in which she had been kept. Her back was so severely arched over it was thought that Halo was even suffering from the possibility of permanent spinal damage.

Thankfully her blood test results showed that operating on her would pose no obvious risk, so she was carefully put under general anaesthetic and spayed. Her uterus showed evidence of one previous caesarian section, and manipulating her hips and legs suggested no obvious restriction to movement, important to assess because of her severely curved spine. Halo also had three rotten teeth extracted, with all her remaining teeth checked, cleaned, and polished. Her ears were cleaned again, and infestation of ear mites treated. When first rescued, Halo weighed just three kilograms, half to one third of what an adult female Cavalier should weigh. But she now had lovely clean teeth, healthy ears, had been treated for all parasites, both external and internal, was tucking into a high quality tasty diet, and had been successfully spayed so her tiny, vulnerable body could never be exploited for puppies again. Halo's details, when first uploaded to the rescue shelter's website, before her legs and hips were assessed under general anaesthetic, read as follows:

'Halo is a 5-year-old ex-breeding Cavalier. She is absolutely tiny for her breed and is very nervous. She will be seeing our vet as her hips appear to be fused and she has a reduced range of movement in her hind legs. Dear little Halo is very worried at the moment,

and will need a kind and gentle dog in her new home
for her to learn from, and help raise her confidence.
She needs plenty of tender loving care.'

It's a heartbreaking description which raises the biggest question
of all. How is it that, in this day and age, dogs like Halo are
allowed to get into this state in the first place? We've already
established that puppy farming is all about making money, and
we know that these breeding dogs are kept hidden from view
where the public can't see them. But surely there are laws in this
proud nation of so-called animal-lovers specifically designed to
protect animals? The Animal Welfare Act 2006 was written over
10 years ago and contains the famous 'five freedoms' to take into
account an animal's needs: suitable environment; suitable diet;
ability to exhibit normal behaviour patterns; to be housed with,
or apart from, other animals; and to be protected from pain,
suffering, injury, and disease. You don't have to be a professor in
animal welfare to work out that the needs of dogs like little Halo
are clearly not being met or protected by this law. Somewhat
shockingly, it was recently revealed in a high-profile case that
a group of campaigners took a notorious puppy farmer to the
High Court, at their own personal expense, only to be told that
dogs kept in large commercial breeding establishments like Halo's
don't appear to be covered by the Animal Welfare Act at all.

What about the local councils and their inspectors? They
must like dogs; doesn't everybody? It would appear not, since
all these legal, licensed puppy farms are visited regularly by

representatives of local councils, including official vets, and the necessary paperwork is completed to ensure these places continue to operate. Furthermore council officials must give puppy farmers sufficient advance warning that they're coming, usually a good few days, which provides the puppy farmer ample opportunity to 'clean things up' – e.g. replace dirty straw and sawdust bedding in their tiny rat-infested pens; hide or destroy all really obviously diseased dogs; fix any broken lightbulbs; bring in extra staff; and generally tidy the place to make it totally clipboard-friendly. Some puppy farms in Wales and Ireland have even invested in electronic feeders and automatic drinkers so they can exist with even fewer staff and therefore make much more money.

Many puppy farms are found co-existing alongside traditional livestock farms too, usually containing sheep or cows. It's not uncommon for the farmer's wife to run the dog-breeding operation to supposedly supplement the husband's livestock farming income, although it often exceeds it, given the price for which they can sell puppies and how much is done via cash transactions with no paper trails, bringing in income that's not disclosed to HMRC.

We cannot therefore rely on the Animal Welfare Act as breeding dogs don't seem to be covered by this legislation. We cannot rely on local government and council inspectors as advance warning of inspections are given to the puppy farmers and their hands appear to be tied with red tape. Perhaps in these tight-knit rural communities the problem is compounded further with council officials being friends, or even family, with the puppy-farming community, thus even looking out for one another? We know we can't ask the public to alert the relevant authorities as they'd never be invited onto these places to even see the breeding dogs. And yet for decades these irresponsible practices have persisted across the UK, Europe, and the rest of the world.

There have been countless campaigns to end puppy farming and smuggling by some of the UK's larger animal charities over the last few years, but it would appear due to the sheer numbers of puppy-farmed pups still being produced here and imported illegally, that they have all proved largely ineffective. There is however one common factor that means most puppy farmers don't have to deal directly with the public: these individuals rely 100% on dealers instead, allowing them to remain unaccountable for the cruelty, suffering, and demands inflicted on these poor vulnerable souls. This prevents any degree of traceability for prospective puppy buyers, less so than if purchasing a washing machine or laptop; it also enables and encourages illegal puppy smuggling and impulse purchases too, as well as puppies sold as commodities in shops rather than seen interacting with their mum in the place they were born. The puppies are often distributed and sold by a network of dealers, sellers with no puppy's mum to show an excited owner-to-be, and sold far away from the place of birth. Dealers that sell to pet shops, or arrange to meet puppy buyers at neutral locations like motorway service stations for 'convenience'; dealers that import smuggled or totally legal pups from Europe or Ireland; or even dealers that sell to other dealers: whatever it takes to sell a puppy without the public ever seeing the mother. That's one of the main reasons puppy farming exists. Halo's pups, and those of every abused breeding dog like her, would have most likely been removed after three to four weeks (not the recommended eight to nine weeks), collected by a puppy dealer, and sent long distances along with countless other puppies in the back of unmarked vans, distributed around the country, and sold by pet shops or dealers making excuses why mum isn't there. Even selling puppies by these third-party dealers is completely legal – a system that permits puppy farming to happen behind closed doors and puppies with impaired immune systems to be transported long distances and sold without their mums, to shortly die or suffer lifetimes of painful disease. A license called the Pet Animals Act permitted it, a piece of legislation drafted back in 1951, way before the internet or the concept of factory farming dogs purely for profit had been dreamt of. So what chances do dogs like Halo have of ever enjoying a normal life as a dog, and not just a nameless breeding machine that's destroyed when she can't make the puppy farmer any more money? Surely something had to happen to change this system and end all the suffering; but by who, and when, and how?

Back at the shelter, Halo was making huge progress surrounded by so much love and care. The volunteers were each noticing a unique personality slowly emerging – a personality she would never have had the opportunity to exhibit before. Halo was starting to trust humans, was becoming gentle and affectionate, and was enjoying human attention; she was starting to show most of the characteristics for which this charming breed is famed. How very sad that Halo had to wait until she was five years old to discover she possessed all these breed instincts and natural emotions.

Every member of staff at the rescue who met Halo, even just to spend a few minutes grooming or walking her, realised she was something extra special, and they knew she'd make someone a cherished best friend one day. Just like the thousands of dogs that had passed through that shelter's life-changing doors before her, that had also experienced this enormous stepping-stone towards happiness, Halo too would soon be ready and well enough to be adopted. But one thing was very clear. Like most dogs rescued from puppy farms, given all she had been through, and with the numerous and largely permanent health issues already diagnosed, Halo was going to need a very special home due to these specific medical and behavioural requirements, a home where she could continue her rehabilitation from commodity to companion.

Less than a week after arriving in their care, Halo had made enough of an improvement to leave the sanctuary of the rescue centre and be placed with a kind, experienced fosterer to continue her epic journey to recovery in a home environment, for the first time in her life.

Chapter 3

❧

As far back as I can remember, I always wanted to help animals. I was a geek. A nerd. A square. I knew I was different from the rest of my classmates, and not in a good way. I behaved differently, thought differently, and even looked different. I was brought up differently from the rest of my class, behaved differently, and even looked different. With my background, a mix of non-British roots as a third-generation refugee, providing me with darker features and bigger lips than most other class-mates, accompanied by what can only be described as 'massive' hair, I was in effect a school bully's dream target. I was always a loner, a dreamer, never really part of the gang, cool or not; preferring, maybe not always by choice, to just quietly slope off and get on with my own thing. This would often mean spending hours gazing into ponds and rivers, or maybe disappearing into local woodland, collecting and bringing back home with me as many things from nature as I could fit in my pockets. For me growing up in north west London, learning and exploring were by far my biggest thrills, and still are very much to this day.

I enjoyed a very safe childhood. Two happily married parents, an older sister, and our pets, all lived in suburban Stanmore, on what my dad used to proudly describe as 'the last road in London', meaning it was just one of the literally thousands of outer perimeter roads that make up Greater London's unofficial border with the greenbelt. It was this close proximity to the countryside and its wildlife that inspired my love of creepy-crawlies and all things animal-related. Thanks to my folks also enjoying and encouraging outdoor life, and taking me with them on walks in the fields near our house, I was incredibly lucky to be regularly exposed to these exciting environments and always made the most of it. The thrill of discovering a hatched-out egg shell, clouds of frogspawn jelly, watching pond skaters taking advantage of the water's surface tension properties, identifying birds by their calls and dropped feathers... Nature was the only friend I needed, and the more I learned the details about all the different species of butterfly, moth, frog, toad, bird, and every other animal sharing my surroundings, the more I felt like I belonged in their world rather than mine. Looking back, it's odd that I never had a dog as a pet; ideally I would've loved to share adventures with *The Littlest Hobo*, and I enjoyed playing with Mum's friend Evelyn's Cavalier 'Scampi', but instead my early years were spent in the company of a succession of cats, tortoises, and the occasional caterpillar brought home to observe even more closely.

My first feline friend was Suzy, and we'd go on all sorts of adventures exploring the back garden, seeing how near we could get to butterflies feeding from the purple flowers of the Buddleia bush, or trying not to disturb moths sleeping on the apple tree trunks, or staring in fascination at the utter panic that ensued when we accidentally disturbed the small brownish mound of an ants' nest. Suzy and I spent our early years together always hanging out. I only remember her as an adult cat, a shorthaired tabby with greenish eyes that I can easily say was my best and, to be brutally honest, only friend. As well as spending weekends and school holidays as a team, hunting for insects and snails in the bushes and hedges, I remember how every evening she'd curl up, tail wrapped around her, fast asleep on my lap, as my mind was, like many millions of kids and adults in those days, captivated by David Attenborough's original *Life on Earth* series. Sadly, my Suzy only made it to 12 years old, regarded as a very decent innings in those days, but eventually she was beaten by failing kidneys, complete with their classic signs of increased thirst and weight loss. I still remember the day I accompanied Mum to our local vet, helping a very thin and miserable Suzy into her wicker basket, and off to Mr Lewis' surgery to help end her suffering.

My first proper experience of the veterinary profession, therefore, was a deeply unhappy one, but one which was necessary to end Suzy's pain and discomfort, as I fully under-stood at the time. Indeed, my first ever test to save an animal under my care took place in my own back garden when I was just three years old. Our tortoise Speedy, a name that was not only hilarious but all the rage in those days, bore an open wound on his leg, left hind leg, if I remember rightly. Admittedly it's all a bit of a blur as I was young, so unsurprisingly my mum recalls this story better than I ever could. But the gash on my tortoise's leg was only half the problem, for deep within Speedy's wound there was a maggot wriggling around, probably the larvae of a bluebottle fly – the same maggots that cause an often fatal condition known as 'flystrike' in rabbits.

On noticing the maggot, Mum proudly recalls, young Marc didn't panic or become squeamish; instead he rushed to find a small enough twig, and then carefully removed the chubby little intruder, before cleaning the area with very diluted TCP on a cotton wool ball. Not only did Speedy's wound heal, but the feeling of helping an animal get better was the single moment I decided that I wanted to help animals forever. Combined with my fascination for nature and wildlife, this meant I just *had* to be a vet. Then as now, veterinary science was one of the toughest courses to get into at university, made even more difficult by the small number of universities that offered the course. But in those early years, I had no idea what universities, GCSEs or A-levels were. I just knew I had to be a vet, and that I was prepared to do anything and everything possible to make sure that happened; chiefly to work as hard as I possibly could until I got into vet school. Back then I guess I was lucky to know exactly which path I wanted to choose at such an early age, and somehow, presumably aided by the lack of distraction from any human friends, always managed to remain focused and single-minded enough to guarantee the best chances of achieving my dream. Signs of a 'going it alone' attitude also surfaced on a family trip to Greece when I decided to slink off, jump off the boat, and attempt to swim to an island. Luckily Dad dived into save me and dragged a spluttering Marc back to safety.

As I got older my friendship circle remained unchanged, usually a combination of pets, butterflies, or tadpoles; I was fascinated by each and every one of them. On day trips to the countryside outside London to spend time with my parents' friends, for example, it was not unusual for me to climb out of the car on arrival, and before even saying 'Hello!' I'd politely ask for a jam jar instead, and then disappear into the meadows and woods for the whole day. I'd meet brand new six- or occasionally eight-legged friends, scoop them up into my glass transporter, and bring them back to show them off to the grown-ups. Because I inherited some of my dad's artistic talents, it wasn't enough to simply collect these new friends or observe them with my magnifying glass; I then *had* to meticulously draw them too, before always releasing them back into the wild, and then climbing back into the car, and heading back home.

Alongside nature and animals, art history also played a major part in my childhood years. I was named after my dad's favourite artist: the Russian-French early Modernist painter Marc Chagall, who is famously associated with being incredibly versatile, creating various artistic styles including painting, book illustrations, stained glass, stage sets, ceramics, even tapestries. As well as carefully drawing caterpillars at primary school age, in secondary school it wasn't uncommon for my diagrams in biology homework to resemble tiny art projects, complete with appropriate layers of crosshatching of course. Nowadays I'll occasionally draw dogs that share their lives with my human friends, and give them as presents.

And I didn't just draw animals in those days! I would spend literally hours drawing anything, from copying highly detailed Ordnance Survey maps with their tricky contour lines, riverbanks, and railway cuttings, to national flags, and reproducing the tail designs on aeroplanes; which perhaps unconsciously, and please stay with me on this one, introduced me to the concept, simplicity, effectiveness, and power of branding. Having a father who worked in advertising ensured I was always around some sort of logo, font, campaign, or original brand design from a very early age. Dad worked for an agency in Baker Street, London, and sometimes as a teenager I'd meet him at his office after school to raid his stationery cupboard, which as you can imagine in a place like that was an Aladdin's cave of specialist pens, rubbers, tracing paper, sheets of Letraset transferable letters, and professional drawing pads. As well as animals, maps, flags, and aeroplane logos, I would also replicate full pages of the *Beano* comic with fine professional Rotring art pens, and joined the Dennis the Menace Fan Club, at which point I remember feeling the rare sensation that I actually, perhaps for the first time ever, belonged to something vaguely 'cool'.

Chapter 3

Visiting Dad at work also helped teach me about another of his qualities that's never left me, and I believe has stood me in good stead in life: looking out for the 'little guys'. One Christmas I remember quietly sitting in Dad's office as his smart Armani-suited colleagues (he *always* wore t-shirt, jeans and trainers) rushed in and out, clutching beautifully drawn advert storyboards, and helping Dad tie up any loose ends before leaving for the festive break. I remember the huge pile of posh wines and whiskies that his best clients had sent him for Christmas, as was the custom in those days. But my dad never drank, not one drop of alcohol ever in his whole life, and what he did next has stayed with me ever since. As the cleaners came around the office emptying the bins and polishing the desks, he asked them if they drank and, if yes, whether they'd like to help themselves to his stash of expensive booze, which they did enthusiastically. Dad always looked out for, and made time for, everyone, no matter what their job, background, age, appearance, or social status.

Mum worked at the local hospital, mainly in their pathology laboratory, and was both a huge people-person and an avid animal-lover; to this day she is absolutely fascinated by the numerous birds that visit the back garden. In fact, growing up I could have actually been forgiven for thinking my name was 'Nuthatch' instead of Marc, such were the levels of excitement reached on spotting one climbing up our tall silver birch tree. Mum also always looked out for the underdog; she loves to help people and make sure they're OK. To this day, she charges a small fee to football supporters who've traveled down to London to park in her driveway for games four tube stops away at Wembley Stadium, and then gives all the money she makes to a local cancer charity.

It wasn't obvious at the time, but looking back as an adult it's not difficult to understand why both parents always remained conscious of looking out for the underdog, as both *their* parents were victims of Nazi persecution; my mum's mother escaped Germany as a teenager on the Kindertransport. As a third-generation refugee, with great-grandparents murdered in the death camps at Auschwitz, it was instilled in me from a very early age that it was normal to always look out for those less fortunate, whether human or animal. I always struggled with identity, which of course helped fuel my reclusive childhood; but it was in my nature to never give up on anything that could potentially help the most vulnerable.

My older sister by four years, Danielle, is also very strong-minded but was never a geeky loser like me, far from it. She was the streetwise kid growing up, hanging out with loads of cool (human) friends and always getting invites to the best parties. There were numerous, often failed, attempts made to persuade me to join kids my own age outside of school. I was an active cub scout, loved going camping, had a sleeve full of badges, and was even made Sixer of the Year, as well as being given the honour of carrying our flag at the St George's Day parade. I also loved playing tennis, especially as my dad's doubles partner. We'd always enter competitions and would occasionally win them; these were some of the happiest times of my childhood. I learned that when people on the same team never give up, anything seems, and often is, entirely possible. Stupidly ambitious on the tennis court, I would launch myself at balls way out of reach, scuffing my knees and elbows trying to return them. Chess too, unsurprisingly perhaps, was another huge part of my younger years, being crowned school chess champion two years running. Little did I realise back then it was probably chess and tennis that taught me most about the importance of teamwork and successful strategy respectively.

Comedy also played a major part in my childhood, and I would often do impressions to get myself out of sticky situations with potential bullies, employing the philosophy that if you make someone laugh, they're less likely to kill you. I loved silly humour like *Blackadder*, Kenny Everett, *Alas Smith and Jones*, and movies like *Caddyshack*, and would watch them again and again, often writing out the lines. When alternative comedy arrived, I did exactly the same for *Young Ones*, *Comic Strip Presents*, and *Friday/Saturday Night Live*, often venturing up to London's *Comedy Store* in my teens on weekends with my best mate Russell to check out the latest stand-ups.

Every school report was peppered with As and A stars, especially in the sciences, positive feedback gushing onto the page from every teacher, and as a result, my parents were always very proud. I loved how pleased they both were, which motivated me further to try and make them happy. Getting good grades meant I loved doing homework, and leaving school every day I must have suffered an early case of fear of missing out regarding my textbooks, as I filled my schoolbag with every single book, dragging them to and from school, ignoring the warnings of backache from my parents and teachers. I was science-mad, not giving any thought or interest to subjects such as history, English literature, law, or anything to do with politics. These subjects were relevant to other people but definitely not to me. I think my only contact with politics growing up was watching *Spitting Image* with Mum and Dad on Sunday nights.

When I'd completed my homework, I'd invent some more for me to do. My life outside school was spent between the local library and my bedroom, with the occasional walk in the countryside to visit my creepy-crawly and feathered friends. All this activity took place in the daytime, but at night I'd set my alarm for the Open University science programmes that were only broadcast in the early hours. I'd wake up at 3am to watch a documentary about the Periodic Table, the nitrogen cycle, or how ammonia was made industrially. I needed to get into vet school so couldn't learn enough science.

I was also fortunate to join school biology field trips, usually to South Wales, and once again, would tend to remove myself from the rest of the group and just wander off on my own, which often meant looking amongst the seaweed and limpets for mermaids' purses (egg cases of lesser spotted dogfish and skate) and crabs, or exploring rock pools. On my return Mum would send my photos off to be developed, and must've been slightly concerned when they returned every time full of pictures of coastal landscapes, animals, nature, and usually a combination of all the above, but rarely a human visible in any of them. When it was time to apply to get into vet school I had accumulated top marks in all my subjects, gained enough experience working with animals in my summer holidays, including spending time on Kibbutz in Israel, and had the best chance possible of being accepted into university, but unlike my cool sister, I was still far from streetwise. In fact, with my geeky background I can safely say I couldn't have possibly been more poorly equipped in social skills to engage with other teenagers or adults.

The best example of my obvious lack of cool in those days was when I was 16 and had met some really interesting people at my interview for Edinburgh University. They were locals, so after we'd all been interviewed, we happily exchanged contact details and they invited me back up to Scotland to stay with them and experience Hogmanay, Scotland's world-famous New Year's Eve celebrations. Even though I was 16 going on 17 years old, I'd still never been in a pub, let alone had an alcoholic drink, but had just agreed to travel to Edinburgh for Hogmanay, notorious the world over for being one of the most drunken nights in any city anywhere in the world. I found myself out with a load of Scottish rugby lads, probably about 10-12 of them, all of a similar age, and all drinking pints of beer. Nothing strange so far. But when I arrived at the pub, and I think it was Deacon Brodie's Tavern on the Royal Mile, everyone already had their drink, so I ventured to the bar to order mine, for the first time ever in my booze-free life. When I returned to the table, full of semi-drunk Scottish lads, and as possibly the only English person in that pub, I was met with stares, silence, and astonished – even angry – looks. For this particular English teenager on Hogmanay, yes that's right, one of biggest drinking nights in the world, had ordered himself not a pint of beer, or glass of red wine, even a whisky on ice, but a refreshing Malibu and pineapple instead. If that wasn't bad enough, it was also for some reason served in a champagne glass. You can imagine the furore that ensued when I returned from the bar to the table of rugby lads, and me desperately trying to defend my choice by explaining that it was *still* alcohol, conveniently leaving out the fact that the only reason I'd ordered a Malibu and pineapple was because it was the only thing I'd ever seen my sister drink. Needless to say when I subsequently got accepted into Edinburgh vet school and spent the next five years there, I quickly learned how to drink properly, and started to become a bit more streetwise.

I spent all my holidays as every other vet student had to, gaining valuable animal-handling experience volunteering on farms, stables, and other animal-related establishments. Many of my classmates seemed to be from solid veterinary or farming backgrounds, so not for the first time, I felt a bit of an outsider: an unusual mix of medical influence and advertising campaign talent, of science and art. All in all, life's building blocks were being laid down: from the birds, caterpillars, butterflies, and moths, to the reproducing of maps and biological diagrams, from hoarding as much knowledge as possible studying atlases, encyclopedias, and capital cities, to learning just as much about science, and, above all it seemed, to always try and protect the most vulnerable. Of course, I had no idea at that time why and where all these early life influences were heading, but at least when I finally qualified as a vet, I was in a much better position to meet, interact, and indeed order the appropriate drinks when in the company of other grown-ups.

Chapter 4

🐾

'How on earth did I get here?' I thought to myself, perched precariously on a dusty raised curb, surrounded by rows of multicoloured homes that comprise the extraordinary labyrinth of one of the largest slums in Mumbai. I'd just found a rare patch of shade, shielded from the scorching midday sun, and was now sitting watching the people, dogs, goats, and rest of the world go by, experiencing what most of us refer to as a 'moment'.

I was on another international dog rescue mission, this time volunteering alongside the phenomenal charity Welfare of Stray Dogs (WSD) India, run by a charming gentleman and graduate-in-hotel-management-turned-canine-hero, Abodh Aras. Abodh had set up the charity in response to the Indian government killing dogs in an attempt to cure rising human rabies cases and dog aggression outbreaks in the slums. He successfully managed to convince the authorities to stop poisoning these dogs, which would leave 'dog vacuums' that would then fill with neighboring dogs, meaning these same problems would continue, and to instead embark on a hugely successful city-wide programme of neutering and rabies vaccination. Abodh is one of the most inspirational people I've ever met and a perfect example of someone whose vision and determination not only changed his career, but also led to him not just helping dogs, but improving human welfare in these unique communities too.

The WSD team and I were frantically trying to track down the dog next on our list for capturing, castrating, and receiving its rabies jab. I was impressed by the WSD's incredibly high level of organisation and was honoured to play a small part in their work that week. In Mumbai these dogs aren't called slumdogs but are instead referred to as free-roaming street pets, belonging to specific neighborhoods in the slums, but with no fixed address. What most impressed me about the WSD, amongst their many other fine qualities, was that they didn't merely prioritise the animals being removed and taken back to their clinic to be neutered and vaccinated, but also returned them to the exact same spot in 10 days' time after their stitches have been removed. And it works. Not bad for a city with a population of around 20 million inhabitants in its metropolitan area alone. Abodh had started all this from nothing and I immediately felt inspired and became one of his biggest fans.

Of course I didn't go straight into international voluntary work after leaving university. My veterinary career started by working at a mixed practice in a place, with the greatest respect, slightly less exotic than Mumbai: Watford, Hertfordshire. Like most new graduates there were many options regarding what kind of vet I could be: small animal vet (dogs, cats, and rabbits, etc), large animal vet (pigs, sheep, cows, goats, etc), equine vet (horses and donkeys), government official, zoo, conservation, scientific research, pharmaceutical, the list goes on. But usually most newly qualified vets are eager to get their hands dirty, admittedly some much dirtier than others, so mixed practice (combination of small, large, and equine) is often the first port of call. It didn't take me long to realise that cats and dogs were my favourite type of patients, with surgery emerging as the most attractive element of my work. I loved operating and always enjoyed doing the relatively simple stuff, such as lump removals, stich-ups, and of course spaying and castration (neutering). Being able to do the basics well will always stand any vet in good stead for their future in clinical practice, able if required to use those surgical skills to tackle slightly more tricky operations like removing infected wombs (pyometras) and fixing twisted stomachs (gastric torsions). Regarding treating anything bigger than an Irish Wolfhound or Great Dane, unless on emergency call, which all vets in my first practice had to do one night a week and every few weekends, I found it challenging working with farm animals because most farmers seemed to already have diagnosed the problem before I'd arrived, so were often more reluctant to call the vet out. And most horse owners just wanted to see the main partner's Land Rover driving into their yard, not some fresh-faced new graduate with tons of enthusiasm but little equine experience to match. In Watford I also started to arrange visits to local schools in my lunchbreaks to teach pupils about caring for animals, enjoying the feeling of educating and raising awareness about animal welfare.

After 18 months of learning the basics as a mixed practice vet I decided to spread my wings and experience working in a few different practices, see a bit more of the country, and so became a locum vet. I'd spend a month in Cardiff, a fortnight in Kent, a few weeks in South West London. When you're in your late twenties, you don't mind living out of a bag or sleeping in strange rooms attached to practices, or being put up in random B&Bs. When I was asked to cover an emergency clinic for a weekend in Brighton, everything changed yet again. That one weekend was all it took to convince me to make Brighton my new hometown, so after working months of night and weekend shifts at my first emergency clinic and being bluntly told by the practice owner that there was *never* going to be any opportunity of promotion or becoming a partner there, I took some time out to reflect by going backpacking around Brazil. After experiencing Carnival in Salvador, living with an indigenous Indian tribe on the banks of an Amazonian tributary for a few weeks, exploring the Pantanal swamplands and waterfalls of Iguassu, and even getting shot at during a 'routine' drive-by shooting whilst trying to save someone who'd been hit in the leg, it was time to return to the UK and decide my future. Unsurprisingly it was Dad who sat me down and advised me to settle down into some form of regular employment, ideally a partner of a vet practice, as I wasn't getting any younger. With that guidance I immediately approached a hugely respected independent vet practice on the outskirts of Brighton, with a view to opening a dedicated emergency out-of-hours clinic in their pre-existing daytime clinic, on condition of becoming their third partner, i.e. part-owner of the whole practice as the arrangement, which we all agreed on.

Emergency out-of-hours clinics differ greatly from a normal vet practice in several ways: they usually open from 6pm until 8am on weeknights, and Saturday afternoon to Monday morning. Surrounding practices who don't provide their own out-of-hours cover subscribe to the nearby emergency clinic and divert their phones or give the emergency clinic number on answerphone; the dedicated night clinic then triages their clients' calls, inviting concerned owners and their pets down to the clinic to be seen by the vet onsite, and operated on, kept in the hospital overnight for observation or treatment if necessary, or sent back home with medication. Back in the day when I set up this venture from scratch, emergency clinics were a fairly new concept in the UK, but nowadays they are the norm for many practices across the country. Advantages of emergency clinics include a dedicated team waiting to see your pet whatever time of night or weekend, ready to examine, treat, and operate, and the worried client doesn't need to wait until routine appointments have finished; disadvantages may include needing to drive further than your normal practice, paying a higher initial consultation fee, and, most importantly for many, seeing a different vet from your usual daytime one.

One of the most important skills as a vet, alongside all the clinical stuff, is being able to effectively communicate with people and their pets. At the end of the day, as with any business or public service, if your clients trust you, they'll remain loyal, and will keep coming back not just when there's a problem, but also for routine health checks too.

Growing up I was fortunate to spend my school holidays and occasional Saturday mornings volunteering at the local vet's, a one-man practice run by Tony Lewis (who had had to put down Suzy for us). Mr Lewis is one of the kindest people I've ever met, and it was this honesty, empathy, and compassion shown to his patients that made sure there was a queue outside his waiting room every time he was consulting. To me it's that simple: show people you care about their pets, and they'll come back, and hopefully even say nice things about you to other pet owners too. This is the foundation for any successful practice, whether it's a day clinic or dedicated out-of-hours emergency service. I really enjoyed working in this pressurised, often stressful environment because dealing with emergency cases, as you can imagine, is very different from your usual vaccinations, flea treatments, and routine checkups. Not that there's anything 'wrong' with those reasons to visit your vet. But when your caseload is full of unpredictable caesareans, road traffic accidents, seizures, twisted stomachs, poisonings, treating hospitalised patients, with sadly higher instances of euthanasia, not only is it sometimes more interesting as a clinician and surgeon, but also you get better at diagnosing and treating cases not normally seen in regular daytime 'office hours'.

Working nights and alternate weekends, and being able to survive on minimal sleep, meant I was now technically free to do stuff in the daytime too. I've always been passionate about educating pet owners about common pet problems and responsible pet ownership, so I approached Brighton's local newspaper, *The Argus*, and asked whether I could write a weekly pet column for them, to which they agreed. There was no money involved, just the buzz of education and raising awareness in order to hopefully prevent disease and suffering for local pets. Furthermore every one of my columns was meticulously cut out and glued into my scrapbook, accumulating into quite a library after a few years' writing. It was about this time that a vet visiting the clinic looking for locum work herself mentioned that the hugely popular *Paul O'Grady Show* was changing TV channel and looking for a new resident vet.

With my growing hunger to educate as many pet owners on the biggest scale possible, surely this was the perfect gig, and what's more it would allow me to keep working nights as well. So, I applied, and was invited up to Soho for my audition complete with scrapbooks in tow, proving I was indeed the perfect candidate for the role. Days later I received the call that Paul had liked what he'd seen and heard at my casting, and that I'd been successful in my application. I prepared for my first ever 'Pet Clinic' on the *Paul O'Grady Show*, which was filmed live for Channel 4 in London the following week.

As a complete television novice this was really a journey into the unknown. I'd been an extra on *Grange Hill* when I was 12 for about three seconds, and even then, struggled to act the hugely complex direction of 'clapping and turning around at the same time' in one of Mrs McClusky's assemblies. I'd also appeared briefly on an episode of Victoria Stilwell's *It's Me or the Dog*, giving medical advice to owners of obese dogs, done the occasional radio interview, and filled my scrapbooks full of pet care newspaper columns, but I'd never been a *regular* guest on live primetime television, and especially not on a show of Paul O'Grady's size and scale.

The first *Paul O'Grady Show* I appeared on was alongside English actress, dancer, and singer Bonnie Langford. It was my job to take Paul and his celebrity guests around my Pet Clinic, usually consisting of four or five concerned owners with their pets, who'd contacted the show asking to be featured. I would then happily explain common diseases and, more importantly, their prevention to the owners in turn, as well as Paul, his dogs, and the celebrity guests, not to mention the live studio audience and five million viewers all watching at teatime.

Working with Paul on his show was one of the most incredible experiences of my life. Firstly, he's an amazing guy, a true animal-lover, and of course a phenomenal stand-up act. Secondly there was the buzz of educating millions of pet owners, while being given free rein to set up Paul's jokes or make my own – it was a comedy dream come true. In amongst my Pet Clinics came World Penguin Day, guest-starring Graham Norton and five Humboldt penguins, in which we all fed them sprats on live TV. Establishing myself as a 'TV vet', albeit completely by chance, would have an even greater advantage I wouldn't be aware of for another few years; and while it could be pretty nerve-wracking at times, the whole experience proved to be lots of fun and I was lucky to meet and work alongside some amazingly talented people.

I was invited onto other TV shows to give pet advice, such as BBC *Breakfast* and *The Alan Titchmarsh Show*, and then to film a six-episode series for Sky One, *My Pet Shame*, which I co-presented with the amazing Joanna Page. Later I would join Philip Schofield and Holly Willoughby as one of the resident vets on ITV's *This Morning* too. I was still penning columns for *The Argus* and now various other Brighton publications, being invited into local schools to talk about looking after animals, and even joined DJ Danny Pike as regular guest expert complete with monthly phone-in on BBC Radio Sussex's *Breakfast Show* answering concerned pet owners' questions. Life really was the perfect mix of emergency vet by night and educating the public via some of the biggest mainstream media platforms as well as continuing my regular animal welfare school visits by day.

And then one morning, Boxing Day 2004 to be precise, the western world woke up to the devastating news that a huge tsunami in South East Asia had killed hundreds of thousands of people. I remember it like it was yesterday. I'd just come off my night shift at 8am and found myself glued to the telly as news from the tragedy unfolded.

On seeing the horrific scenes of devastation and destruction 10,000 miles away, I made a few enquiries with animal charities I'd heard of over there. They confirmed this was an animal disaster as well as human, so without waiting for an answer, I asked my fellow vet partners to please find cover for me while I was gone, and booked the first flight out to Thailand to help those poor animals affected by the disaster.

It was still the festive period and there were no travel clinics open to arrange necessary inoculations, so I boarded a bus to Heathrow and was in Phuket within 24 hours, ready and eager to offer my veterinary skills to help the Soi Dog Foundation. Our work mainly consisted of treating dogs and cats affected by the waves and utter chaos they had caused in Phuket, Phi Phi Island, Khao Lak, and surrounding fishing villages. Working with the charity, we were able to offer food, set up makeshift operating theatres in Buddhist temples, and over the next few weeks locate and capture stray wounded and injured pets, often having to blow-dart them from the back of speeding motorbikes as the only way to physically even get anywhere near them! Helping animals meant not only saving the dogs and cats, but also the humans too, as so many survivors were dependent on the company of their pets to help them deal with this level of grief and what had just happened. This was definitely one of the proudest missions

I've ever been involved with, and I'll never forget some of the disturbing sights, sounds, and smells I encountered there.

A recurring pattern was emerging in my veterinary work: as well as volunteering in the Mumbai slums and post-tsunami Thailand, other places I enjoyed visiting out of my comfort zone included the Peruvian Amazon to neuter dogs and cats, rescuing a dancing bear in the Ukraine, a mission to save cruelly treated working donkeys in the Middle East, a trip to the incredible Animals Asia sanctuary in China to help operate on a moonbear, and most recently helping to close down a dog meat farm in South Korea with Humane Society International. As a fully fledged TV vet with a growing media profile, back then I was also being invited by various animal charities to help judge their fun dog shows around the country: the novelty ones featuring Waggiest Tail, Best Rescue, and Child's Best Friend, rather than the more serious-looking championship pedigree dog shows. Obviously, having never owned a dog, I'd never been to many dog shows, but found them fascinating on many levels. I loved interacting with the owners, identifying the dog breeds (heaven for a geek like me), and was always impressed by their popularity and turnout, whatever the weather.

Life in Brighton was fun, and I was enjoying working nights and weekends at my emergency vet clinic, as well as judging fun dog shows around the country on weekends. Then one fateful Friday night in May 2009, early on in my nightshift, eight puppies were brought into the clinic by eight worried owners registered at eight different subscribing vet practices respectively. These poorly pups not only looked very similar, all Jack Russell crosses, and also appeared to be of similar age, most likely around six or seven weeks old. But it was the smell that hit me first. Anyone who's ever worked at a vet's will know this distinctive odour: pungent, stomach-churning, and usually that first indication of parvovirus – the killer disease commonly picked-up from environments with poor husbandry, typically those breeding establishments known as 'puppy farms'. For those of you who've never seen, smelt, or had to deal with a case of parvovirus (or 'parvo' as it's often known), it's possibly the cruellest of all the diseases to affect puppies. It destroys their guts in seconds, rapidly leading to and causing the characteristic vomiting and bloody diarrhoea symptoms as the virus ravages their tiny bodies. It's painful, overwhelming, and often challenging to treat, not to mention expensive for the new puppy owners too. Parvovirus is easily one of the most serious and contagious infections, and we vets recommend vaccinating all dogs against it annually. It can affect dogs of all ages, but puppies with compromised immune systems, like those born on puppy farms, will usually always be at greatest risk.

On that Friday night, those eight puppies were admitted, hospitalised separately in isolation, dripped with intravenous fluids, injected with various drugs including the strongest painkillers and anti-vomiting medication, and guarded prognoses made to each individual owner. My team and

I worked hard through the night; sadly we lost two but managed to save the other six. What no one could possibly have known at the time is that those eight puppies were the start of a long journey to change UK animal welfare history forever; but I had no knowledge, background, or interest whatsoever in campaigning, law, or indeed politics, so surely I wasn't best equipped to make any real, or indeed lasting difference. Was I…?

Chapter 5

❧

I often think of what would've happened since that evening if I hadn't worked that nightshift, or was away on holiday. A few days later, after those six surviving puppies had been given the all-clear and discharged from the practice, I did some serious thinking about the whole scenario. It wasn't just the sad circumstances in which the puppies had been sold, already loaded with a deadly virus; I was also shocked at the situation the owners had been put into, one minute their families excited to get a new pup home and introduce it to his or her new toys, the next having to shell out thousands of pounds on the same tiny pup that could well die in agony. Where was any accountability of the seller or breeder? Where was the justice for the pups, or indeed their poor mums? My tendency to look out for the most vulnerable was strongly kicking in, so I spent a few hours calling each of the eight puppy owners to confirm exactly where and from whom they'd purchased their sick pups.

The owners were all pleased to hear from me. It's not always easy ringing people soon after their pets have been seriously ill in hospital, or worse, have died, but I got the feeling they also *really* wanted justice for their little ones, so they were very forthcoming with the information. Unsurprisingly all eight pups originated from the same puppy dealer, located about 45 minutes by car outside Brighton. I had to visit them immediately. So on my next free day, I made an appointment with the dealer pretending to be interested in buying one of their pups, and drove over to see and hear for myself what was going on. I was aware I might be recognised, as I was on the *Paul O'Grady Show* quite regularly in those days, so I swapped my contact lenses for glasses, put on my beanie hat, and kept my head down. As I drove up the muddy driveway, I was immediately struck by how untidy and messy the whole place looked, with lots of dogs and kids running randomly around. My first impression was that this was not a responsible, high-welfare breeder's home. It was all a bit chaotic to say the least.

Parking my car this side of the gate in case my cover was blown and they locked me in, I was immediately met and taken to a large wooden stable, one of those with a stable door that makes it easy for horses or humans to peer over. There were plenty of puppies in there, all displaying various states of energy, from lethargic and sleeping to those few tearing around the sawdust, almost showing what I would even call 'normal puppy' behaviour.

Most pups I could see were Jack Russell crosses like the ones I'd seen at the clinic, though there were also other breeds like Westies and Cavaliers too, but no obvious mother to be seen anywhere. I started down my list of questions: 'Have they been vaccinated?' 'What happens if they get ill? 'What if things don't work out, do you take them back?' And of course, the all-important golden question 'Where's Mum?'

I have to say I was impressed with the answers that seemed to roll off the dealer's tongue. 'Of course they've been vaccinated'; 'they won't get ill'; 'of course they take them back'; and 'their mums are at the vet's'. I knew he was lying, and the place definitely felt sinister, but I assumed that no matter what he said to any prospective owner, the sight of these cute puppies, all roughly six or seven weeks old, in various stages of play, or sleep, was enough to make anyone want to buy one, or more than likely feel the need to rescue him or her from this horrible environment.

I politely thanked the dealer for his time and told him I was going away to discuss with my girlfriend which puppy to come back for the next day. With that, the overall mood changed very quickly and quite considerably. Happy sales patter turned into aggressive selling tactics, like someone had just flicked a switch. The desperation to sell me a pup was intense, almost nasty, but I stuck to my guns, calmly got into my car parked on the other side of the gate, and sped off.

As I drove back to Brighton, I thought about the last few days. The sick and dying pups, the stench of parvovirus still in my nostrils, the pups that didn't make it, and now this undercover investigation to try and find the root of the cause, and most importantly to try and find a solution to prevent this happening to any more dogs or owners. I'd just come face to face with a puppy dealer selling pups of various breeds without their mothers, and becoming pushy and insistent when I didn't agree to the immediate sale. I knew what needed to be done with regard to changing the public's buying behaviour. There are only two options to consider when choosing a dog: either buy direct from the breeder so you can see the pup's mother and the seller is accountable, or better still visit a local rescue shelter, and adopt a puppy or more mature dog instead. I had a decent media profile, and was spending my weekends busy judging on the fun dog show circuit, usually for charities; so it was just a case of transforming public behaviour with the few resources I had. Metaphorically I was about to embark on the longest game of chess of my life, but with the potential result, if I did eventually manage to crack it, of improving and protecting millions of dogs' lives.

As an expert of the fun dog show circuit, in order to understand the *whole* dog world, I needed to get to grips with the pedigree-owning and showing community too, especially if I was to attempt to engage them in any future campaigning. After sitting next to the owner of *Our Dogs* newspaper (official weekly newspaper for pedigree dog breeders) at a veterinary awards do in Birmingham, the brilliant Mr Vince Hogan invited me to write a monthly column for his paper. This inspired me to visit some of the Championship dog shows around the UK including Bournemouth, Windsor, and Mid-Wales for the Welsh Championship Show. These dog shows couldn't have been more different to the novelty shows I'd judged, but everywhere I went people would recognise me from my columns and take me under their wing. All of a sudden, I was being invited for posh lunches on judges' tables, wearing jeans, trainers, and t-shirt; but people like Ann and Graham Hill, Chairs of the Welsh Kennel Club, and Julia Isles-Hibbert, President of the Bournemouth Association didn't mind and welcomed me with open arms. I learnt so much about this other canine world, and would also attend Crufts every year as it was a useful place to network and I enjoyed being surrounded by so many dogs, especially all the different breeds as well as charities, and campaigns too. Being a friend of the pedigree dog world, as well as monthly columnist for *Our Dogs*, was to stand me in good stead and proved very useful for my campaigning years later.

In December 2008 I was invited to appear on BBC *Breakfast* for the first time, one of the most nerve-racking telly gigs I'd done yet. I was on to discuss puppy farming, the pros of rescue pet adoption, and of course cons of buying a puppy for Christmas, with those two options surfacing again: choose a dog from either a responsible breeder or a rescue shelter. Persuading the British public to choose either of these two options by changing their behaviour was the desired end-result, but I'd only just started my journey to get there. Understandably the pedigree dog owners attending championship dog shows were well aware of the first option: after all, they were often the responsible breeders supplying these puppies alongside their mums in the place they were born; and the dog owners supporting the fun dog shows usually seemed more aware of the other rescue option, but what about the rest of the estimated nine million dog-lovers in the UK – how on earth could I possibly reach them? With my brand-new, extensive knowledge of *all* aspects of the dog show world, fun and serious, and a rapidly developing media profile, there seemed only one way forward: to start my own fun dog show and invite celebrities and well-known personalities to be the judges, which would surely then attract media interest, raise awareness, and eventually create the required behaviour change!

The following spring I heard about a special day in the American animal welfare calendar, a designated Puppy Mill Awareness Day ('puppy mill' is the US term for puppy farm). That's right: a specific day in September had already been established stateside in order to help educate the public about puppy farms and the signs to look out for when buying a dog, as well as promoting rescue dogs too. So, in the spirit of joined-up thinking, I decided to start my own puppy farm awareness dog show in autumn that year, on exactly the same weekend as our friends across the pond. Apart from a Sussex Pet Friendly Awards event I'd organised as a PR stunt for my newly opened emergency clinic at a venue just outside Brighton, I'd never actually organised a dog show or outdoor event before. But that wasn't going to stop me from trying!

I'd already decided that this new dog show concept would include recognisable and well-known judges, but it needed something else too, something more to make people stay longer, and also to attract non-dog-lovers who were maybe thinking about getting a dog. Preaching to the converted is one thing, but reaching those who've not yet decided is often much more challenging. To this end I had a meeting with my mate Milton, about which we still laugh today for its sheer incredulity. I say meeting – it was more like a few pints up the road in the beer-garden of a Blues-themed pub called The Ranelagh. Milton, originally from Sweden, was a music producer, dog-lover, and one of the first friends I made when I moved to Brighton, so we hung out a lot. At the pub I pitched him my idea: 'How about we make a dog show with a difference... but as well as celebrity judges, we have live music too?' Now Milton is one of the coolest people I know, so it was unsurprising that without even pausing for one second mid-drinking his pint he replied, 'Sounds crazy enough, sure, let's do it!'

And so the first puppy farm awareness day dog show, complete with celebrity judges and live music, was now in its early planning stages. Drawing on all my past experiences with fun and pedigree dog shows, I knew I needed a venue with an outside space that was safe and secure for dogs, was easily accessible, had ample free parking, and plenty of room for stalls to sell doggy-related stuff, served food and drink, and of course could provide a small stage for our musicians to perform (not too loud of course, as there were dogs coming: acoustic singer-songwriters only). With only a few months to throw this all together, I rang around some suitable venues which were all already reserved, so finally settled on Brighton Racecourse, using their paddock as the dog show ring. Looking back, a venue dedicated to horse racing wasn't the best choice for an animal welfare awareness event, but with all the emergency vetting by night and media vet stuff by day, not only did I not have time to shop around, but I also paid the price – quite literally.

As well as venue hire, I also had to book the specific shell scheme infrastructure for the stalls too. Since they knew this was a dog show, with dogs allowed inside the Grandstand, the venue then insisted I provide carpet cover for the whole of the indoors to protect against any accidents. So, before I'd even attempted to design a flyer or contact some local personalities to help judge, I was already thousands of pounds out of pocket. There was no going back now. While Milton was booking our singers and guitarists, I was pulling everything else together: PR, judges, stall holders, and of course the all-important rosettes. The awareness day was called 'The World's Biggest Puppy Party' in order to attract as many dog-lovers as possible. I made the event free entry too as I believed asking for donations on the door would help me pay for my overheads and initial outlay, and I could then give the rest to a few different charities. This assumption proved to be wishful thinking, with hardly anyone donating a penny, and I ended up losing an absolute fortune, but looking back it was definitely worth it. The World's Biggest Puppy Party was fairly well-attended, considering we had minimal budget or PR company helping us. I had managed to convince pet food company Eukanuba to donate some useful sponsorship money which definitely helped ease the pain of the final amount lost personally. One of the event highlights was having former British professional boxer Michael Watson there to judge Best Boxer Dog! It was perhaps the first time the theme of a dog show class had been specifically tailored to the judge. Other judges included actors from *The Bill*, *EastEnders*, and local politician Caroline Lucas.

The World's Biggest Puppy Party was ticking its boxes nicely regarding attendance, music, and atmosphere. Even the weather was perfect: dry, no wind, and not too warm for the dogs. But it was mainly about raising awareness of puppy farms and rescue dogs, so I'd printed literature to hand out which listed tips on buying a puppy responsibly, recommending rescue pet adoption, and including signs to spot if a pup has been bred irresponsibly. As well as leaflets, between each class, information announcements were made, again educating all dog-lovers enjoying the day about the correct way to choose a dog, by going direct to the breeder or rescuing instead. If only this message could be amplified and shared with everyone in the UK.

What came next was the *pièce de résistance*, the big moment of the day, the shock factor. While everyone was enjoying themselves, I took the microphone, thanked everyone for coming (for the twentieth time), then proudly introduced the parade of invited rescued ex-breeding puppy farm dogs. There was silence. From one second to the next, it was as if someone had pressed the 'mute' button. The dogs now on show in the ring weren't the fluffy, shiny, athletic, stylish, uber-groomed pooches with expensive collars and designer leads outside the paddock: these were the sorry, slow, delicate, tired, fragile souls that, although in various stages of rehabilitation, still clearly bore the emotional and physical scars of their previous painful puppy farm lives. Their ears and eyes down, swollen exploited tummies with exhausted mammary glands, and elongated teats dragging along the grass, they shuffled slowly and without confidence, certainly not wagging their tails or walking like normal dogs with their heads held high. From the silence came a few surprised gasps, long sighs, even tears of realisation. People were being confronted with the facts, the evidence of puppy farming cruelty right in front of their own eyes; this was how to raise public awareness. I could feel change was starting to happen.

The World's Biggest Puppy Party proved to be an over-whelming day for me. Despite the financial hit I took, I felt a feeling of immense pride. I'd organised a relatively successful event at short notice in a city in which I was a relatively new inhabitant, amid running my emergency clinic and spinning all the other plates in my professional life. Sure, looking back maybe I should've charged an entry fee, or hired an event or PR company to do it 'properly', but none of that mattered. That momentous day I still remember looking around at the celebrity judges, musicians playing acoustic music, stall holders selling leads, collars, and treats, everyone and their dog having fun, and of course, the emotional parade of hard-hitting puppy farm survivors; and it struck me that maybe, just *maybe*, this event had the formula to become one of the main campaigning tools to raise awareness, change public behaviour, and perhaps even help end puppy farming cruelty in the UK?

Chapter 6

Carol Reeves was a dog fosterer. A rather special dog fosterer. To give you an idea of how special, here's a brief description of her family of dogs who she once fostered but who she now permanently shares her life with in the Channel Islands. There's Inca, a Cocker Cavalier mix, and Kabie, a Blenheim (brown and white) Cavalier who suffered from pulmonary stenosis, a serious heart condition that affects humans as well as dogs. There's Micky and Minnie, brother and sister Cavaliers, who were both born blind and destined to be put to sleep. Dylan is an orange Pomeranian rescued from a shed in Wales, and so unbelievably emotionally traumatised that he never really came out of his shell, and often panics, unable to cope with his surroundings. Little Dylan is also blind; Carol is unsure if he's ever been able to see and he can only manage to walk on three legs, as his fourth leg is fused and locked in one position. Cassie is another rescued Blenheim Cavalier, plucked from a council dog pound, who suffers from severe separation anxiety. Finally, there's Galli, Carol's first ever foster dog, adopted at just eight weeks old as a partially blind puppy with a very poor prognosis. Not only do all these dogs have very complex medical, surgical, and behavioural needs, like most puppy farm dogs, but Carol decided to adopt them herself, elevating them to the level of permanent pets, to become part of her own family. In so doing she became the best example of one of my favourite expressions in the animal rescue world, a 'failed fosterer'.

But when reading all those descriptions, please don't assume these dogs aren't happy. Far from it. Carol informs me that both Inca and Kabie live very normal lives, while Micky and Minnie have had complex eye surgery and new lenses fitted, so can now see. Little Dylan the Pom has now had both eyes removed and happily hops around in his safe garden on three legs. Cassie is very settled with the rest of her friends and spends a lot of time sitting on Carol's knee. And finally, Galli, who's also had both eyes removed, runs around on those long sandy beaches very happily indeed. All these severely disabled dogs, most of them rescued from Welsh and Irish puppy farms, have been successfully rehabilitated by Carol, and are now all happily living their best lives together.

Carol hasn't always lived in the Channel Islands. Before moving there she lived in the south of England. She's the niece of Betty and Bernard Davidson, founders of their own charity trust whose animal welfare aims and activities include promoting 'kindness and preventing cruelty to animals,' as well as 'protecting animals and improving their condition.' Uncle Bernard passed away when Carol was just 19 years old, but Aunty Betty wanted to leave their fortune to help animals when she passed, and Carol gladly agreed to run the charity once it was formed after her death. With so many animal charities desperately needing financial help, and already having donated substantial legacies to larger, more corporate charities, this time Carol searched for some smaller organisations, thinking any financial grant donated would make an even bigger difference to the animals in their care. Uncle Bernard's sister had previously worked with the world-famous nun and missionary Mother Teresa, so already had strong connections with India, leading Carol to choose an amazing charity based in Rajasthan, called TOLFA, to be one of the foundation's first lucky recipients. TOLFA stands for 'Tree of Life for Animals', and to this day it runs a busy animal hospital and rescue shelter, as well as working hard to eradicate rabies, sterilise street dogs, and much more.

With TOLFA in India now the happy beneficiary of significant funds from the Betty And Bernard Davidson Trust, Carol was keen to identify another similarly suitable candidate in the UK, subsequently meeting a woman running a rescue centre in Wales, a smallish organisation (which has requested not to be named) specialising in rescuing and treating dogs from Welsh and Irish puppy farms, and at that time, she recalls successfully rehoming about 50 dogs per year. Carol enjoyed running her aunty and uncle's trust fund; being a small charity Carol and the trustees felt more agile and able to do things quickly, like making important decisions on the spot. Together with her daughter Natasha, she didn't just donate generous amounts to this Welsh rescue but actively got involved with them too, helping computerise their records and database, as well as design, and write content for, their website. But it still wasn't enough for Carol, who was noticing a lot of dogs coming out of these puppy farms in Wales and Ireland with serious and painful eye problems. Shortly after, she started fostering for the rescue, taking these damaged rescued dogs into her own home to rehabilitate, before they found permanent families to live with. Over the next 10 years, Carol watched this smaller rescue, with its strict no-kill policy, grow from rehoming 50 dogs per year to around 4,000, and always providing not just veterinary treatment, but also sometimes lengthy rehabilitation in foster homes. Carol's home became a haven for more and more sick, damaged, and broken ex-breeding dogs, as well as puppies with health issues that were unlikely to be sold.

In all her years fostering, Carol can recall taking in approximately 200 puppy farm dogs, losing only four, and she made sure every individual dog was looked after, and given the very best chance of survival and happiness. With some of the worst cases, Carol even managed to negotiate deals with her local vets, who then kindly offered much-reduced rates, to ensure these dogs received the best treatments and surgery if required. Carol's foster dogs were always made immediately comfortable, with blind dogs suffering debilitating eye problems such as cataracts, helped by life-changing operations so they could see, often for the very first time.

Looking back, Carol thinks at least 85% of the 200 dogs she successfully rehabilitated when she lived in England were Cavaliers. Her soft spot for this unique breed stemmed from her time living in Central London and the obvious impracticalities of owning a big dog which come with that. Carol's dream dog breed, a giant Bernese Mountain Dog – with their distinctive brown, white, and black markings – was just not an option, and so Carol's first ever tricolour Cavalier, a brown, white, and black dog called Lady, was in her words a 'shrunken-down Bernese!' Lady was soon joined by brown and white Blenheim Cavaliers Tiggy and Lacey, and a second tricolour Cavalier called Mitzi. When Carol's aunt Betty passed away, her Golden Retriever Gus came and joined the Cavalier gang in London, and it was obvious Carol now needed more space.

As a fosterer for this particular smaller rescue, Carol enjoyed the freedom she was given to talk directly to the applicant when she received their application from the rescue centre; she was able to assess their lifestyle and home environment, and have the final say in whether that dog was placed in that home or not.

Living with her existing family of rescue dogs, Carol got to know the various problems and individual quirks of these puppy farm ex-breeding dogs, just like the hundreds of other amazingly dedicated fosterers out there, so could be satisfied they were going to the right home to suit their individual needs. Rehoming rescued puppy farm dogs gives them something they've never experienced before: a secure and happy place to call home. Carol always makes a point of warning prospective adopters that they might have to pay for the treatment of long-term medical problems and potentially expensive vet bills. She informs people looking for these most damaged dogs that many rehoming stories end in lot of heartache, so 'if in any doubt', Carol cautions them, 'then this may not be the right dog for you.' Carol is proud to be the spokesperson for that dog and rescue shelter, talking on their behalf and prioritising the welfare of that particular dog, and doing her very best to match him or her with their perfect owner. As exhausting and emotionally draining as this extremely tough process sounds, Carol sums it up rather neatly by telling me, 'you just do your best.'

What makes a good rescued puppy farm dog adopter? There are many characteristics that rehoming organisations and their fosterers look for. Interviews for who's right to take on one of these special dogs are often extremely in-depth, designed to establish roughly what type of dog or breed the prospective owner is looking for, and whether they fully understand, and have researched, or have already lived with that particular type of dog. Fosterers are experts in detecting people with empathy, have the necessary time to commit to rehabilitation, accept that these dogs have come from such a difficult place that they would benefit from a calm home, and that of course they already have a 'normal' dog to educate the new arrival. Carol, like most fosterers, posts updates to the rescue shelter's website every week containing as much information as possible, e.g. 'started to walk on lead'. This gives any potential dog adopter looking online a good feel of exactly what these dogs can, or more often can't do, and of their specific medical, surgical, or behavioural needs, including whether they've been successfully house-trained yet. There are many different stages and levels of rescued puppy farm dog rehabilitation, and carefully matching these brave canine survivors to their new owners is an exceptional skill. After the adoption paperwork is signed, if things don't work out – after all, these dogs can prove a real challenge, even to the most experienced dog owner – the rescuer takes the dog back, and previous fosterer where possible, and patiently waits for the next enquiry.

Given there's such a wide range of potential problems and issues from which these particular dogs can suffer, it's no surprise that the time taken to be rehabilitated in foster, to a point where that dog is finally ready to continue their journey and be rehomed permanently, can be extremely variable. But how do the dogs picked up from puppy farms even reach their fosterers in the first place?

In most cases dogs are collected from the organisation's kennels on a weekend, having been already checked over, put on any necessary medication, fully vaccinated, neutered, teeth cleaned, bathed, nails clipped, and treated for parasites such as worms, ticks, lice, and fleas. It's worth noting that some of these specific puppy farm rescue organisations have the unenviable position of knowing exactly who and where the worst offenders are, and over the years have formed delicate trust relationships, purely just to get these dogs out to safety and allow them to experience any possibility of normal life in the outside world. If the rescue reported the puppy farmers, their relationship would be immediately compromised, and the lifeline of these dogs would be gone for good; so they can't, won't, and don't, so as not to risk the safety of the dogs. They continue to be these dogs' only chance of a decent life away from the pain, misery, and exploitation. The rescue shelter's very carefully coordinated foster network is updated with which group of dogs are next available for rehabilitation in a home environment, and the fosterers then submit their applications – in Carol's case usually for any Cavaliers.

Then a fully air-conditioned van transporting these dogs, all about to begin the next stage of their new lives in the safety and freedom of a foster home, will usually set off from the shelter on pre-planned coordinated runs, sometimes for long distances right across the UK. Fosterers and volunteers will already be waiting at agreed destinations for these poor, broken dogs to be handed over; it's a well-organised, well-oiled operation, with committed rescuers and fosterers around the country all working together giving their spare time, weekends, and years of expertise just to help these delicate souls. The volunteers involved in this whole rescue and foster network are, to me, the unsung heroes; they don't have to do this week in, week out, but all *choose* to. Of course, not everybody is in a position to pay for dog food and medicines, so these folk will always do whatever they can to help, including collecting towels and newspapers for the van to take back to the shelter.

On one of Carol's regular visits to a motorway service station to collect more dogs to foster, she clearly remembers picking up a very small dog that she'd specifically requested; and it's no surprise that this particular ex-breeding dog was her favourite type of rescue dog, a tricolour Cavalier who'd already been named 'Halo'. The main reason Carol remembers Halo isn't just because she had her favourite black, tan, and white markings, but because online Carol had noticed that Halo had an obvious severe curvature of her spine, appeared emaciated, and was described as being terribly quiet, or 'shut down', a powerful phrase used by rescuers and fosterers that best describes the mental state of a recently rescued puppy farm breeding dog. There are different degrees of 'shut down' observed by fosterers like Carol, depending on the dog's individual personality, breed, age, and how badly they were treated; but in many cases, once safe in a nice home, these dogs still won't come and greet you, wag their tails, or even look at you. It's not uncommon for them to panic and bolt in search of a 'safe space', making themselves as small as possible huddled in a corner, under a table, in their bed, or behind a sofa, not wanting to move a muscle. This is one of the biggest differences between 'normal' rescue dogs and those escaping a life of puppy farm suffering. Some will just stand there staring at you, almost statuesque, watching everything, determined not to move from their safe space. Often this will be the first proper bed they've ever been given; many prefer their beds placed in the corner of a room, with walls on both sides providing the feeling of extra security. Dogs who have only had food pellets thrown at them, perhaps cheap kibble scattered amongst their filthy straw or sawdust, will often look blankly at their new food bowl without moving towards it, without a clue what it is, or what it's used for.

Those dogs that appear 'food-driven', meaning they respond positively to edible treats offered to them, are more easily coaxed than ones that are not, and this is often related to their breed (e.g. Labradors can be easier to get eating than some other breeds or crossbreeds). But Carol developed a system that gave the best chance of success for all types of dog entering her warm, friendly house: smelly sardines. And if the sardines failed, (which, Carol admits, they occasionally did) she'd offer milk or yoghurt next to tempt them instead, as many of these high-volume dog breeding establishments are run alongside dairy farms, meaning dogs are often already familiar with the taste of dairy products. Carol also played calming music, often mindfulness and yoga albums, to help relax the most fearful dogs, trying to quickly remove any tension from this new, often terrifying, alien situation in which they've suddenly found themselves, that environment all dogs should only ever know: a simple, kind, safe, loving home. Carol also used large children's playpens to give these dogs a smaller safe space that also encouraged them to socialise with other dogs, as well as Carol and her family. Even the most basic tasks like teaching them to walk around the garden in a harness, or going to the toilet outdoors could take weeks, as these dogs have never had to go anywhere, and have just urinated and defecated within the same four walls of the crate or pen they've been standing, lying, sleeping, and living in since the day they were born. Carol will often choose liver paste for this type of training, and always preferred harnesses to collars, to make sure no undue pressure was applied to their delicate windpipes when they inevitably started to pull away in fear.

Our little Cavalier Halo was so frail when she joined Carol, her spine so rounded, that when she stood up, all hunched over, the paws on her skinny back legs almost touched her tiny front paws. Carol sought to address this problem immediately, organising a local vet to visit every week to give Halo acupuncture and physiotherapy treatments. Over the next few weeks it worked a treat, and Halo's arched back actually started to straighten out. Painfully thin, Halo began cautiously picking at tiny amounts of food, an appetite not uncommon for a just-rescued breeding dog, and she was still itching and scratching and looking rather flea-bitten, most likely still suffering from the effects of mange, an all-too common issue that can take weeks of treatment to fix. When she came into Carol's care Halo was both emaciated and clearly feeling February's cold temperatures, so Carol dressed her in a bright red knitted doggy jumper to keep her nice and warm. She also posted a picture of Halo wearing an oversized pink t-shirt online, along with some other photos, even though she wasn't yet up for adoption. As Halo's spine continued to loosen up, straighten, and appear less painful, so her appetite and general health improved too. Carol would post new detailed progress reports, refreshing Halo's profile on the rescue's website, so that potential adopters could keep a close eye on her progress.

In February 2013, while still in foster care, Halo suffered what appeared to be a collapsing episode. She was rushed to the vet for a full check-up, where it was discovered Halo was also suffering from possible neck pain. The vet decided to give her an MRI scan, to form detailed pictures of the anatomy affecting the physiological processes of her body. Results showed that Halo's right cerebral hemisphere, the part of the brain that controls muscle functions on the opposite side of the body, was smaller than her left cerebral hemisphere, the part of the brain that, in humans, controls speech, thought, emotions, reading, writing, and learning. From the MRI the vet also diagnosed a very common condition seen in Cavaliers called 'Chiari-like malformation', in which their brain tissue extends down into their spinal canal. As with most cases of infrequent seizure, owners are often advised to observe and only seek treatment if the fits become more frequent, so Halo wasn't discharged with any specific anti-seizure medication, and it was treated for now as a one-off, possibly stress-related event. On Wednesday 13 February 2013 Carol updated Halo's status on the website, accompanied by some pictures of Halo with some of her other dogs:

> *'Halo needs a calm adult environment with someone who has lots of time to give her. She definitely needs canine friends and would love nothing more than a couple of other Cavaliers to curl up to. She loves lots of cuddles on your knee. She has been to our groomer for a bath and was very good. She travelled well in the car, and she is 90% housetrained. She has seen our vet who feels she may have been restricted badly in the past and so walks with a slightly rounded back, but this has improved greatly since she arrived, with the regular short walks and now she is less frightened. She is still underweight, but otherwise we have found no problems. She has a T-shirt on at present as she feels the cold and she has a coat when she goes outside. She is just adorable!'*

That same day, Carol received an email from someone called Lisa Garner who ran her own online pet clothes boutique, based in the West Midlands. Having read the update on the website and seen Halo wearing the T-shirt (which was unsurprisingly very baggy on her little body), Lisa decided to contact Carol offering to send little Halo some clothes from her boutique to keep her warm, as well as some other goodies. A few days later a big bright pink box arrived at Carol's house addressed to Halo. It contained warm clothes, a doggy raincoat, and some tasty treats. Over the next few days and weeks, emails between Carol and Lisa became more frequent, even though Halo still wasn't up for adoption; her health problems and socialisation issues from her past life on the puppy farm still needed lots of work, but nevertheless, with each email exchange, Carol became more and more impressed with Lisa's kindness, positivity, caring attitude, and the fact that she was clearly watching Halo's progress very closely. Carol knew that if Lisa chose to adopt Halo, she'd have no doubt that Lisa would provide the perfect forever home. Carol's daughter Natasha sent Lisa some photos of Halo clearly happy in her new clothes, including a soft comfy pink fleece with hood, fashionable pink t-shirt, and padded green anorak. In some she was even showing interest in her paw-shaped lollipop treat. The email from Natasha arriving in Lisa's inbox with the photos read:

'Hi Lisa, Mum asked me to take some photos of Halo in her wonderful new clothes!! You will see from the photos that even her friends think this is wonderful as they can now rest their heads on her snuggly jumper. This morning Halo went for a walk in the field with the others and she didn't shiver or cry thanks to her wonderful jacket. Thank you so much for your kindness, your jumpers and coat have made a big difference to Halo, especially given the very cold weather. All the best, Natasha.'

With all this amazing progress it was just a matter of days until Halo was ready for adoption, and almost as soon as her status on the rescue website changed, it came as little surprise whose was the first application Carol received, enquiring about finally coming to meet her.

Chapter 7

Lisa Garner has always been a West Midlands girl; I'm sure she won't mind me saying she has the accent to prove it. Born into an animal-loving family living south west of Birmingham, Lisa was the youngest of three children. The family's pets in those early years growing up included a Welsh Springer Spaniel called Bella, a grey dwarf rabbit named Benito, two gerbils, Gertie and Bubbles, and three guinea pigs who all, Lisa recalls fondly, followed one another across the garden in single file. There was black-and-white Twinkle, ginger Thumper, and a black one called Malu (named after Matt and Luke Goss from 80s pop sensation Bros, obviously), who once crawled into a bowl of porridge. The family also enjoyed gazing at the cockatiels, zebra finches, and quail in their aviary, as well as observing fish and other wildlife in their pond at the back of the garden. Every animal was very well looked after, cared for, and played with by Lisa, her older sister Sarah, and her older brother Stephen.

From before the age of 12 and for most of her teens, Lisa continued to develop her strong connection with animals, and was always happier when surrounded by all her four-legged and feathered friends, but there still didn't seem to be enough animal contact to satisfy her. So she enrolled in some horse-riding lessons, and spent the remainder of her spare time at a local livery yard, pretty much every weekend. Lisa loved spending time riding her loaned horses starting with Percy, and then followed a few years later by another called Star, named after the distinguishing white marking between his eyes. As well as taking her various equine companions out on cross-country hacks, Lisa also enjoyed helping out at the yard, mucking out the stables, and grooming the horses. For an animal-obsessed teenager growing up in the West Midlands with so many animals in her life, it's no surprise that from an early age Lisa knew she wanted to learn more, read more, and spend her life in the company of her four-legged friends. As Lisa's passion for helping animals grew and grew, any free time was divided between entertaining her pets in the garden, including being fascinated by how the goldfish came to the surface when she fed them bread, and riding horses around the beautiful Worcestershire countryside. Lisa finished secondary school and felt the need to embark on some further education. But after a few weeks of A-level lessons, which included Media Studies and English, Lisa decided to leave studying for good, and find a permanent job instead.

In her late teens Lisa sought employment locally, mainly taking admin roles, and after over 10 years of office work, and with her love of animals getting stronger and stronger still,

Lisa decided to set up her own dog-walking and pet-sitting business. As sole charge of her first proper company, Lisa also took a course in dog-grooming too, so she could offer all three pet services to her clients. After a while it became obvious that dog-sitting and dog-walking were by far proving the most popular, with Lisa now developing a loyal customer base.

Lisa puts the popularity of her dog-walking and pet-sitting business down to offering that personal touch – for example, only walking a single dog at any one time, and only occasionally choosing to walk more than one dog when they are owned by the same person. As well as pet-sitting at her clients' houses, Lisa will be out exercising Greyhounds to Springers, Cavaliers to Crossbreeds, whatever the weather. Lisa walks every size and shape of dog imaginable, paying extra special attention to those dogs requiring slightly more care, such as anxious dogs like rescue dogs from cruel backgrounds. With this level of care and kindness it's really no surprise that her dog-walking and pet-sitting business became so well-liked, enjoying an excellent reputation; and to this day, a good number of years since Lisa ran her business, local dog-lovers are *still* requesting her bespoke walking and sitting services.

It was well over a decade since her family brought their first dog, Bella the Welsh Springer, home as a puppy, but now Lisa was old enough to have her own puppies, Izzy the brown and white Blenheim Cavalier, and Daisy the Lhasa Apso. When Izzy passed away, along came Lady, a deep reddish-brown or ruby-coloured Cavalier, also purchased as a puppy. In those days Lisa and her family had never even considered rehoming, not because they didn't want to, but because even the concept of rescue dog adoption had never really appeared on their radar, and being a fan of smaller, mainly toy breeds like Cavaliers, there would be no point even looking in rescue shelters as such breeds would surely never be given up and abandoned…?

Lisa's dog-walking and pet-sitting business continued to enjoy its success well into 2011, when one day she was shopping online for doggy clothes for her own family of small pooches. She couldn't find the exact items or sizes she was looking for, so she thought she may as well start ordering them in and stocking and selling them online herself. As soon as Lisa started to go down that avenue and appeal specifically to the small-dog-owning demographic, her first ever business venture into e-commerce struck a chord with consumers and began to steadily grow. But very soon her online dog boutique began to experience some of the common pitfalls of small businesses, notably lack of discoverability. So she signed up to a training course, and began learning how to compete with the bigger, more established brands in this sector.

Lisa concentrated on providing that personal touch, offering a niche service to owners of small dogs only, and in true Lisa style, doing it very well. So well, in fact, that Lisa was even willing to take a risk by stocking some of the more unusual doggy fashion brands on her pet boutique website. And, as every business owner knows, the better the customer service you provide, the more likely you are to enjoy success, which was proved time and time again with excellent online reviews, customer testimonials, and of course, lots of repeat business.

Of all the emerging social networking platforms fighting for our attention back then, encouraging users to set up accounts and begin entering their personal details online, Facebook seemed by far one of the best suited, preferred, and trusted marketplace. Without a huge amount of money to invest like her rivals, Lisa started teaching herself more about understanding how Facebook worked, and in very little time at all, became very skilled at how best to employ this particular platform to achieve optimal business results.

Lisa's online pet boutique's top-selling products in the winter of 2012-13 included regular harnesses (always popular with smaller dogs), jumpers, and collars, as well as two types of coat: practical waterproof anoraks with reflective piping for that 'dog about town' look, as well as more fashionable puffer-type jackets too. But as well as endless webpages listing specialist clothes and accessories to keep your little dog warm in these colder months, Lisa also decided to stock more random outfits too, such as dog wedding dresses and tuxedos, even hair bows. Customers loved it all and were even clicking on multiple outfits and styles to buy for their petite pooches. Lisa's online venture was even recognised and awarded a Small Business Sunday national business award in Birmingham, presented by *Dragons' Den* entrepreneur and spaniel-owner Theo Paphitis.

Anyone running a business knows that winning an award can prove to be a very useful endorsement indeed, not just to add the business award badge to your company's website, but to generate local news stories and media coverage too. As Lisa's pet boutique's profile continued to grow, more eyes were focused on Lisa's website, and it was really no surprise to anyone what happened next.

It was February 2013, and even though it was cold outside, business was ticking over nicely inside. Lisa was working from home, kept company by Daisy and Lady, both bought from responsible breeders. Lhasas are usually pretty bombproof, and though Cavaliers should have their hearts checked regularly for a specific cardiac disease called Mitral Valve Disease (MVD), these issues, although serious, can often be spotted early, and usually respond well to medication even months before any obvious symptoms of serious cardiac conditions such as congestive heart failure arise.

At that time Lisa had never really considered getting a dog from a rescue shelter, and only had very limited experiences with rescue dogs from her pet-sitting and dog-walking days. The summer before, though, Lisa had enjoyed attending a fun dog show in London which was different from other dog shows she'd previously attended, in that it had invited celebrities to judge the classes, many of whom were taking part with their own rescue dogs, all competing for a red winner's rosette. This dog show had also raised awareness of buying puppies responsibly, as well as the benefits of rescue dog adoption. But

Lisa already had two dogs already; there was no way getting a third was *ever* going to happen.

Lisa's popular online dog boutique's page on Facebook was quickly becoming the obvious virtual meeting place for owners of small dogs. People would chat, leave comments, post pictures, generally share stories of their dogs, and like posts from others. One day someone shared a link from a rescue centre, complete with rehoming details of a few dogs, including Cavaliers, which appeared to be from a different background compared with other rescue dogs. Lisa loved Cavaliers, but surely there couldn't be these dogs in rescue? 'Who in their right mind would ever buy a Cavalier and then abandon it?' Lisa thought to herself, confused. She knew from first-hand experience that Cavaliers were the friendliest and sweetest of all breeds, so what on earth could be going on?

Out of curiosity, and desperate to discover a good enough reason why Cavaliers were listed on a rescue shelter site looking for new homes, Lisa clicked on that link. As the webpage started to load, Lisa was expecting to see perhaps one or two random Cavaliers surrounded by breeds and mixed-breeds sadly more commonly associated with rescue or being abandoned, for example Staffies or Greyhounds. But that didn't happen. She was shocked and surprised to see pages and pages of Cavaliers up for adoption, on this one rescue centre's website. On closer inspection, Lisa realised that this wasn't a link to any normal rescue shelter. These dogs weren't coming from bored families, separating couples, or even broken homes; they weren't discarded Christmas presents, causing allergies to children, or costing their owners too much money. It appeared that all these Cavaliers listed here online had originally been used for breeding even more Cavaliers; for some reason unbeknown to Lisa, they were now apparently totally useless, surplus to their breeder's requirements, and perhaps using up valuable space and food.

But it wasn't just Cavaliers on this website. There were other small breeds too, like Bichons, Miniature Schnauzers, Westies, Cairns, Pugs, Beagles, Chihuahuas, and Cocker Spaniels; there were bigger breeds such as Labradors, Mastiffs, Newfoundlands, Bulldogs, St Bernards, Boxers, Border Collies; and of course the fashionable crossbreeds such as Puggles, Cockapoos, Labradoodles, with every other weird and wonderful cross in between. With one innocent click of her mouse, Lisa had inadvertently discovered another world; so she kept on reading, and clicking on more links, shocked and saddened at all these different types of dogs needing homes, and after a while she felt like she was being constantly drawn back to a particular Cavalier's face in one of the links, almost hypnotising Lisa from behind the screen.

Listed on the website as 'Halo' was a startled but very beautiful and vulnerable-looking tricolour female Cavalier. Though she was on a rescue centre's website, Halo was not yet ready for adoption; there were no reasons given why. Lisa quickly printed out the webpage containing Halo's details and basic information, and over the next few days repeatedly went back to check on her status. Soon enough another picture was posted on Halo's page, this time with the little Cavalier sat in a bed in an oversized pink t-shirt. Lisa was hooked. Who was this little face peering out from her computer screen? Where even was she? Whose house was that? Why was she so thin? Lisa's list of questions grew. But still the website said Halo wasn't yet up for rehoming, and anyway Lisa wasn't even looking for another dog. But as the days went on, Lisa became more and more obsessed with checking Halo's online profile.

Halo update 27th Feb

Halo has had a difficult two weeks; you will probably have noticed we changed her status to 'Not Available'. She developed a very sore eye and after a visit to the Ophthalmic Vets we were told she had chronic dry eye. She had a very bad infection. This has been treated and her eyes have been checked and are much better. However, her dry eye will require treatment with eye drops am & pm for the rest of her life to keep moisture in her eyes.

Halo during this time has been very low, her condition was very poor, and she was exceptionally underweight. She had a short fit/faint which was very worrying. Since this happened, she has had several tests and the neurologist/cardiologist looking after her has ruled out a major illness. We are hoping this was a one-off problem, as it has not happened again.

Halo is a very special little girl, she is a real fighter and, despite her sad life, she is a trusting lovable soul. She has learnt to walk on a lead, she is housetrained, she travels really well in the car. Halo is probably a Cavalier X (possibly a Chihuahua) and as she is a Toy breed size (now 3.8kg) she still needs to build up her muscle and gain a little more weight slowly. She loves to be cuddled and out on walks round our garden she stays close to me. She is a very delicate little dog and we feel a calm adult home will suit her best. Halo adores our other dogs, she is always curled with a couple of them, so she definitely needs at least one small friend. Halo will not be able to get full insurance cover so please consider this when making an application for her.

From her listing on the website, Lisa knew that Halo was also badly feeling the cold. Lisa still had no desire to actually adopt Halo, but felt the need to make her happy in the best way she knew how, so she sent an email enquiring about Halo, and asked for her girth and back length. Being an expert in providing clothes and treats specifically for small dogs, Lisa wanted to send Halo a special bundle of hand-selected goodies from her online dog boutique. Halo's foster carer, a nice lady called Carol, immediately replied, and sent Lisa Halo's measurements so Lisa could get her clothes' sizes absolutely spot on, which of course she had no problem achieving. Once Halo's special package had arrived, which included a green jacket, pink jumper, t-shirt, toy gingerbread man, and vanilla-flavoured yoghurt lollipop, all packed into a big pink gift box, Carol's daughter Natasha emailed some semi-professional photos to Lisa of Halo in her new clothes. Lisa thought Halo was deliberately posing for these pictures, and every time she looked at Halo smiling back at her from behind her computer screen, Lisa felt a stronger and stronger connection with the Cavalier, and it wasn't long before she sent one of the most game-changing emails in animal welfare history. Lisa enquired about adopting Halo.

For the previous few weeks, ever since Halo had gone into foster care at Carol's house, Lisa had been keeping a very close eye on her updates, already aware that any delay in Halo being ready for rehoming was most likely due to health issues, possibly because of her eyes, or perhaps her funny turns. Carol and Lisa emailed each other back and forth, with Carol really trusting her instincts that Lisa was the experienced dog owner she appeared, so already felt more than comfortable with Lisa rehoming Halo if she ever decided to. When Carol changed Halo's online status, unsurprisingly she heard Lisa had already applied to adopt Halo via the rescue, so she quickly arranged some West-Midlands-based home-checkers to visit Lisa's house and ensure a happy, safe, and loving home awaited little Halo. Lisa passed the home check with flying colours, with the home-checkers thrilled to meet Daisy, Lady, and Dolly too, not just because they're all lovely dogs, but because a strict condition of rehoming a dog with a past like Halo's is that she lives with at least one other dog, so they can teach her the basics of how to be a dog. Carol and Halo lived about 100 miles away from Lisa, who wasn't the most confident long-distance driver, so she hired someone with a dog-walking van to take her to Carol's house. On her way to meet Halo and Carol, Lisa was so excited, her heart beating fast in anticipation. She'd never had a rescue dog before, and knew that there were most likely many challenges ahead, but she'd spent the last few weeks building a strong dialogue with Carol over email, fueled by adorable pictures. Lisa really had fallen completely head over paws in love with little Halo.

Lisa remembers going into the house as if it was yesterday, seeing Halo for the first time, and Carol picking up this tiny little dog, and then carefully placing her into Lisa's arms. But Halo didn't want to sit with Lisa at first, preferring instead to just get back down on the carpet and rejoin Carol's other dogs, a very common trait in previously abused rescued breeding dogs. But with a glowing report from her home-checkers, and Carol and Lisa liking each other from way before they'd even met, it wasn't long before Halo was curled up on Lisa's lap, already on the way back to the West Midlands.

Lisa hadn't seen all of Halo's medical records and vet reports yet. She was sure just from looking at her that there were some serious ailments common with puppy farm breeding dogs, such as emaciation, dry-eye for which she'd been given some tubes of treatments from Carol, and her very unusual stance when just standing still at rest. These were some of Halo's more obvious health problems, but in the short time of Halo being collected from Carol's foster home, Lisa hadn't yet had a chance to appreciate the extent of Halo's epilepsy and separation anxiety, as they slowly made their way up the motor-way towards her new life, well out of any more harm's way.

Chapter 7

Clutching Halo tightly in her arms, it was impossible for Lisa not to contemplate the whirlwind nature of the last few weeks. She'd never ever expected to see such a popular and unique breed like the Cavalier, and so many others, up for adoption on a rescue shelter website. All this had started with that urge to send warm clothes and stop little Halo feeling the cold. Lisa had just wanted to use her online pet boutique to help another little dog in need. However, as it turned out, Halo wasn't the only vulnerable dog that Lisa would eventually help out.

Chapter 8

❖

On Tuesday 12 March 2013 all the i's were dotted and t's crossed, as Halo's official paperwork was finally completed, and her brand new life began. In rescue circles they call this date the 'gotcha day', and as well as her new postcode in the West Midlands, Lisa thought it apt that Halo's fresh new start deserved a fresh new name. After all, Halo had only been called Halo for the last couple of months, and before that, she'd never been called anything. And there was one name that Lisa had always really admired, a name which also had two syllables and was thus unlikely to confuse the new arrival too much. Just like that, Halo became 'Lucy'.

Lucy learned her new name quickly and, much as she had done in Carol's home, Lucy started following Daisy and Lady around the house. But unlike when she had first met Lisa and immediately scuttled away to rejoin the other dogs, this time Lucy was now firmly attached to Lisa's side. Within just a few days of exploring her new home, Lisa was quickly becoming Lucy's security blanket. Despite this Lucy would always look apprehensive when Lisa went to pick her up, and also appeared fearful of doorways – both phobias that are very common with ex-puppy-farm dogs, because neither experience in their past ever led to anything pleasant or positive. But as the days became weeks, and the weeks became months, it was clear that as long as Lisa was there, Lucy seemed to be able to cope with life. What's more, she was also starting to put on weight, and even began to appear outwardly happy.

Lucy seemed to get on very well with both Daisy and Lady too, who very graciously accepted her into their family group immediately. And when she wasn't sticking to Lisa's side like glue, Lucy was gradually learning from Daisy, Lady and now also Lisa's mum's dog, a Shih Tzu called 'Dolly', how to behave and act like a dog. Things were going very well, with all four dogs getting on very nicely indeed, so Lisa decided to celebrate Lucy's most recent identity and brand new start, by ordering her a shiny metal identification tag, complete with phone number and new name proudly engraved upon it.

As the weeks passed, and as all the dogs became even closer friends, Lisa started to feel a bit guilty. She wished that she'd rescued before; she started to wonder why she'd ever thought of doing anything *but* rescue. Even in the early days, Lucy really was different from any other dog Lisa had ever known, not just on an individual level; and with Lisa's expanding knowledge of social media, coupled with her desire to spread the word about how amazing it felt to rescue a dog, she was very keen to share her story, hoping her experience of adopting would encourage others to consider opening their homes, and hearts, to welcome a rescue dog into their lives as well.

Lisa thought that rescuing a dog, especially from such a cruel ex-breeding background, might prove challenging, but she actually found the complete opposite was true. Lisa and Lucy's shared journey together was definitely a rewarding one that improved daily, sometimes hourly. Lisa noticed subtle differences and decreasing anxiety levels, all signs that indicate a growing confidence, together with improved mental health. Many of these positive factors, Lisa admits, like most owners who'd purchased dogs as puppies, were usually taken for granted. In Lucy's case however, and in the cases of most dogs rescued from puppy farms, these little changes to us are very major to them. When Lucy arrived, her skin was still quite itchy, presumably caused by it trying to heal itself after the mange and flea infestation contracted back in the puppy farm, so Lisa would give her regular baths to soothe her. Probably as a result of her poorly skin and mistreatment, Lucy also started off rather smelly, her coat still giving off a slightly pungent odour from the urine scalding and related burnt flesh, so Lisa's frequent bathing of Lucy not only helped these issues, but did wonders to strengthen their unique bond too.

Furthermore, due to her previously poor diet and parasite burden before she was rescued, Lucy's coat was understandably thin, but with Lisa's remarkable home nursing, and foster Carol's TLC before her, together with Lucy enjoying a highly nutritious diet, Lucy's coat began to improve, and the ammonia-like smell, a horribly sad reminder of her miserable past, eventually disappeared. Even the hair covering Lucy's little rat-like tail, together with her scrawny ears and feet, was now being allowed to grow freely, perhaps for the first time ever, and it was being expertly maintained by the local groomers, helped along of course by Lisa's own professional grooming skills that she'd learned a few years back, when she set up her dog-walking and pet-sitting business.

With little Lucy's weight, body condition, and coat all rapidly improving, she was starting to resemble a normal dog more and more. Something else Lisa couldn't fail to notice in those early days, was that in just a few weeks Lucy appeared more grateful towards her and was forming a stronger attachment with her than Daisy, Lady and Dolly, even though they'd all been with her since they were puppies. Lucy seemed to be a lot more emotionally invested and much more dependent on Lisa than the other dogs ever were.

Dogs that have experienced a similar background to Lucy's are not like normal dogs and must always be treated very differently. Routinely, and thanks to all the dedicated non-profit organisations, many of them run by volunteers, that rescue them in the first place, these ex-puppy-farm dogs are usually already neutered. Greeting a rescued puppy farm dog must always be done slowly and sensitively as they are likely to cower in fear, a fear that can be so deep-rooted and imprinted that it often never completely goes away. How does a prospective dog rescuer even start to deal with these potentially serious behavioural issues?

As we saw with Carol's sardine trick, offering tasty treats can be one of the very first steps to gaining trust and confidence. It can often work wonders, as many dogs rescued from puppy farms are food-motivated, usually because minimum amounts of low-quality food have been their only diet, and even then usually only just enough to keep them alive to breed. Another feature of 'normal' dog ownership, wearing a collar and harness and going for a walk, is also completely alien to most of these ex-breeders. Responsible socialisation of puppies should always start weeks before going off to their new homes. This is not simply a matter of making sure they've spent quality time in the company of humans and other dogs, but also that they're familiar and unfazed by daily sounds in the home such as a TV, washing machine and doorbell, as well as the physical sensation and practice of wearing a collar or harness if more appropriate, and the basic experience of just walking on a lead.

Lucy was very slow to walk wearing her harness. She'd take a few nervous steps and then stop, only to be bribed into completing another few steps with some more treats. A few steps more and treat. Then a few more. Treat. Lucy was five years old when she learnt to walk on a lead, and not only that but, having been imprisoned her whole life, she'd most likely never been outside either. Imagine how scared and confused she must have felt when she initially experienced weather?

Every single raindrop, gust of wind, or snowflake must have been terrifying to start with. Compared with pups reared and socialised by people that *actually* care, it's understandable why dogs rescued from puppy farms are incredibly anxious, needing very special care, attention, and a lot of patience.

Just as with human anxiety, canines often have triggers too, with the role of the fosterer and then adopter being to spot, observe, deal with, and try to anticipate these sources of potential panic, with the sole aim of reducing the chances of recurrence; and if they do, then to help lessen the dog's stressed behavioural response. Annabelle, another ex-puppy-farm Cavalier adopted after Lucy, suffered from a phobia of flashlights, possibly a result of being kept in the dark and any stressful interaction with her puppy farmer, for example being forced to mate, preceded by her being located in amongst the straw of her pen by the farmer's torch. This is precisely why dogs rescued from puppy farms almost always benefit from living with responsibly bred dogs, as they learn not to react to potentially stressful situations from observing the reaction, or lack of it, from the calm resident dog. What a sorry situation it's become when adult dogs have to teach another adult dog how to even be a dog.

Lucy loved treats. The more the merrier. Lisa's constant supply of them was positive reinforcement at its very best, and Lucy's speedy progress a testament to Lisa's natural skills of patience and rehabilitation. Using the tastiest, most nutritious treats over the months that followed, Lisa was able to help

Lucy to shake off some of her anxieties and to realise normal life wasn't the scary day-to-day mixture of long periods of boredom, hunger and solitary confinement, interspersed with horrible episodes abuse and mistreatment, which had sadly become her norm. Lucy was experiencing love for the first time in her life. She was safe, able to sleep deeply, and at the same time perfected the art of snoring loudly, something that would always make her human friends smile from ear to ear.

Lisa promised herself that from now on she would only rescue the most vulnerable dogs, either ones rescued from puppy farms, those with disabilities, or both. They'd require a lot more work than a normal adult dog which already recognises a food bowl, or knows what their owner jingling their harness and lead means; but Lisa's huge heart had realised how much it enjoyed the feeling of helping the less fortunate, the true underdogs, and especially as she worked from home it meant she could give any rescue dog all the attention, time, and space for healing they so badly needed.

Health-wise, Lucy had a whole list of issues to live with. Although discussed at the time of adoption, it's often not until these problems properly manifest themselves that their true extent and impact is fully known. For example, Lucy's eyes, although relatively clear early on, soon became cloudier. Even with regular visits to an eye specialist, Lucy's left lens developed into a very obvious and opaque full-on cataract, resulting in most likely total blindness on that side. But that wasn't the only serious problem to affect Lucy's eyes. As already diagnosed by

Carol's ophthalmic vet, with appropriate treatment prescribed and then given to Lisa to take home, Lucy also suffered from 'dry-eye', which can prevent dogs from producing tears. Some dogs with dry-eye may just be able to produce a small amount, but others won't be able to produce any at all. If these are left untreated, the affected eyes gets much worse over time, and can result in dogs developing debilitating corneal ulcers. If *these* are left untreated the eyes may even have to be surgically removed.

'Idiopathic' canine epilepsy was another of Lucy's serious health issues that in many cases like hers, had no obvious cause. Although it remains the most common cause of seizures in dogs, and is widely understood to be an inherited disorder, its exact origin still remains a mystery. Unknown causes of serious medical conditions such as epilepsy call for carefully calculated treatment plans, often seeing if one medication works and how effective it is, before tweaking dose rates or adding or replacing them with an alternative drug. With such a wide range of treatments available to vets for controlling canine idiopathic epilepsy, we usually end up prescribing a course of long-term tablets, explaining to the client that there's a certain element of trial and error, sometimes requiring different drug combinations and dose rates. This fine-tuning also benefits from owners keeping a diary, and unsurprisingly this scenario was also true for Lucy. As well as constantly changing her tablets to find the most effective and safest dose, Lisa also reached out to a specific canine epilepsy charity who advised that the protein levels in Lucy's food and treats were possibly too high, so they recommended offering a lower-protein diet instead, which seemed to help a lot.

Just days after adopting her, Lisa first experienced one of Lucy's epileptic fits, albeit a mild one. She was panic-stricken, as anyone who's ever witnessed a seizure, either canine or human, would be, and felt an immense feeling of helplessness as she watched her tiny friend suffering right in front of her eyes. Lucy's seizures got worse as time went on.

With no previous experience of living with a dog with this condition, it's extremely challenging, as not only is it difficult to control, but with no obvious trigger Lisa constantly found herself on red alert. Like most cases of canine idiopathic epilepsy, Lucy's seizures often happened when she was fast asleep in the early hours. So Lisa would sleep with her arm around Lucy, so she could tell as soon as something was wrong. It would start with a few tremors, progress to more violent shaking, before causing backward arching of the head, neck, and spine at its worst. As soon as Lisa could tell she was having a seizure, she would bundle the quivering Lucy into her arms, run into her mum's bedroom, and wake her up to hold Lucy steady while Lisa quickly administered the emergency rectal valium tubes. Lucy would then suddenly seem to come out of it, and appear blind and disorientated for the next hour or two. As the treatment kicked in, Lisa would line the room with soft duvets and cushions so little Lucy, in her half-sedated state, wouldn't hurt herself walking into walls and doors.

Chapter 8

One of the most frustrating aspects of treating canine epilepsy is the unpredictability, never knowing if or when that next seizure will strike, and Lucy's fits were weeks, sometimes months, apart. Even on treatment these episodes can still happen, such is the randomness of this disease. As well as medication and diet change, Lisa also added a natural tincture to Lucy's meals, which she thought also helped control and prevent her seizures. Lisa already knew from the initial vet report that Lucy was thought to have 'Chiari-like malformation', commonly seen in Cavaliers, a developmental fault causing part of the brain to protrude from the opening at the back of the skull; often characterised by the mismatch of size between the dog's brain and skull. Symptoms can include behavioural signs of pain such as vocalisation, head-scratching or rubbing, reduced activity, decreased stair-climbing or jumping ability, spinal pain, altered emotional state to become more timid, anxious or aggressive, sleep disturbance, and touch aversion. Chiari-like malformation, with its direct involvement of Lucy's brain and spine, could potentially have contributed to Lucy's epilepsy, and these days it is a condition so widespread in toy breeds that it's thought up to 95 percent of Cavaliers may even be suffering with this disease. As well as affecting thousands of dogs, it's thought that a similar condition affects hundreds of thousands of children every year too.

As if eye problems and epilepsy weren't enough for Lucy and Lisa to deal with, Lucy also suffered from arthritis, painful chronic inflammation of her little joints. Her skinny legs would shake underneath her, barely strong enough to hold her body upright, and severely lacking in any muscular support. Lisa started taking Lucy on lots of short walks to build up her muscle mass. With such poor body condition it's no surprise that Lucy would often tire easily with even the slightest of exercise, so Lisa usually chose a very local park not far from Lisa's house in which to walk her – a very dog-friendly park with its own designated areas for play and recreation. As Lucy's body became stronger her muscles started to fill out, and she began running around the park in her pink harness and coat, usually off lead, which she always enjoyed. These short walks progressed over time to one long 45-minute walk, with Lucy stuck close by Lisa's side. From those shocking initial pictures of her curved spine, fused hips, and tiny emaciated frame, it's not hard to imagine the likely strain on those joints and resulting arthritic changes that had developed inside them over the last few years. And if you think there's a confusing number of treatment strategies for epilepsy, these days our range of arthritis treatments is even more varied, with a whole spectrum of drugs available, all with their particular advantages and disadvantages. Lisa wasn't keen to add to the many potential side effects of Lucy's existing medications – after all, just like with human medication, most prescription drugs will usually have some detrimental effects on fragile internal organs, and with her background Lisa could only assume Lucy's insides were still very delicate. In order to deal with Lucy's joint issues, Lisa focused on feeding her an appropriate diet, complemented with gentle routine exercise and natural joint supplements, which all appeared to be very effective in keeping Lucy both asymptomatic, and most importantly, pain-free.

Those were just some of Lucy's life-threatening medical problems. None of them, sadly, are uncommon amongst the thousands of poorly bred Cavaliers and other ex-breeding dogs like her that are either rescued, or used for breeding even more genetically damaged Cavaliers and so-called designer crosses like Cavachons. Initially Lucy was in a worse physical state than other dogs Lisa has since adopted, especially as she was only five years old, but unlike other Cavaliers of her background, Lucy's heart was strong, and thankfully she wasn't too 'shut down' psychologically either. Lucy would sleep on Lisa's bed and bark at her every morning, always appearing impatient when she wanted Lisa to get up for breakfast time.

Severe separation anxiety meant that every time Lisa left the house without her, to pop to the shops for example, Lucy would cry and whimper behind the kitchen door, and then fell asleep when she returned, most likely out of sheer exhaustion. One of the most complex and difficult behavioural conditions to treat in any dog, Lucy's separation anxiety proved very hard to crack; sometimes toys left around can prove a useful distraction, but Lucy had never had toys in her past life; occasionally she'd pick one up but had no idea what to do with it, and she never reacted to squeaky toys either, totally uninterested. As a result it was easier, and admittedly far less stressful, for Lucy to never leave Lisa's side. They went *everywhere* together, and over the weeks, months, and years of rehabilitation that followed, their bond became stronger and stronger. Lisa and Lucy became mutual comfort blankets, completely dependent on each other.

As Lisa worked tirelessly and successfully helping Lucy emerge from her shell, the little rescue Cavalier's food obsession grew and grew. When Lisa invited her two- and four-legged close friends and family round to celebrate Lucy's arrival, she knew that not even a canine party is complete without a special cake, so she ordered a specially made dog-friendly gateau for her little canine sidekick, and some matching party hats for everyone present to honour the occasion. Lucy would patiently pose for a picture in all sorts of tasteful outfits, giving a look to camera that made Lisa think back to those initial photos of Halo sent by Carol's daughter Natasha, taken by the pink gift box – that very same intense stare down the lens that made Lisa send that email, make enquiries, adopt Halo, rename her Lucy, and give her the very best chance of happiness. Lucy, now growing in confidence, would happily sit on the stairs alongside the other canine guests, all wearing their party hats, and posing for pictures. Of course there was no way anyone could have possibly known at that time, but when Lucy dressed up for a party like this one, or any other occasion during those early months since her Gotcha Day, the resulting images would be the start of something that would eventually help change history forever. Just like Lisa, Lucy seemed to be drawn to the colour pink, a bright candy pink, indeed the same colour pink of the t-shirt and fleece Lisa had originally sent for Halo to keep her warm when she first made contact with Carol. The number of albums of pictures of this highly photogenic Cavalier in all sorts of hats and outfits, usually in various shades of bright pink, were now growing quickly, so Lisa started to post them on her personal Facebook page, for all her friends and family to enjoy. But as their bond continued to strengthen, and with Lucy seemingly keen to pose for more and more pictures, it gave Lisa a burning desire to start up a *dedicated* page in order for people to follow Lucy's excellent progress, as well as spread the message of how amazing rescue dogs can be, given the chance.

Lisa had minimal resources, yet here she was in a small town in the West Midlands not only totally transforming this little Cavalier's life, but also determined to make a difference, starting to raise awareness of the effects of puppy farming, her experience adopting and rehabilitating Lucy over the last six months, and hopefully encouraging others to do the same. Lisa thought long and hard about what would make the most impact and how best to inform the most people possible; eventually she decided to set up a page on Facebook specifically devoted to little Lucy. It was an online space allocated specifically for fellow animal-lovers around the world to join in, get involved, to 'like' Lucy's page, and virtually meet one very special dog. Whether you lived in Birmingham or Brazil, Solihull or South Africa, everyone was welcome to connect with little Lucy, get to know her unique character, marvel at her huge personality, as well as witness for themselves the phenomenal strides her health, confidence, and ultimately happiness were making every single day.

Lisa was already experienced in effective branding techniques, so like many successful brands decided to keep the name of Lucy's page nice and simple. In September 2013, just six months after Lucy was adopted, the 'Lucy the Rescue Cavalier' page went live on Facebook, and no one could have ever predicted what an enormous impression it would eventually have on the world and future of dog welfare.

Chapter 9

❧

With a substantial Cavalier community already very active on Facebook, it wasn't long before the 'Lucy the Rescue Cavalier' page gained its first followers and Lucy's pictures and story were being shared by like-minded people.

Lisa would upload images and videos of Lucy's most recent adventure, at least once daily, usually containing at least one smiling Lucy pic, and usually with her tail happily in mid-wag. Lisa chose her main cover pic carefully, an opportunity for visitors to learn the basics within a few milliseconds of landing on the page. For this she used Lucy's before-and-after rescue photos: the sad one with the red top covering her tiny emaciated body and curved spine next to the happy smiley one taken just six months later. This, Lisa hoped, would give new followers a visual representation of her past, without being too graphic or gruesome, as well as showing just how far Lucy had come, both mentally and physically, in just half a year.

Lisa's first proper post commented on Lucy's stubborn 'serious face', and attracted a total of 56 likes and 13 comments, not bad for a brand new page. Lisa was thrilled with the reactions her first few posts were receiving from her followers, commenting for example on how pleased they were that 'they could see [Lucy] happy in her forever home'. It quickly became obvious that the combination of Lucy's infectious smile, shocking backstory, and overall positive demeanour were all helping to make others feel happy too, mainly Cavalier fans in the UK to start with, but soon further afield from all corners of the globe.

Lisa always tried to engage with Lucy's fans as much as she could, whether replying to comments, or just liking nice remarks to acknowledge their positive interactions. This had always been incredibly important to Lisa right from the start, so anyone connecting with Lucy's page didn't feel like they were merely one of thousands of fans, but instead knew that a real person managed the page, and often responded to them individually too.

Lisa's 'Lucy the Rescue Cavalier' page remains to this day one of the most influential and successful pet-related pages on Facebook; it not only continues to raise awareness of puppy farming and has changed people's behaviour when choosing a dog, but has also helped alter the course of dog welfare history too. It's one of the most remarkable and inspiring lessons to any wannabe or existing animal welfare campaigner out there: just how much one single individual can achieve, working full time, with no resources apart from a smartphone, a dog, and boundless creativity and imagination.

Chapter 9

Lisa had her own strict rule that although she was keen to use this page as a platform for promoting rescue dog adoption and raising awareness of puppy farm cruelty, she would only very rarely share more hard-hitting images. This proved to be a clever balance that seemed to work well. Her experience in running her own award-winning businesses had taught Lisa that maintaining a popular social media page was similar in many ways: at the end of the day you want people to enjoy what you had to offer, to keep coming back, and to hopefully spread the word by telling others. And sure enough, back they came, and they invited all their friends too! Cavalier-lovers, small dog-lovers, any type of dog-lovers, animal-lovers: Lucy's Facebook page was fast becoming a beacon of hope for its fans, a safe, happy, positive place to visit which guaranteed its followers a welcome relief from the chaotic outside world.

It didn't take long for Lucy to start making a positive difference to people's lives; posts of upbeat lighthearted pictures were popular, attracting supportive comments and encouraging messages from all around the world. Some of the more iconic images, like the one of Lucy in her black jumper with 'Stop Puppy Farming' in bright pink letters were shared by *literally* thousands. And it wasn't just the pictures. In 2013 Lisa even shared a 'Ban the sale of young puppies & kittens without their mothers being present' government e-petition which I'd created when I first started campaigning, and she generously asked Lucy's followers to sign and share it – long before Lisa and I had even met!

Lucy's page wasn't just bringing people together; it was starting to create change too, and trying to reverse the horrors that had left little Lucy in that crippled state, with possibly just a couple of months to live. There was continual demand for *more* Lucy, so Lisa wrote and self-published 100 copies of a children's picture book called *Adventures of Lucy the Rescue Cavalier* to help raise even more awareness and educate kids at the same time. All monies raised from Lucy's children's book would be split between various non-profit organisations involved with rescuing dogs from puppy farms or campaigning against them. Such was Lucy's popularity that the book sold out very quickly. After the book Lisa's next tactic was to pose a question: if Lucy had a birthday party, would anyone come?

Lisa was soon inundated with excitable Lucy fans, all desperate to come along and meet canine royalty, but the only venue that was both suitable and available was the local village hall. Due to the unprecedented number of responses, Lisa decided that it would be safer to divide the RSVPs into two groups, hiring the hall once for Lucy's birthday party, and then a second time for her book launch. Lisa's next project was a 2015 calendar featuring Lucy enjoying a different activity for every month. Before long, a photoshoot was arranged with a local photographer which saw Lucy posing in front of a white background with all sorts of props. For January, the month of New Year's resolutions, Lucy was dressed in a pair of bright red leg-warmers with matching headband, sitting next to her gym weights and a tape measure. August saw little Lucy getting ready for her summer holidays, sitting in an opened suitcase with her bucket and spade, sun cream bottle, sunglasses, and passport. September's back-to-school month showed Lucy sitting at a school desk, wearing her school tie, complete with textbook, pen, spectacles, and schoolbag. The calendar story was even picked up by the *Mail Online*, the biggest entertainment website in the world, and shared over 500 times. Lucy's story had now crossed over to the mainstream; she was starting to raise awareness of puppy farming and rescue dog adoption on a much bigger scale.

Over 100 copies of the calendar were sold to raise much-needed funds for a campaign group trying to end puppy farming called Pup Aid, as well as a small non-profit organisation rescuing puppy farm dogs. Lucy's story was now being showcased and applauded by some of the world's biggest media titles, alongside more niche magazines like *Dogs Today*. Lucy was also starting to win local awards for her bravery, which helped her fame continue to grow even faster, and of course provided even more useful content for Lisa to upload and share. It wasn't long before she'd accumulated 30,000 followers; every day another few hundred dog-lovers were discovering Lucy's page. Facebook analytical data suggested that some of Lucy's posts were now reaching over a million people around the world, inviting hundreds of comments, likes, and shares; it was becoming a struggle for Lisa to keep track of them all, let alone respond to comments, or attempt to like them all herself, as she'd always prided herself on doing.

Such was the extent of 'Lucymania' that if a day went past where Lisa hadn't posted a picture yet, her followers would start to get worried. They'd begin writing concerned comments, asking 'What's wrong?' 'Where's Lucy?' 'Is she OK?' Lucy's fans were becoming more dependent on Lucy's antics and personality, so Lisa decided to post more frequently, and naturally Lucy's popularity and audience grew even stronger still.

The follow-up 2016 calendar was based on popular movie posters, and featured Lucy's friend and fellow Cavalier Annabelle in some of the months too: behind the wheel of an American car in a *Thelma & Louise* tribute, with Lucy wearing sunglasses below the caption 'Friendship that lasts a lifetime'; Lucy riding a broomstick as Harry Potter; holding a lightsaber and wearing Yoda ears in *Star Paws,* complete with strapline 'May the woof be with you'; one with Lady and Annabelle as *Rescued Angels* instead of *Charlie's Angels*, and other classics inspired by *ET*, *Romeo and Juliet*, *It's a Wonderful Life*, *James Bond*, and *The Wizard of Oz*; even their friend Reggie appeared in the *Lady And The Tramp* scene with Lady! These calendars all sold out within days to fans of Lucy, some living as far away as Hawaii and Australia! Lisa had already accumulated over 50,000 followers, and Lucy was now being described as an 'internet sensation', fast becoming one of the UK's first ever canine influencers, helping educate about the horrors of puppy farming, whilst at the same time, persuading thousands of prospective dog owners to consider adopting from rescue. She was winning prestigious awards, was being invited to glittering events, and was usually enjoying being snapped whilst having cuddles with lots of dog-loving celebrities too. Everything Lucy did was recorded, photographed, and posted for her legions of adoring fans. She was now a celebrity in her own right.

The first time I met Lucy and Lisa was in September 2013 at Pup Aid dog show in Primrose Hill, when she was taking part in the parade of rescued ex-puppy-farm breeding dogs. I immediately felt there was something special about these two, so I went over to introduce myself, and we briefly chatted. A couple of months later I met them again at the Kennel Club's Discover Dogs event in Earl's Court, London, where I was giving a talk on puppy farming. Lucy, Lisa, and I immediately hit it off and of course I reciprocated by liking and sharing Lucy's page as soon as I got home. The third time we met was at Crufts dog show in Birmingham in March 2014, where we were invited onto a radio show to give a live interview about puppy farming, rescue dogs, responsible breeding, and Lucy's story. The interview seemed to go down well, and we hung out together all afternoon. We meandered around the many showrings and stalls of the vast aeroplane-hangar-like halls together, realised we both knew a surprising number of the same people, introduced each other to new people, and even got photographed together in the Press Office. Though we didn't know it then, the three of us, Lisa, Lucy, and I – two humans and one dog – had already begun what was to become a very special and unique journey together.

With Lucy's popularity increasing by the day, sometimes even by the hour, people at these huge indoor dog events would spot her, often from across the vast halls, and scrabble through the crowds just to meet her and have their picture taken, usually a selfie. Lucy was a heroine, a survivor, evidence of an abusive system that was failing the UK's dogs. She was now the poster girl for victims of the puppy farm trade.

Lucy's social life was often hectic, but always in a good way. She loved meeting new people, traveling to and from London by train, and sharing adventures with her personal bodyguard and comfort blanket Lisa. As well as Discover Dogs, Crufts, and various pet shows around the country, Lisa and Lucy would always attend the Pup Aid puppy farm awareness fun dog show in Primrose Hill and take part in the emotional yet powerful parade of rescued puppy farm breeding dogs. Lucy's numerous debilitating health problems meant she wasn't the fastest walker, so Lisa would often pick her up and carry her around the show ring, curled up and content to be back in her arms. Lisa rarely entered Lucy in the classes themselves, for example Best Rescue or Golden Oldie, because she was too competitive and feared taking home anything less than the red winner's rosette Lucy always deserved! As a trio, we attended many glamorous events together, including the Hearing Dogs for the Deaf Awards at a beautiful venue in London, with special guests including none other than Princess Anne. Lucy was now mixing with royalty!

Chapter 9

The roll call of all the famous people Lucy met is nothing short of impressive, and could easily be mistaken for the guest list at the National Television Awards afterparty. Glitterati Lucy mingled with included Paul O'Grady, Peter Egan, Rachel Riley, Pasha Kovalev, Ben Fogle, Lucy Watson, Tim Vincent, Meg Mathews, Michelle Collins, and many more. Some of these encounters were more than just selfies taken at events; for example when bodybuilder and model Jodie Marsh met Lucy, she was holding her in her arms whilst giving an interview to the BBC's *Daily Politics* show outside the Houses of Parliament with me, about puppy farming and how the government urgently need to do something about it. Lucy was also lucky enough to meet rock legend Brian May several times. On one of these occasions, she, Lisa and I joined campaigners at a game-changing meeting with one of the UK's biggest animal charities who we felt were being unsupportive in our quest to end puppy farming. Mid-meeting Lucy sadly suffered a seizure. Looking back, it was as if she was just using every power she had in her tired, frail body to ask the various people present to please help end puppy farm cruelty, and to convince them that debilitating health problems stemming from puppy farming conditions, like her epilepsy, were all too real. It wasn't long before any resistance around the table evaporated and they eventually gave their support. When she began fitting and shaking, Lisa and I whisked Lucy away to a quiet corner with her carry bag, which always contained a few doses of valium, and waited for Lucy to recover, which she did quickly.

If you ask Lisa about the most memorable event she and Lucy attended, she'll most likely tell you it was 6 September 2016. Lisa and Lucy were invited down to another glittering awards ceremony in Mayfair: the very prestigious *Daily Mirror* Animal Hero Awards. These annual awards celebrate the *crème de la crème* of the animal welfare world, and once again Lucy had been nominated. Lisa was understandably nervous and emotional, but also incredibly proud of where their journey had taken them. As she listened to the nominations being read out for her category, and watched the accompanying videos played on the big screens around the room, featuring our dream team, as well as the four other nominees, Lucy, wearing her best outfit, sat on Lisa's lap waiting patiently. Lisa had absolutely no idea Lucy was going to win, so when the announcement came that Lucy had indeed won Rescue Animal of the Year, Lisa burst into tears, dropping her phone as she tried to film what was happening onstage!

Lucy had won a prestigious Animal Hero Award for overcoming adversity since starting life in a puppy farm, as well as her huge awareness-raising for rescue pets with her incredibly popular 'Lucy the Rescue Cavalier' Facebook page. Lucy got to meet even more celebrities that night, as her award was presented by *EastEnders* actors Richard Blackwood and Danny-Boy Hatchard, while TV presenter and *Britain's Got Talent* judge Amanda Holden was hosting the awards, and as Lisa and Lucy went up to collect their impressive silver and blue trophy, Amanda enjoyed sharing a cuddle with the newest, and smallest, winner in the room.

As the afterparty continued well into the night, there was a queue of guests and celebrities eager to meet the prize-winning Cavalier, all hungry for that precious selfie, and all of them now well aware of not just her incredible story, but also the enormous impact she was making on the world via her Facebook page. But even in the noisy bar area of the Grosvenor Hotel on London's Park Lane, Lucy was already fast asleep and snoring away, tucked up in her comfy pink carry bag; it had been a day full of excitement, and she was now snoring away loudly, content in the knowledge that she'd now been crowned Rescue Animal of the Year.

Chapter 10

✿

I don't know about you, but for me the best ideas seem to come from either being completely submerged in water – taking a bath or swimming or scuba-diving – or at 35,000 feet in the air on a plane. I'm guessing that's because being suitably mentally or physically detached from the rest of the world, most notably without access to mobile phone distraction, makes space for creativity to pop in and temporarily fill that gap. Also, it's not like I've got a great deal of hair to wash, which I guess frees up even more time to think! Following the World's Biggest Puppy Party at Brighton Racecourse in September 2009 I couldn't stop thinking about how I could improve on this relatively successful first attempt at a puppy farming awareness day. How could I repackage the event in order to make it snappier-sounding, and call it by a better name, referencing both the music and dog show elements, and basically give it more public appeal? One day, after much puppy-related wordplay had taken up a fair bit of my imagination quota, I was soaking away in the bath and the two words 'Pup Aid' arrived in my cerebrum.

The irony of renaming the World's Biggest Puppy Party 'Pup Aid' must now be shared; and it is possibly one of the best examples of how nerdy and geeky I was as a teenager. I kept this story quiet through my twenties and thirties out of sheer embarrassment, but these days I'm actually, in a weird way, quite proud of it.

When I was at school one of my friendly classmates in the cool gang was a boy called Jeremy Goldsmith, who was related to Harvey Goldsmith, the promoter of what is widely regarded as the greatest and most iconic rock concert of all time, Live Aid. Jeremy was Harvey's nephew, and my parents were good friends with Jeremy's parents. In July 1985, when Jeremy and I were both 12 years old, I was generously offered a ticket to Live Aid by Jeremy's family, which would've most likely meant not just attending, but most likely venturing backstage and meeting all the bands. As you can imagine being offered a ticket for Live Aid at that age would be anyone's dream come true, let alone a pre-teen like myself. To see live performances by some of the planet's biggest artists including Status Quo, Phil Collins, David Bowie, The Who, and of course the most memorable and show-stopping of all, Freddy Mercury with Queen, plus two of my favourite comedians, Mel Smith and Griff Rhys Jones. In many ways this invite made Charlie's golden ticket to the Chocolate Factory look like little more than an all-zones One Day Travelcard. But guess what, I turned it down. I said 'no' to my free ticket for Live Aid, complete with backstage pass!

Why did I dismiss this unique once-in-a-lifetime opportunity to witness the most historic rock concert of all time? What could possibly have been more important? Well, it clashed with my school's prizegiving day, and I was collecting my chemistry prize, which to a square like me was clearly *way* more important. Imagine that diary clash as a 12-year-old, attending Live Aid or receiving a chemistry prize, and then going with the latter?

And so the phrase 'Pup Aid' was born. It was now just a case of taking it from its warm foamy bath surroundings to the many dog-lovers of Brighton, surrounding areas, and perhaps eventually beyond. Regarding finding a suitable venue, I definitely wanted to move away from Brighton Racecourse and was already friends with a girl called Rebecca Weller, or 'Bex' for short, who was the event organiser at a nearby venue called Stanmer House. This stunningly restored Grade 1 country house on the outskirts of Brighton is set in acres of peaceful, open-access Sussex woodland and countryside – basically a dog-walkers' paradise.

I discussed Pup Aid with Bex, another huge animal-lover, herself owned by two cats, Chili and Pickle, and we decided to hold this rebranded puppy farm awareness event in the large gardens of Stanmer House. It would be held exactly one year on from the World's Biggest Puppy Party, keeping with the original month of Puppy Mill Awareness Day over in the States.

In early 2010 Bex and I started to plan the inaugural Pup Aid puppy farm awareness day for that September. First on the agenda, in common with any public event, was the need for a flyer, a logo, and a brand. As a homage to Live Aid, and keen to make the flyer design as both dog- and music-related as possible, I decided to draw from Live Aid's iconic poster design concept, which for those of you who don't remember, or weren't even born, featured a guitar's headstock (that knobbly bit at the top of a guitar housing the pegs that hold the strings), which then morphed into the map of Africa via the capital 'i' in 'Live', and capital 'i' in 'Aid'. However, for our Pup Aid version, my Swedish friend Milton and I swapped the African continent with the thick end of a dog chew instead!

The inspiration for Pup Aid's original poster was even showcased when I was booked to appear on the *Alan Titchmarsh Show* to discuss microchipping, lost pets, and GPS pet trackers. Whenever appearances on these daytime shows are in the diary, they're always preceded a few days beforehand by a lengthy phone call with one of the show's researchers, to chat through the item and give them an idea of what I'll say. From my *Paul O'Grady Show* days I learnt to always ask which celebrity guests would be appearing too, partially out of interest, but mainly to recruit them to help spread the word, raise awareness, and/or judge our fun Pup Aid dog show. During this particular call, I was very pleasantly surprised to hear which personalities were also booked to appear on the show with me that week. 'Well we've got confirmed Mel C, AKA Sporty Spice,' said the researcher. 'Ah cool,' I replied, and since I knew there were usually two celebrities on at a time, I asked, 'Anyone else?' The researcher continued, 'And Sir

Bob Geldof from Live Aid as it's their 20-year anniversary'. What a coincidence! Of all the celebs to be on the show with! As you can imagine, I ran around my house in Brighton like an excited schoolboy. Perhaps this is how excited I *should've* been when I was actually offered a free ticket to Live Aid 20 years earlier but turned it down? On the morning of the show I grabbed some Pup Aid posters and flyers to take with me to London, to show the actual co-founder of Live Aid what his campaign had inspired some two decades later. I'll never forget what happened next.

The *Alan Titchmarsh Show* was always recorded live and my item was first up. Alan and I shared the stage discussing the important issue of pet theft, as well as sharing tips on how to prevent your pet being stolen, promoting microchipping, with a few seconds dedicated to high-tech GPS collars which, in those days, had only just become available to buy from retailers.

I still hadn't met Bob Geldof yet as he was on a bit later than me, but when I returned to the green room there he was in all his scruffy glory. Everything around you moves fast in a live TV environment: there's a quick turnaround of guests and lots of anxious-looking production crew frantically running around with clipboards. I knew all that, so not wanting to delay Bob, and also conscious to keep the crew happy, and the show running as smoothly as possible, I only had a few seconds to show him the Pup Aid posters and flyers that were so clearly inspired by his own work a generation ago. As I unraveled one of the posters Bob's eyes lit up. He asked me if I'd just been promoting Pup Aid on the show? I replied no, I was just talking about lost pets and microchipping, and with that, as it was now time for his interview, he grabbed all the posters and flyers out of my hands, and hurriedly walked towards the set to get settled into position for his interview with Alan. Right at the start of his interview segment, Bob Geldof said to Alan, 'The guy who came on in the surgeon's outfit, I didn't quite know what he was doing, he was a vet,' to which Alan confirmed 'Marc the vet, Marc the vet!' Bob nodded and then held up one of the flyers to the camera, 'And he was out the back and just showed me this "Pup Aid".' *Cue audience laughter* 'It's a dog chewy bone in the thing [logo] and he's using it as an animal protection thing or something, so the idea has resonated down.' Moments in animal welfare campaigning don't really get more surreal than that! Speechless, mouth open, I watched Bob on the monitors in the green room. This was one of the first moments that Pup Aid had not only just been endorsed by a huge celebrity, no less than the co-creator of Live Aid itself, but Pup Aid had now been mentioned on primetime telly too. It was being recognised in the mainstream media.

After Sir Bob Geldof came singer and 90s legend Jay Kay from Jamiroquai, who mentioned Pup Aid in his blog soon after. The celebrity dust had started to sprinkle down nicely, with more and more well-known personalities now beginning to support and endorse Pup Aid's campaign to end puppy farming. This TV vet media platform was the only thing I had at my disposal to try and get the message out there about puppy farming and influence public behaviour. In particular, I wanted to reach prospective dog owners so they would be encouraged to only go directly to a breeder and see a puppy interacting with its mum, or better still visit a rescue shelter and consider adopting instead. Whenever I mentioned or invited celebrities and well-known personalities to support Pup Aid's campaign and dog show, I always did my best to represent as many walks of life as possible, so as to try and reach every possible demographic of the British population, from highbrow to tabloid, young and old, dog-obsessive to never-had-a-pet. As long as you agreed that dogs should either be bought direct from the breeder or adopted from rescue, Pup Aid was the campaign for you: totally inclusive, free to support, and an exciting animal welfare campaigning vehicle that everyone, anyone, even their dogs, could enjoy getting involved with.

That September's Pup Aid fun dog show in Brighton was to be a golden opportunity to join together with fellow animal-lovers in person, to enjoy being around lots of lovely dogs, a few celebrities, and acoustic music; it would be an event that anyone could have fun at, while raising awareness about the serious animal welfare issues of puppy farming at the same time.

A special mention must at this point go to Stuart Vernon who, as a friend of another friend, attended the World's Biggest Puppy Party the year previously, and immediately wanted to get involved. An avid dog-lover, Stuart joined Bex and me to help ensure the planning and logistical organisation of Pup Aid was always watertight. Stuart was an expert in doing everything right in terms of contracts, health and safety, and all the other important stuff that must be meticulously planned and signed off behind the scenes: basically all the stuff I was totally useless at! Stuart and Bex's hard work and commitment made Pup Aid's first and subsequent fun dog shows all huge successes, so much so that we were advised to turn Pup Aid into a Community Interest Company (CIC), which by definition is a 'limited company, with special additional features, created for the use of people who want to conduct a business or other activity for community benefit, and not purely for private advantage'. Pup Aid was now a legally bound, volunteer-run, non-profit organisation that was trying to do some good in the world with minimal resources. Bex, Stuart, and I were all equal Directors. Most importantly, our campaign which included the annual fun dog show, complete with celebrity judges, trade stands, live music, a have-a-go agility course, and a parade of rescued ex-breeding dogs, was starting to make an impact.

Celebrities and well-known personalities that came to Brighton to support the first two Pup Aid fun dog shows at Stanmer House included *EastEnders'* Patsy Palmer, actor Mark Williams, and Jasmine Harman, presenter of Channel 4's *A Place in the Sun*. Amongst the many bands and singer song-writers that performed at Pup Aid we were fortunate to host local hip hop duo Rizzle Kicks, a month before they released their first album. Just like Michael Watson's 'Best Boxer Dog' class at the racecourse, we thought up a few relevant classes here too, including 'Best Chocolate Labrador' judged (and featured on their own subsequent TV series) by local chocolatiers Choccywoccydoodah. There was also 'Most Stylish Pooch', judged by local celebrity-tailor and Pug-owner Gresham Blake, alongside style-icon Meg Mathews, whose involvement in Pup Aid would soon prove to be completely game-changing.

Anyone who's ever read or seen an interview with Meg Mathews will already know she's one of the most passionate supporters of animal welfare out there, so when a friend of mine passed Meg's contact details on to me, I was quick to get in touch. It didn't take many email exchanges for us to realise that we were on the same page regarding our views on our four-legged friends. But more relevant was the fact that her Boston Terrier Oscar was thought to have been born on a puppy farm. Shortly after purchasing Oscar, he became very poorly, as we know only too well that most low welfare and irresponsibly bred pups are. Oscar was so ill he required thousands of pounds worth of abdominal surgery just to fix his insides. Thankfully he made a full recovery.

Meg was keen to help us end the terrible conditions that dogs like Oscar were being born into, and asked what she could do to support Pup Aid. I invited Meg to be a judge at both dog shows at Stanmer, which she kindly accepted and for which she travelled down from North London. At the end of the second Pup Aid she took me to one side and suggested we move our dog show up to London, in order to attract more of her celebrity friends, and raise even more awareness. Growing up in north west London I had already thought this one through, and at the same time, as if we'd rehearsed our lines, we both looked at each other and said out loud those two words: 'Primrose Hill!' I invited Meg to be our Patron and she accepted.

Primrose Hill is a super-exclusive and very dog-friendly area of London. Just bordering the upper edge of Regent's Park, the neighbourhood has an intimate village-like feel but is also home to many celebrities, politicians, and successful businesspeople. It has a large park attached containing a famous hill with an iconic viewpoint on top, delivering the most incredible views over London. My parents used to take me and my sister there when we were kids to climb its summit and enjoy pointing out and identifying the various buildings and landmarks that make up the unmistakable London skyline, such as Big Ben and the Houses of Parliament.

What with Pup Aid's forward momentum, at the event itself, online, and in the media, it made sense to move the fun dog show to London, and thankfully Stuart and Bex didn't need much persuasion. But organising a fun dog show in the private garden of a big house in Brighton is slightly different in scale and workload from putting on a Pup Aid fun dog show in a Royal Park. Undeterred, Stuart and I ventured up to London to meet the person we'd now have to convince, Nick Biddle, Park Manager of Regent's Park and Primrose Hill.

Stuart and I explained our campaign to end puppy farming and what we'd already achieved over the last two years back in Brighton. Stuart went into detail about the all-important logistics: litter-pickers, public toilets, first-aiders, security, insurance, and so on. Primrose Hill isn't just a normal park; it isn't even just a normal Royal Park. It is the jewel in the crown of *all* London's parks, if not the UK's. No one had ever put on a big event there; those were generally accommodated by fellow Royal Parks, notably neighbouring Regent's Park, or Hyde Park instead.

Our meeting felt like one of the toughest we'd ever had. Nick is an incredibly charming, friendly man, a dog-lover through and through, and he totally 'got' why holding Pup Aid in Primrose Hill would not only be ideal to promote animal welfare, attract celebrity dog-lovers, but also good for the local community too. But as Park Manager, being confronted, in a nice way, by two compete strangers from Brighton wanting to organise a huge celebrity-judged dog show with music in one of the UK's most exclusive open spaces, Nick was understandably concerned about protecting the grass, benches, trees, lampposts, as well as the park's impeccable reputation.

And then something quite magical happened. As Stuart was busy showing Nick our proposed and very detailed event plan, Nick's recently adopted rescue lurcher pup Dobbie grabbed my woollen beanie hat from out of my bag, galloped across the office, and started chewing a big hole in it. We all looked at each other and laughed. It was as if Dobbie had made Nick's mind up for him. Pup Aid was given the go-ahead for Primrose Hill. I quickly grabbed my half-eaten hat, Stuart and I breathed a huge sigh of relief, and we headed back to Brighton.

Unsurprisingly, Pup Aid in Primrose Hill had to follow certain strict conditions. We now had to play by the Royal Parks' rules. Our flyers and posters needed to change from the Live-Aid-style design to a more English country fête theme. The dog show ring itself had to be a smart, white picket fence, all stalls and branding had to face inwards, and the site had to be cleared of all activity and litter by 6pm on the day. We were more than happy to respect every rule; after all, we had just been given the green light to put on a fun dog show of a size London had probably never seen before. Bex designed the new artwork and invited the stallholders; Stuart got stuck into fulfilling all the guidelines; and I cracked on with inviting celebrities and planning the first Pup Aid London. It didn't take long before September 2012 came around and it was upon us. Being a one-day dog show we didn't have the luxury of getting things delivered the day before and stored in the park. Instead we had everything either dropped off on the day, or sent to Primrose Hill Pets instead – the pet shop and dog groomers in the village that don't sell animals, where Gail and her team very kindly stored everything in their biggest grooming room for our team of volunteers to collect at 5am on the morning of the show.

The first ever Pup Aid in Primrose Hill was a huge success and very overwhelming. With perfect weather we hosted 36 trade stands, a mix of stalls selling doggy accessories, as well as a few smaller animal charities and campaign groups represented too. Our have-a-go agility course was generously provided free of charge by North London doggy daycare Halo Dogs, and just like the last few years in Brighton, the day featured a celebrity judged fun dog show, live music, and of course the parade of rescued ex-breeding puppy farm dogs. Public entry to Pup Aid London was always free, made possible over the years by some very generous sponsors including Barking Heads, Specsavers, Agria, Zoflora, Leucilin, Leivars Design, Pets Pyjamas, and most recently Nutriment.

Celebrities who turned out that day included Ricky Gervais with partner Jane Fallon, Brian May, Peter Egan, Liam Gallagher, Nicole Appleton, Joanna Page, Sarah Harding, Matthew Wright, and of course Pup Aid patron Meg Mathews and her daughter Anais Gallagher to open the show. As the years went on the event grew and grew. Celebrities would arrive, often with their families, help judge the dog show, take part in the assistance dog demonstrations, have a picnic on the grass, and then hang out there for the rest of the day. The paparazzi would also inhabit the VIP area from 10am until 5pm, happily snapping away at celebrities like Elle Macpherson, Sue Perkins, Anna Richardson, David Gandy, Gail Porter, Susie Dent, Peter Crouch, Abbey Clancy, Elle Macpherson, Tony Robinson, Tim Vincent, Sinitta (who famously once arrived wearing an outfit and clutch bag made entirely of dog biscuits), Alice Beer, Lizzie Cundy, as well as various representatives from reality TV shows like Debbie Douglas, Lucy Watson, Callum Best, Kirk Norcross, and in later years stars from *Love Island* too. The wonderful Rachel Riley, one of our biggest supporters who attended numerous times, would arrive with partner and *Strictly Come Dancing* dancer Pasha Kovalev, as well as very kindly promoting Pup Aid on *Countdown* the day before.

Not one celebrity *ever* asked for money in order to attend. They were all happy to give their time and donate plenty of activity on their highly influential social media channels to Pup Aid and raising awareness of puppy farming. They'd post about the signs to look for when buying a responsibly bred pup, as well as the benefits of rescue pet adoption too.

The parade of rescued ex-puppy-farm breeding dogs was an emotional showstopper every year, with individual cruelty stories, each passionately read out to accompany the dog by friend of Pup Aid, the Welsh-toned Leigh-Catherine Salway.

Teams of volunteers would help us every year. We had displays by the Southern Golden Retriever Display Team and Hearing Dogs for the Deaf, to the doggy act finalists from *Britain's Got Talent*, Trip Hazard and Pippa and Buddy. Our compère, owner of rescue Jack Russell Teddy and pub quiz question master extraordinaire, Simon Happily, was always brilliant and highly entertaining; PR companies Belle PR, Borne Media, and celeb-liaison officer Laura Critchley, all worked pro bono, invited their celebrity contacts, and organised photographers. We had created a one-day festival for dog-lovers. In the last few years our friends Owen and his 3-legged dog Haatchi would cut the ribbon to officially open the show. I would make my big speech before the rescued breeders' parade, a rallying cry updating all those present how the campaign was progressing in Westminster. People loved the feeling of being part of change. The stallholders didn't care how much they sold, or how much money they made. The atmosphere was unique; we were all just in it for the dogs.

From its early days in Brighton until 2018 in Primrose Hill, Pup Aid was one of the proudest concepts I've ever come up with. It started with no resources as just an idea shared over a pint, but formed the foundation stone of the whole campaign. Pup Aid made sure puppy farming was talked about by the relevant celebrities and in the mainstream media. Pup Aid made sure puppy farming reached the masses whatever the demographic. Pup Aid provided somewhere for animal-lovers to feel like they were part of a movement, all doing something to improve animal welfare in the UK. Pup Aid was free, inclusive, and could be enjoyed by everyone and their dogs.

Pup Aid also attracted a very special lady to come all the way from the West Midlands each year, a lady accompanied by a tiny black, brown, and white dog: a very important Cavalier King Charles Spaniel by the name of Lucy.

Chapter 11

✿

In those early years of campaigning I had absolutely no idea about lobbying, politics, or what really happened in Westminster. But deep down I was aware that we needed something else to make an impact on this disgusting puppy farming industry. Furthermore, with an exponential rise in popularity of photo-sharing platforms like Twitter and Facebook, and with Instagram close on their heels, the significant noticeable impact and influence that certain celebrities from Lady Gaga to Jonathan Ross, Paris Hilton to Gok Wan were making on pet-purchasing patterns to encourage large-scale breeding like puppy farming was becoming scary. Pictures of cute pedigrees and designer crossbreeds were, and still are, very shareable, especially the flat-faced 'brachycephalic' breeds, such as Pugs and French Bulldogs.

The increased demand for basically any cute purebred dog such as Cavaliers, Labradors, or Miniature Schnauzers, or mixed breeds such as Cockerpoos, Maltipoos, or Schnoodles, was all helping to effectively fuel the greed of puppy farmers who would watch these trends and then breed the most sought-after dogs, both in the UK, and for smuggling in from abroad too.

After five years of working nights and weekends, the out-of-hours work plus the daytime campaigning and media work was taking its toll; it was time to sell my partnership and leave the emergency clinic I'd helped set up. I was happily back to doing locum work around the UK and vetting in the daytime, and no matter which consulting room I was in, in whatever town in the UK, I was constantly seeing and treating the victims of this cruel industry: sick, diseased puppies. It wasn't always the owners' fault for buying these poorly, often dying pups either. Like the vast majority of dog-lovers, they were desperately trying to do the right thing when purchasing their puppy by sourcing them responsibly; here was one of the first major issues that was repeatedly being flagged by distraught owners of these damaged pups.

'We tried to do it properly,' they'd tell me, often through floods of tears, before collecting their thoughts and continuing, 'We visited a licensed pet shop, who assured us that their puppies came from licensed breeders.' And everything about those comments was in fact correct. Pet shops are licensed by the local authorities to sell puppies, kittens, rabbits, fish, and all the rest of the pets we see for sale as disposable commodities on the high street, in garden centres, or from gigantic pet superstores in retail parks across the land. And they do, on the whole, source their puppies from licensed breeders. But puppy farms *are* licensed, and 'licensed' in this case doesn't mean 'good' in terms of animal welfare, merely totally legal, routinely inspected, and officially regulated.

I pictured those sick and dying Jack Russell cross puppies I'd treated in my Brighton emergency clinic a few years back. They were all from a legal licensed dealer that I'd visited just outside Brighton, buying in pups from a legal licensed puppy farmer in Wales. Legal it might be, but the system was broken, definitely wasn't working for the animals, and worse still, it was being abused on a massive scale.

Looking ahead, it was clear something more than a celebrity-judged fun dog show was called for, and it wasn't just me saying that. Other concerned, like-minded individuals and animal welfare organisations were now reaching out and starting conversations, all keen to do something about this increasing puppy farming problem. I remember being invited to attend a meeting at the British Veterinary Association (BVA) that brought together similar-thinking individuals for a proper brainstorm; I'd been invited for creating Pup Aid and had a useful media profile as a TV vet. Looking back nothing really came of that particular meeting, except that I sat next to a very confident Australian lady by the name of Linda Goodman who'd founded a Wales-based campaigning organisation called C.A.R.I.A.D., which stood for 'Care And Respect Includes All Dogs'. 'Cariad' also means 'beloved' in Welsh. And Linda didn't just live in any part of Wales; she was based in Pembrokeshire, surrounded on all sides by licensed legal puppy farms, just like the ones Lucy was born into. I'd already heard of the good work C.A.R.I.A.D. was doing, including Linda spending seven days and seven nights in an outbuilding, livestreamed 24/7 on Facebook, to help raise awareness of the sensory deprivation experienced by breeding dogs in puppy farms. It takes a real character to not only think outside the box and come up with ideas like that to raise awareness, but also to actually then go through with it *and* make it a success. Unsurprisingly, Linda was not only a huge dog-lover but also had a background in creative advertising as well, so naturally, with the influence of my dad's career as an advertising executive, we got on very well, quickly becoming firm friends. We agreed back then that we could probably achieve more by all these individuals and organisations present at the meeting working together for the same goal; or so Linda and I innocently thought. We would chat every night on the phone for hours; we were kindred spirits living hundreds of miles away from one another, desperate to find a way, a path, *something* to help end puppy farming with. Over the next few weeks and months, the late-night chats and hundreds of emails backwards and forwards, we came to the conclusion that there's one single thing that the majority of puppy farms have in common: their extensive dealer network.

In the spirit of trying something different campaign-wise, I cautiously dipped my little toe into a completely new world, a world with very different surroundings from any consulting room operating theatre, dog show, or TV studio I'd ever worked in, a place found on the banks of the River Thames called Westminster. Back then Westminster was little more to me than a gothic, intimidating cathedral-like group of buildings full of real-life *Spitting Image* puppets; oh, and Big Ben was there too. My first few visits to Westminster were all very different and you'll laugh at how inexperienced I was when it came to meeting a politician. One of my first meetings in those days was with a certain Mr Neil Parish, Conservative MP for Tiverton and Honiton. I'd contacted Mr Parish after meeting him at the annual MPs' Westminster Dog of the Year fun dog show, which I'd been invited to help judge. Taking place in Victoria Tower Gardens, in the shadow of the House of Lords, Mr Parish's Labrador Wilberforce won the trophy. We briefly chatted about puppy farming and he generously invited me to contact his office to arrange a meeting with him. When the date of our meeting arrived, as well as my notes and a memory stick containing my well-rehearsed PowerPoint presentation, I also took in with me my mum, grandma, and her friend and fellow Holocaust survivor Otto Deutsch. It was like we'd entered a competition on the back of a cereal packet to 'meet an MP', and now here we all were, gathered in Central Lobby, all waiting to receive our prize. Mr Parish was very kind to us all, a perfect host who made us feel very welcome. He watched and listened to my presentation, gave his honest opinion, and even entertained us all with drinks on the Commons Terrace afterwards.

I was also contacted by one of my local MPs, Mrs Caroline Lucas. Caroline had attended and helped judge at the World's Biggest Puppy Party at Brighton Racecourse a few years back, so we had actually met before. She needed some advice about which dog to choose for her family, so she invited me around to her house for a cup of herbal tea and a chat. After agreeing that adopting was the best way forward for her circumstances, a rescued black Labrador soon became the newest member of the Lucas family. Caroline was keen to repay the favour, and was genuinely interested in how far my campaign had progressed. She invited me up to her office in Westminster for a proper meeting. In those early days Westminster was so alien to me, and I always compare going there to that scene in *Gladiator* when the slaves first enter the Colosseum, and are gazing up in awe at the high walls and imposing architecture.

Just like Neil Parish before her, Caroline made me feel very welcome, listened to what I had to say, and then asked if I'd considered starting something called a 'government e-petition'. Being so inexperienced in all things political, I had no idea what that even meant! Caroline explained that one of the most effective ways to get a campaign on the 'political radar' was using this fairly recently devised and free online tool. If, after a year (it was a year in those days – it's six months now), your petition collected 100,000 signatures, then the subject of your petition would be considered for debate in Parliament. I immediately thought that, what with my media profile and celebrity contacts, surely collecting 100,000 signatures was not only very doable, but would probably only take a few days. After all, in just a couple of weeks, Brian May's badger petition had just collected hundreds of thousands of signatures, presumably from attracting a similar animal welfare crowd, so how hard could it be? How naive! I wrote the petition and submitted it, and on 2 May 2013, e-petition number 49528 was published on the government's website:

Ban the sale of young puppies & kittens without their mothers being present

Puppies & kittens mass produced in horrific puppy/kitten farms are separated from their mothers too early, transported long distances & sold via pet shops, newspaper ads, websites & private dealers.

These puppies/kittens suffer:

Impaired immune systems
Painful diseases requiring costly treatment
Shorter life spans
Poor socialisation leading to behavioural issues

Prospective owners should always:

Ask 'Where's Mum?'
Insist on seeing puppy/kitten & mother interacting
Be aware of scams e.g. fake/no mother present

In summary, and aided by a very strict character count (not even word count), this is what was being asked of government as the first major step in solving the UK's worsening puppy farming crisis. I even used ampersands to save on characters and fit in even more info in. By clicking submit and seeing the petition go live after a few days waiting for approval, the campaign was now onto the next level of trying to make a difference, even though I had absolutely no idea how huge this step would prove to be, on so many levels. By nicknaming the petition the 'Where's Mum?' petition, as it was mentioned in the text, the resulting #wheresmum hashtag became a vital tool in what was shaping up to be a very important political campaign.

At that time I was working at a clinic in Southwick, near Brighton. I'd been employed to set up a branch practice belonging to an independent local chain. As it happened planning permission hadn't yet been agreed for external signage, so as well as vetting I was also using my PR, branding, and marketing skills to bring clients and their pets in. I was giving branding and PR lectures at all the big vet conferences so relished this challenge. Needless to say the combination of school visits, weekly newspaper columns, social media, and events made sure we were kept busy in the daytime, and proved that I could apply the basics of branding to anything, which was a good rehearsal for what was to come. Furthermore one of the events I organised was a talk on puppy farming, attended by a representative of the local free newspaper that advertised a pet shop selling puppy farm pups. Off the back of that meeting I was invited to the paper's headquarters, so took with me three ex-puppy-farm dogs. They were so shocked by the state of the dogs that they agreed to put a big warning sign that I designed in their paper amongst the pet adverts but alas, after just five weeks, it was removed. I presumed money was more important than stopping puppy farm cruelty.

Throughout 2013, I travelled up to Westminster every Tuesday on my day off from vet work; I felt the need to meet with MPs, discuss and explain to them the puppy farming issues and the solutions my petition put forward, and hopefully recruit some more MPs to support the campaign too. I would always have the petition open on my laptop in my consulting room back at the practice, and it wasn't long before clients coming to see me with their pets were asking about it, what it all meant, and how they could also get involved. My clients loved being part of the campaign, signing and sharing the petition and feeling part of positive change for animal welfare. It's an amazing energy to observe radiating from someone standing in front of you with their pet, and these moments definitely helped inspire me to continue the campaign with even more passion.

The petition quickly collected signatures, aided by numerous clients of my clinic, readers of my columns, and various high-profile celebrities like Ricky Gervais who I'd had the pleasure of meeting privately to quietly explain the campaign to, just before an afternoon charity tea party in Hampstead in aid of Mayhew, arranged by animal welfare legends Angela and Martin Humphery. I would tweet the petition link multiple times a day, and share it on my Marc the Vet and Pup Aid Facebook pages too – always including the signature #wheresmum hashtag. Just a few weeks later, the petition was recognised in Westminster in an actual debate for the first time by Luciana Berger MP. In June 2013, roughly one month after the 'Where's Mum?' petition went live, Members of Parliament were debating 'Dog Control and Welfare' in Westminster Hall, and Luciana generously acknowledged that the petition had already quickly gained over 30,000 signatures, saying:

'Does my honourable Friend wish to join me in congratulating Pup Aid, which put together the petition, and Marc Abraham, who is the vet leading the charge? I hope the Government will sincerely respond to the need to consider dog breeding, particularly the need not to separate pups from their mothers too soon.'

To be mentioned by an MP in Hansard was, and still is, a big deal for a grassroots campaigner like myself. 'Hansard' is the name of the official transcript and report of every single debate that's ever happened in Parliament going back hundreds of years, either in the Main Chamber of the House of Commons (the one you see on telly with the green benches), the House of Lords (red benches), or their smaller sibling, Westminster Hall. To be mentioned in Hansard means you've been noticed, you're making a difference. Caroline Lucas was right: we were starting to appear on the political radar. Trying to get the 'Where's Mum?' petition to 100,000 followers was easily one of the hardest, most stressful things I've *ever* done; I was so inexperienced and optimistic when I submitted it. But what with the amount of repetition on social media, sending begging emails to organisations like online vet pharmacies and pet insurance companies with huge databases and bigger reaches, from friendly charities and other non-profit organisations to other like-minded campaigners, animal-lovers from all corners of the pet sector appeared to be coming together and embracing something potentially game-changing for the future of dog-breeding and selling in the UK.

To my surprise, not every animal-loving brand or organisation you'd expect to get involved was keen to play a part in this campaign for positive change. Pathetic excuses were offered from certain pet brands and even animal welfare organisations, such as 'We never get involved in politics,' or 'We don't sell puppies so it's not relevant to us,' which I found a bit odd at the time, considering these same brands were claiming to prioritise animal welfare! What could be simpler than all coming together and making change happen, even if it just meant getting the subject aired and debated by MPs in Westminster?

At that time, I was so preoccupied with thanking those animal-lovers actually helping the campaign, that I just ignored the naysayers, pressed on, and tried to engage others, always out of sheer desperation – almost an obsession – to reach that 100,000 target. During the high 80-90,000s, when it was looking very likely we were going to reach our goal, I received invitations from two of the UK's largest animal welfare organisations to visit their rescue centres and have a picture with one of their rescue dogs, which I accepted. They both then made accompanying statements via press releases offering their full, committed, unequivocal support for the campaign. Another of the UK's big charities, the same one that called for a total ban on the sale of puppies in pet shops in 2009, then shared the petition on their Facebook page too; it seemed like everyone was united by the 'Where's Mum?' petition, finally working together, from big animal welfare charities to the pet owners in my consulting room.

In order to collect more signatures, Pup Aid supporter Steve Fletcher, who runs a TV production company, kindly asked one of my favourite comedy actors Mark Heap (*Big Train, Green Wing, Friday Night Dinner*) to star in a short YouTube video with the petition link attached, which he agreed to do for free. This helped us accumulate thousands more signatures, and was another good example of having limited resources and making the most impact. You can watch the video, based on an old Yellow Pages advert, and which still makes me laugh, by searching for 'Crazy Puppy Party'. Enjoy!

Finally we did it! It took everyone who supported it six hard months, but we did it: we'd reached 100,000 signatures on what was one of the largest ever government e-petitions for domestic pets of all time. It was an amazing feeling of achievement and incredible relief! But then it dawned on me: what the hell do I do next? It's one thing having no knowledge of how the parliamentary system works, but another to have a debate there that you've instigated by drawing on the support of tens of thousands of animal-loving members of the British public. I couldn't possibly let everyone down, and especially not the dogs. So I started putting some feelers out. Apparently, there were experts called 'public affairs consultants' out there that specialised in this kind of thing, i.e. changing government policy and laws using various tried and tested methods, formulas, and parliamentary know-how. My increased presence in Westminster led to various invites to high-profile gatherings in London in the evenings, such as political fundraisers, charity events, even animal-related movie screenings. I was still vetting near Brighton in the daytime, but now also on the lookout for a public affairs consultant in London by night. All pretty normal, right? I was desperate for a contact, a business card to pursue, any link or recommendation – basically any hook that would help me get to the next level of this brand-new parliamentary game in which I'd found myself.

Every Tuesday on my day off I'd meet representatives from all different parties, attend receptions inside the Palace of Westminster, and even speak at rallies outside in Old Palace Yard, or on Parliament Square itself. I was now being labelled a 'TV vet and animal welfare campaigner' and got invited to speak at various events inside Parliament too, honoured and proud to support a range of campaigns and organisations I believed would help improve animal welfare, both domestic and wild. On topics from fox-hunting to wild animals in circuses, dog-fighting to puppies sold in pet shops, I was quickly becoming more active in Westminster and better at public speaking. The invites arrived to speak at various party conferences across the UK, spreading the word about animal welfare, getting my face known by meeting more MPs, and gathering further support for my Pup Aid campaign.

But I still desperately needed that public affairs contact. It finally happened at the close of a political fundraising event in London, when a nice lady who had been sitting across from me and who had clearly been listening in to my conversations handed me a small piece of paper with a mobile number and the name 'Jo' scribbled on it in pencil. Shoving it into my palm, the woman leaned in close, said 'She'll help you!' and with that, almost like a fairy godmother in an old Disney movie, she disappeared.

The next day I nervously called the number on the paper, Jo answered, and yes, it turned out she could in fact help me. We arranged to meet at one of the coffee shops near Wimbledon Station the following Tuesday. After explaining where the campaign had got to so far, with 100,000 signatures on a government e-petition that was pretty much guaranteed a debate in Westminster, Jo, who confessed to being owned by two black cats which she proudly showed me on her phone, told me about this public affairs consultancy run by her partner Mark, called Bellenden Ltd (now Newington Comms).

An even bigger world was opening up. My first meeting with Bellenden was fascinating. I explained the whole 'Where's Mum?' backstory and goals of the Pup Aid campaign: to ban third-party puppy dealers, make all breeders accountable, promote rescue, and ultimately to end puppy farming. Mark and his general manager Nikki, both experts in the finer details of parliamentary procedure, were also both huge animal-lovers so naturally very sympathetic to the campaign; as a result they very generously offered to work with me pro bono, absolutely free of charge. This helped to save the campaign thousands and thousands of pounds, which of course we didn't have. I was effectively turning up on their doorstep with a lump of campaigning gold in the form of a 100,000 signature e-petition, and remember my first meeting so clearly, particularly Nikki's reaction to the progress made by the campaign in Westminster so far: she exclaimed 'You're ripping up the Parliamentary rule book!' to which I replied, 'I wasn't even aware there was a rule book?'

Nikki and Mark would set me homework. First up I had to find an MP to champion the petition and lead our debate in Westminster, while Bellenden would help prepare the briefings and arrange a 'drop-in' event for MPs. All of a sudden, I was starting to do things properly, translating the campaign into a language used, understood, and spoken by the decision-makers themselves. Briefing documents were prepared (briefing documents are basically one to two pages of A4 summarising the campaign objectives, facts, and possible solutions, to which MPs will often refer to in debates). Parliamentary 'drop-in' events happen in rooms in Westminster, booked or 'sponsored' by an MP, and usually colleagues from all different parties are invited to attend to learn more about the campaign. MPs collect literature (usually briefings), and sign a pledge or have their picture taken with the campaign placard and/or banner which can then be used on their social media channels, local newspaper articles back in their constituencies, or on their own websites and blogs. From a campaigner's point of view these drop-in events mean the support of various MPs and political parties can be quantified, any questions or issues from MPs addressed, as well as the photos taken used on the campaign's social media platforms too.

But you can't just book any old room in Westminster for a drop-in, so I had to find an MP who would agree to lead the campaign in Parliament. Back in my very early campaigning days I attended a meeting in the rather ornate surroundings of the Jubilee Room in the annexe of Westminster Hall, hosted by the then Labour MP for Stoke-on-Trent South, Mr Rob Flello. Mr Flello, inspired by his handsome rescued German Shepherd called Diesel, had invited interested parties to come together for a discussion about puppy farming and, more importantly, what could be done to help put an end to it. I was particularly impressed with Rob's sensitivity and determination towards this subject, so I stayed behind after the meeting had finished, introduced myself, and we exchanged contact details. Rob and I continued our dialogue, and, impressed with his passion and commitment to ending puppy farming, I invited him to join me for lunch during the Labour Party Conference in Brighton. I nervously asked if he'd consider spearheading Pup Aid's campaign in Westminster and leading the 'Where's Mum?' e-petition debate in the

Commons. After less than one second Rob graciously agreed. We became a close-knit team, and before long, good mates. We met regularly in Westminster to share campaign updates, and I'd happily travel up to his constituency of Stoke-on-Trent, and judge fun dog shows for his local rescue shelter, Animal Lifeline, from where Rob's beloved Diesel was adopted.

Back in Westminster the Backbench Business Committee, the group of MPs responsible for deciding when and in which debating chamber e-petition debates are held, offered me debate dates in the smaller Westminster Hall chamber. But Rob and I had made an unconventional pact: namely, that the plight and future of puppy farm dogs deserved to be discussed in the debating chamber with the *highest* profile. So we kept refusing Westminster Hall, determined to wait for the Main Chamber of the House of Commons instead. To give us and the dogs our best chance of this ever happening, I needed to convince the Backbench Business Committee that a substantial number of MPs from all parties would be interested in attending. With that, I temporarily stopped working as a vet, and took advantage of my best mate Russell's empty flat in Surbiton as he'd just moved in with his girlfriend. For the next two months I travelled up to Surbiton every Monday night and stayed for three nights, going into Westminster every day by train; then I'd return to Brighton late Thursday evening, deliberately matching most MPs' working week in Parliament.

In order for the 'Where's Mum?' debate to be heard in the Main Chamber I needed to guarantee to the Backbench

Business Committee that a significantly higher number of MPs would attend than a typical e-petition debate in the smaller Westminster Hall. I was now determined to enlist even more MPs to back Pup Aid's campaign. It was necessary to engage with them, meet them in the flesh, explain the whole backstory, and ask for their support. With a total of 650 MPs to potentially connect with in just a few weeks, you can imagine this was a pretty daunting task, especially with zero experience in the art of 'parliamentary lobbying'.

To improve my chances of connecting with the most appropriate MPs, I read old Hansard reports, noting exactly who'd spoken out in animal welfare debates in the past, and began reaching out to those Members. I contacted their offices, and the majority of resulting meetings were arranged in the atrium of Portcullis House, the modern-looking building opposite Big Ben.

With security in Parliament understandably strict, visitors are only allowed to sit in the atrium if accompanied by either an MP or an MP's member of staff. So apart from a few meetings in MPs' own offices, and a few in the various ornate tea rooms over in the Palace, I arranged back-to-back meetings in the atrium in order to be able to stay at the same table, always accompanied by a pass holder. It meant that I could save valuable time by not having to keep going out and coming back in, repeating the whole security process again and again. MP after MP arrived at my table, we'd chat about the campaign, and if supportive I'd invite them to attend the 'Where's Mum?' debate, hopefully taking place in the Main Chamber soon.

Over the next eight weeks, I arranged lobbying meetings in Westminster every Tuesday, Wednesday, and Thursday. All in all, during that time I managed to successfully persuade and convince over 90 MPs from different parties to support Pup Aid's 'Where's Mum?' campaign. Now I just needed to let the all-important Backbench Business Committee know, to try and persuade them to let us have the petition debated in the Main Chamber rather than the less prestigious Westminster Hall. This was a huge task, especially for someone with no background in politics, with minimal resources or PR opportunities in Westminster.

One such opportunity soon presented itself. I would always watch *This Week* on the BBC, hosted by much-feared Scottish journalist Andrew Neil. Occasionally Andrew would bring on set his own dog, a beautiful Golden Retriever called Molly he'd nickname 'hashtag Molly the dog'. One night, I had a silly idea that I hoped might just work. Just after midnight, when the show had finished, I emailed 'Molly the dog' using the contact details on the programme's website and explained the campaign.

The next morning I was pleasantly surprised to see I'd already received an immediate reply. The email had found its way into the producer's inbox, and now one of the BBC's highest-profile political programmes was keen to highlight, support, and feature my Pup Aid campaign to ban puppies sold without their mums, to help end puppy farming, and discuss our all-important 'Where's Mum?' petition debate. The daytime version of the show, the hugely popular *Daily Politics*, was prepared to give us valuable airtime on a programme closely watched and forensically examined by political commentators and parliamentarians. Over the next few days I worked closely with the production team and even filmed a short video with a litter of eight responsibly bred two-month-old chocolate Labrador pups at a vet practice in North London. This video, together with some disturbing puppy farm footage, was to be shown on the live *Daily Politics* episode on which I had now been invited into the BBC studios in Millbank, Westminster, to be their guest contributor!

There I was sitting on the expert panel, alongside Labour MP Maria Eagle, Conservative MP Mark Harper, and hosts Andrew Neil and Jo Coburn. Our segment was shortened because of a slightly extended Prime Minister's Questions so I didn't have much time. They played the film with the chocolate Labrador pups and the clip of the undercover puppy farm footage, then proceeded to ask me about Pup Aid's 'Where's Mum?' campaign and petition. I voiced my concerns about overproduction of dogs, celebrity and social media influences on puppy buying, and responsible dog breeding, before pointing out the hypocrisy of the government ignoring their own guidelines by telling prospective puppy buyers to always see the mum with the pup, yet still giving out licenses to puppy dealers to sell pups without mum present. 'Effectively,' I said, 'government is warning people against its own licensing system.' And it was *that* comment, apparently, that proved to be the straw that broke the camel's back with the Backbench Business Committee's, because the next day after my appearance on *Daily Politics* I received a private message on Twitter from that Committee, demanding an urgent meeting with me in Westminster. So with trepidation I met with the MP who chairs the committee, and she admitted that my comments the day before accusing the government of hypocrisy had caused a bit of a stir. So far so good.

It was now eight weeks since I'd stopped vetting and moved temporarily to Surbiton to start the mammoth task of lobbying as many MPs as I could. I knew the question was coming and had the answer ready. 'How many MPs are now on board with your campaign?' she asked, quickly followed by 'And how likely are they to attend the debate?' It's worth noting at this point that the average number for MPs attending an e-petition debate in those days was around six to ten, hence the smaller Westminster Hall chamber was more than appropriate for these debates. 'About 90,' I replied, proudly unravelling a piece of paper containing the full list of names of cross-party Members of Parliament I'd engaged with in the last two months. '90?!' asked the Chair of the Backbench Business Committee, 'Well that's a three-hour debate in the Main Chamber then!' With that she picked up the phone and immediately dialed her diary team, reserving us a three-hour slot at the earliest opportunity 4 September, the first Thursday back after the summer recess. Not bad for a silly idea.

We'd done it! All that lobbying had paid off, as had the pact with Rob Flello MP to stay firm and repeatedly, and always respectfully, refuse offers of Westminster Hall. Pup Aid's 'Where's Mum?' petition was going to be debated in the most famous and prestigious room in the world, the Main Chamber of the UK House of Commons. And it was nothing less than this country's dogs deserved.

Chapter 12

❦

September 4, 2014: a sunny, crisp autumnal day in London, MPs were back in Westminster after summer recess, and the day of the 'Where's Mum?' Main Chamber debate had arrived.

We were asking the Government to 'ban the sale of young puppies & kittens without their mothers being present' and had overwhelming support from the public, many of the UK's largest animal welfare organisations, over 90 MPs, and numerous high-profile celebrity animal-lovers too.

Our pre-debate drop-in event for MPs in Westminster, hosted by Rob Flello, and organised free-of-charge by Bellenden, was hugely successful in attracting dozens of cross-party MPs, all keen to pledge their support, and confirm that they'd attend the debate and speak out for the dogs and cats. I travelled up to Media City in Manchester the Saturday beforehand for a five-minute interview on the famous red BBC *Breakfast* sofa to discuss the campaign and forthcoming debate. We'd made the front page of the *Independent*, and were to be broadcast live on both the BBC

Parliament TV channel and online for the whole world to watch. With over 90 MPs that we knew of all committed to supporting the motion to ban cruel puppy dealers, and none that we knew of voting against, this impressive stage was *surely* set for a massive landslide animal welfare victory.

As our 'Where's Mum?' debate was scheduled for the afternoon, I thought it would make sense to hand the petition into 10 Downing Street first. Over the previous few months, while my interest in politics was developing, I'd noticed other campaigners and petitioners pictured outside that famous black door, proudly holding a print-out or fake ballot box symbolising a petition that had also collected 100,000 signatures. So a few weeks in advance I made some enquiries, filled in the necessary application paperwork, and booked our slot. Understandably Metropolitan Police and Downing Street security need enough time to run any necessary checks, and confirm our authorisation and access to this most special of addresses. Groups of individuals are only allowed a strict, set number of people for petition hand-ins too, so naturally I was joined by fellow Pup Aid directors Bex and Stuart, along with actor and animal welfare campaigner Peter Egan, Pup Aid official photographer Julia Claxton, and my mum! None of us had ever stood outside the famous Number 10 door before so you can imagine how excited we all were – and with our 100,000 signature petition it felt like we'd earnt the right to be there. Visiting Downing Street for the first time is an experience that I'll never forget, as a grassroots campaigner getting the opportunity to take my campaign to the front door of the chief decision-maker, but also as the culmination of a very personal effort. Being allowed through those gates, walking up Downing Street, and then seeing *that* door for the first time was overwhelming; it felt like the best reward for what had so far been achieved. After a few photos taken with us proudly holding a mounted printout of the online petition displaying its 100,000 signatures, we knocked on the knocker, and the door slowly opened. The police officer inside politely shook my hand and took the petition from us, and we spent the next few minutes taking as many selfies and group pictures in front of the door as humanely possible, all of us grinning from ear to ear like excited kids, as you do when outside such an important iconic landmark; we knew it was unlikely for any of us to return to Number 10 ever again in our lifetimes.

We left Downing Street, turned right down Whitehall, and headed towards the Houses of Parliament. This was just the beginning of what was to be a huge day for many reasons. I was nervous but excited: it's not every day you get to attend a three-hour debate in the House of Commons that you've literally *made* happen. We met up with Rob Flello who was putting the finishing touches to his opening speech, grabbed a snack, and waited for my dad and grandma to arrive.

Watching the 'Where's Mum?' debate on 4 September 2014 from the Public Gallery was one of the most fascinating experiences of my life, not to mention another huge learning curve for how politics works. I had no real previous knowledge about debates and parliamentary procedures and as such I was still like a big sponge – but that's how you learn the fastest, by being in the thick of it. Every single MP I'd met in the previous few months showed up, honouring their commitment from our numerous meetings in the Portcullis House atrium, elegant tea rooms of the Palace of Westminster, and successful drop-in session. Rob's opening speech was excellent, covering every point and giving credit to individuals and organisations that had been constructive with our Pup Aid campaign to date. On a lighter note, the debate provided a rare opportunity for Members to mention their own much-loved pets, such as Rob Flello's dog Diesel, just to make sure their names appeared in Parliament's permanent Hansard records! The three hours allotted for our debate passed incredibly quickly, with all MPs instructed by the Speaker to keep their speeches within a specific time limit so everyone could be heard. It was apparent that other animal welfare organisations had also sent in their briefings from which MPs read aloud extracts, as well as Pup Aid's. Once the opposition bench had summed up, it was time for the eagerly awaited vote and final statement from the Minister. Desperately hoping we were about to witness one of the greatest moments in animal welfare history, we all held our breath, anxiously waiting to hear that cruel puppy dealers who enable and encourage puppy farming to happen behind closed doors would now be banned by the government, thus making all dog breeders accountable.

Chapter 12

At this point I must declare a deeply personal reason why this debate and its imminent vote and decision were even more important and significant to me. On 21 November 1938, just over 76 years and 2 months before Mum, Dad and Grandma found ourselves sitting in the Commons Public Gallery, debate was held in this very same Main Chamber to discuss whether Britain would be prepared to accept more Jewish refugees escaping from Germany, including unaccompanied children. The Hansard report from that debate is an exhilarating read. At 9.35pm, Sir Samuel Hoare, Home Secretary of the day, took the stand and confirmed that as a result of a meeting that morning, with the promise of the Jewish community providing funds, the Home Office would waive visas so that child refugees could be brought to Britain on what would become known as the 'Kindertransport'. Watching the 'Where's Mum?' debate and sitting next to my grandma, a child who herself escaped on that very same Kindertransport, it hit home that she was only alive – and therefore I was only alive – because of *that* debate here, in the same Main Chamber. And here we were, listening to a debate in the Main Chamber which was largely down to me, inspired by my grandma's story, not being prepared to give up, and fighting for every one of those 100,000 signatures. Talk about things coming full circle! It was a moment of profound emotion and realisation for both of us. If you ever visit the Houses of Parliament, do make sure you check out the plaque commemorating the Kindertransport children, and salute Britain's act of generosity to Jewish children in Nazi-occupied Europe; it can be found just off Central Lobby before the stairs up to the Public Gallery.

Our three-hour 'Where's Mum?' debate was almost over. Every MP had made their speech, most had read from our briefing and mentioned their pets, with every MP overwhelmingly supporting the motion, and then all subsequently voting for a ban on the sale of young puppies and kittens without their mothers being present. Surely, we must've done it. But as the Government Minster rose to his feet to sum up and give the government's response, I remembered a private meeting with some familiar faces I'd briefly glimpsed on the way to the Chamber, and thought that maybe, just maybe, not everyone wanted this to happen. The next few minutes were some of the most disappointing I'd ever experienced. Not only did the Government fully reject the motion, despite an overwhelming 'Aye' vote in the Chamber from every single MP present, but the reasons given by the Minister for rejecting the ban were not only clearly a result of serious misinformation, but they were also devoid of any actual evidence and based on pure speculation instead. The penny dropped. There were forces working behind the scenes to make sure our proposal for the ban didn't happen, and it was my next mission to find out who it was.

Chapter 12

The pet industry's stance on puppies sold in pet shops was an interesting and slightly confusing one. They appeared to oppose the concept but were downright against a ban, so much so that it appeared it was their briefing, later shared with me by a friendly MP, which appeared to have been solely responsible for the Government's rejection of the debate. I presumed the reason why the pet industry opposed a ban on puppies and kittens sold in pet shops was that it might eventually lead to a ban on rabbits, guinea pigs, gerbils, fish, and every other animal that's sold off the shelves as commodities, especially from those big retail pet chains across the country. It was a slippery slope down which I, as an animal-lover, would be incredibly proud to start the ball rolling down.

A few weeks after the dust had settled following the disappointing debate result in Westminster, it was important to gather my thoughts and try and regroup with other campaigners fighting for the same thing. I'm often asked if I ever considered giving up during the campaign, especially at moments like this. The thing is, when you've met up with so many MPs, know all the facts and evidence with which to provide them, and are starting to build strong relationships with these key decision-makers, you feel as though your brain starts to resemble one of those crazy murals in crime thrillers like *24* or *Homeland*, one made entirely of post-it notes, newspaper cuttings, photos, quotes, and pins, all somehow linked together with random pieces of string and elastic bands. That's what it feels like inside a campaigning brain. Everything, from

MP's pets' names to statements made in debates, is related to something or someone else. Besides, bailing out would mean giving up on the dogs, and let's face it, that was *never* going to happen. I was determined to see this through for them, however long it took. And I wasn't alone in this; thankfully there were a few others out there with exactly the same goals and ambitions.

In the autumn of 2014, roughly one month after the 'Where's Mum?' debate had been rejected in the Commons, a handful of us met at the Twickenham office of Mark Randell, an ex-police officer who was now CEO of Hidden Insight, an undercover investigations agency specialising in animal welfare crime. Also present meeting was my friend Linda and her colleague Sue Davey, both from C.A.R.I.A.D., Julia Carr from Canine Action UK, Philippa Robinson from Karlton Index, and Jennie Rudd from Gloucester-based animal welfare charity Naturewatch.

As we sat around the table with our tea and biscuits, I reflected that the enthusiasm and sheer passion was breath-taking – as was the knowledge-base. We all had the same dream: to carry on the campaign to eliminate the selling of puppies as commodities by third-party traders and to bring the exploitation of those poor invisible puppy farm dogs like Lucy to light. Little did we know, sitting around that table on that rainy day in South West London, that from this meeting a core group of campaigners would emerge as the coalition that would ultimately make that change happen.

Before taking on the corridors of power, this time as a campaigning team, it was important to get all our ducks in a row. We really needed to be singing from the same hymn sheet, and all agreed the terms used in the existing legislation regarding puppy breeding and selling were confusing. For example, what was a 'pet shop'? If you asked a hundred people that question, most, if not all, would suggest it's a shop that sells pets. But legislatively speaking, a pet shop is much more than simply a bricks-and-mortar building on the high street. A pet shop means anyone in the possession of a pet shop licence. This outdated piece of legislation is what has allowed puppies to be bought and sold either to the public, or to other pet shop licence holders, for decades. Puppies could be sold from premises such as the sitting room of an ordinary everyday house, or a garden centre, or a riding stables as well as traditional high street pet shops. Pet shop licenses have been widely used by puppy dealers to dupe the public. These middlemen and women have made it impossible for buyers to know exactly where a puppy has originated, and is a route to market that has enabled puppy farming to continue to flourish because it allowed both dealers and puppy farmers to keep breeding dogs like Lucy well hidden from public view. The pet shop licenses used by puppy dealers are what has kept the low welfare and unscrupulous puppy farm trade *legal*.

As a result of these early discussions it was agreed that continuing to use the misleading term 'pet shop' was out of the question; I think it was Julia who first coined the phrase 'commercial third-party puppy dealers' to avoid all ambiguity. The use of 'commercial' i.e. for profit, wouldn't affect non-profit rescues, while 'third party' referred to puppies being sold away from their place of birth, as well as their mothers. The next few months were a bit of a blur. I was visiting Westminster to lobby MPs up to three times a week. Lobbying this frequently meant my vet work was becoming sparse to non-existent and, once again, I took the hit financially. Although Pup Aid fun dog show had its generous sponsors, the extra train tickets and occasional overnighters in London were adding up. At one point I remember being so skint that I collected a load of coppers from around my house, including from behind the sofa, and fed the Coinstar machine in my local Morrisons, one of those machines that noisily converts loose change into a voucher to spend instore, just to afford some beans on toast for dinner. It was like being a broke student again, except now I had a professional veterinary degree. The growing financial stress certainly made campaigning tougher, but it also strengthened my resolve to keep fighting for the dogs.

These were some of the darkest days personally speaking, but they were about to get much darker. Being a campaigner with no resources is hard enough, but when trusted old friends become brand new enemies, things get very interesting, and unsurprisingly, a lot tougher and much more depressing.

Our tiny coalition of voluntary campaigners was about to encounter reminders that perhaps not everyone was on the same side after all. This was particularly disturbing as to me dogs weren't just pets, confidants, and best friends. They were also the one animal we humans had chosen to domesticate over thousands of years to look more appealing or to do jobs that we couldn't ever do, like rounding up sheep, keeping guard, guiding the blind, sniffing out cancer or anticipating seizures, relaying vital messages to troops in the trenches, detecting explosives, and locating dead and injured soldiers and civilians.

We knew, and had proven time and time again, that legal, licensed third-party commercial puppy dealers were the main issue. But in order to change laws the government department responsible for any change in legislation usually looks to the same old key opinion leaders in that sector for guidance and advice – in this case the biggest animal welfare organisations and industry representatives, collectively known as 'stakeholders'. The government tries to achieve a general agreement, seeks a 'consensus', and only then is it usually in a position to move forward. Without consensus, we were told repeatedly, there would be no chance of changing the law. Consensus would surely be easily achieved, we had thought, giving the Department for Environment, Food & Rural Affairs (DEFRA) absolutely no choice but to agree with us all and ban third-party puppy dealers. But was something else going on behind the scenes?

At that time one of the charities launched a high-profile, expensive-looking campaign determined to scrap the puppy trade. What was meant by the 'puppy trade'? The legal licensed third-party trade in puppies which we wanted to stop too? It didn't seem like it to me. I looked deeper and the campaign seemed to end only part of the puppy trade. It intended only to 'scrap' the illegal unlicensed trade. This would effectively protect the very same legal licensed third-party commercial puppy trade which was directly responsible for puppy farming and smuggling.

Another campaign focused on the irresponsible breeding of puppies and abuse of breeding mums. Great, we all thought. However, the campaign seemed to highlight backyard breeding, a very different type of dog breeding and selling, often taking place in inner cities and usually of bull breeds. My concern with this was that it didn't look at puppy farming on large commercial breeding establishments in the UK, Ireland, or Eastern Europe. What we needed was an organisation with significant resources, and, more importantly, sway with the government department responsible for animal welfare, that would fight to to ban the route to market for the legal licensed puppy-farmed pups and their poor mums left behind.

I was pleased to see a campaign that focused its attention on illegal puppy smuggling. This is a big issue, but in my opinion one which could be greatly reduced by banning the only legal route to market for these pups when they arrive on our shores: those legal licensed third-party puppy dealers. We knew that it was also the licensed third-party dealers selling pups away from their mums who effectively provide cover for illegal activity and who have been known to purchase unchipped puppies from illegal breeders to hide their origins. By banning legal dealers, it would become pretty obvious who the illegal ones were. The campaign would describe, again and again, the horrendous conditions on foreign puppy farms, the horrific journeys these pups would endure, some even dying en route. These same descriptions applied equally to the legal licensed third-party trade in the UK that was again being ignored, and thus by default, actually being protected.

These presumably expensive campaigns, reports, and 'shocking' investigations appeared to us guilty of effectively protecting the legal licensed puppy dealers responsible for enabling and encouraging puppy farming and smuggling in the UK. We racked our brains to try and figure out why. These organisations had appeared to be on our side just weeks ago, and now the only consensus being fed to the government was to retain the legal puppy trade, effectively propping up puppy farming and permitting the selling of pups without their mums as long as you were licensed and regulated.

2015 arrived and my coalition of campaigners found ourselves with our work cut out. I vowed to continue fighting. I was invited to give lectures on animal welfare, campaigning, and 'how to make a difference' at respected London and Glasgow vet schools. Back in Westminster, which was quickly becoming my second home, the lobbying wasn't slowing down either, especially with a General Election looming. I got to know even more helpful and supportive cross-party MPs, including Zac Goldsmith, Kerry McCarthy, Alex Chalk, David Amess, Justin Tomlinson, Paul Monaghan, Tracey Crouch, Matthew Offord, Cheryl Gillan, Sheryll Murray, Henry Smith, Roger Gale, Jim Fitzpatrick, and many more. Each party released its election manifesto and I was encouraged to read Labour, Greens, and Liberal Democrats all flagging issues surrounding puppy farming, irresponsible pet breeding and sales, even puppies sold in pet shops.

From speaking at events here and abroad, various TV appearances on Crufts and *The Wright Stuff* here, I was becoming the main media spokesperson against puppy farming and the campaign to ban the dealers that enable it. Other animal welfare events I was involved with around this time included the anti-fox hunting rally, an anti-trophy hunting event I spoke at in aid of murdered Cecil the lion, and the high profile 'March for the Animals' which I helped lead with Brian May and Peter Egan. We walked from Oxford Street to Parliament, calling on politicians to do what's right for animal welfare, with soapbox speeches at the march's final destination in Old Palace Yard.

But still the underlying frustration grew. Whatever was being said in public, by campaigners, MPs, celebrities, small-mid size organisations, and the public themselves, it was all being ignored by the decision-makers and most noticeably their advisors. It was time for a radical move, this

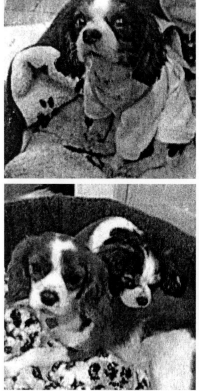

ABOVE Some images that Lucy's fosterer updated to her profile while Lucy was in foster care.
BELOW Lucy when she had not long been rescued from the puppy farm.
RIGHT Lucy enjoying a walk and the sunshine, shortly after her adoption by Lisa.

A PUPPY FARMER THOUGHT I WAS <u>WORTHLESS</u> WHEN I COULD NO LONGER PRODUCE PUPPIES !!! THANKFULLY, I WAS RESCUED & MY FAMILY THINK I'M <u>PRICELESS</u>! STOP THE CRUELTY — <u>STOP</u> PUPPY FARMING!

ABOVE LEFT Lucy raising awareness in her famous 'STOP PUPPY FARMING!' T-shirt.
ABOVE RIGHT Lucy with another one of her awareness raising social media messages.
LEFT My first ever 'Pet Clinic' on Channel 4's Paul O'Grady Show, with guest Bonnie Langford, Paul, and Paul's dog Buster.

Pic: Shutterstock

ABOVE Me as a young boy on holiday. I'm happiest when surrounded by animals, this time some macaws.
RIGHT Lucy and I hanging out at a big pet event in London.
BELOW Lucy, Lisa and I at Pup Aid fun dog show, London.

RIGHT Comedian Ricky Gervais lending his support to the Lucy's Law campaign before one of his SuperNature warm-up gigs in London.
BELOW LEFT Lucy at the Mirror Animal Hero Awards with Paul O'Grady
BELOW RIGHT Lucy at Pup Aid with actor Peter Egan

ABOVE Lucy's Legends celebrate in Downing Street just after their garden party.
LEFT Rachel Riley with Penelope, Pasha Kovalev with Lucy, and I, at Pup Aid fun dog show, London.
BELOW LEFT 'We've done it!'. The front page of the *Daily Mirror*, August 2018.
BELOW RIGHT From L to R: Marc, Linda Goodman (C.A.R.I.A.D.), Dr Lisa Cameron MP and Peter Egan, celebrating passing of Lucy's Law into English legislation in front of the picture of the Borzois in St Stephens Hall, House of Commons.

THE LIFE OF LUCY

TOP LEFT One of the photos sent to Lisa by Lucy's fosterers showing Lucy with a gift Lisa had sent after seeing her picture and write-up online. It was these pictures that made Lisa fall even more in love with Lucy.

TOP RIGHT Lucy with her Superdog rosette after winning a national award.

ABOVE Lucy enjoying a hearty breakfast at St. Pancras Renaissance Hotel London.

RIGHT One of the final pictures Lisa took of Lucy when she was in the hospital, shortly before she passed away.

THIS PAGE: Lucy and Lisa, the dream team!

ABOVE Lucy, Lisa's little angel. Living her best life and wearing a flower garland during a photoshoot at one of Lisa's local parks.

time by Linda Goodman from C.A.R.I.A.D. in Wales. We were still talking with each other every day, sometimes up to four times a day, maybe more, and we were fed up; we'd had enough of the games. How can these big organisations back a campaign to ban cruel puppy dealers one minute, yet appear to convince the government to keep them legal and therefore protect them, the next? Breeding dogs like Lucy were still being bred to death in horrible licensed puppy farms and their sick pups sold remotely via licensed dealers to the unsuspecting public. It was time to try and sort this mess out once and for all. To this end, Linda wrote an email to the CEOs and public affairs officers of all the relevant stakeholders, inviting them to Swansea to meet with our coalition of campaigners for a roundtable discussion. And to our great surprise, they came.

This well-attended meeting allowed us to present all the evidence needed to persuade them to U-turn again, and re-start supporting a ban on third-party puppy dealers. Common ground and consensus of agreement would, you'd think, be easy for everyone round that table, supposedly all under the same umbrella of animal welfare. We had printed out reams of information, data, and evidence to talk through with them. We shared everything we'd ever learned over the years in a last-ditch attempt to bring everyone together to help the dogs. We did everything to put the needs of these dogs on their agenda. We placed gut-wrenching photographic evidence right there in front of them: Linda had made a deeply disturbing film about dogs that had been rescued from a fully licensed Carmarthenshire puppy farm. It seemed to move some, but not others, although the paperwork and evidence we'd amassed did at least seem appreciated. We felt that although there was no immediate acceptance at that meeting that we were right, it was acknowledged that they had underestimated us and our work. We held out hope that this meeting could lead to something substantial in terms of working together from then on. We began holding conversations every few weeks in London under the title of 'puppy steering group'.

After only a handful of meetings, however, the atmosphere became toxic. It seemed that they believed that what we were seeking was pie-in-the-sky thinking, an 'ideal world' scenario that could be dreamt of but scarcely achieved.

What was truly astonishing is that all our expertise and evidence seemed to fall on deaf ears. We did, after all, have lots of experience and knowledge of puppy farming, but were all made to feel like we were just 'emotional' campaigners.

2015 drew to a miserable close after another full-on year of intensive campaigning. Our coalition of volunteers felt exhausted and deflated. It was well over a year on from the excitement and hope of the 'Where's Mum?' debate in Westminster, but any success now seemed further away than ever before. The annual Pup Aid fun dog show in Primrose Hill was getting still bigger and busier, with public appetite for change at an all-time high, but on the flipside puppy farming, puppy dealing, and smuggling were all also increasing too.

I won an Animal Hero Award for being Vet of the Year, as my profile continued to rise, which definitely helped endorse the campaigning. Media headlines, TV coverage, and endless interviews and articles were useful, but didn't amount to bringing about legislation that could effect change.

December 2015 also saw another huge endorsement of our campaign. Months beforehand I was contacted by a US movie documentary producer, Christopher Grimes, who was planning a feature-length documentary on puppy mills and the corruption that enables them to exist. We chatted and DogByDog was released and premiered in NYC and Philadelphia which I attended, took part in Q&A after each screening, was named one of the producers, and also met comedy hero Larry David. I was keen for the movie to be shown in the UK so I organised it to be premiered in the biggest committee room in the Palace of Westminster, to a full house of animal welfare campaigners, making it the only animal-related movie premiere in Parliament! DogByDog is one of the most exciting projects I've ever worked on and whilst in NYC Christopher also taught me one of my favourite, and most inspiring and relevant quotes for any campaigner: 'The arc of the moral universe is long, but it bends toward justice' – Martin Luther King Jr.

More meetings in Westminster followed and on Christmas Day, exhausted and frustrated from all the campaigning, I was invited onto the Sky News sofa with Peter Egan to discuss rescue dog adoption and puppy farming with presenter and Irish setter-owner Kay Burley. I was able to make a heartfelt plea to everyone watching, animal lovers, organisations, politicians, celebrities, and anyone else up that early on Christmas morning: namely, that we are the voice of animals so we all need to step up, and prove that welfare is more important than trade, industry, or whatever other vested interests appeared to be preventing progress to deliver improved health and happiness for our nation's dogs. We must all work together in 2016, I said, to remove these obstacles and make change happen; and with that rallying cry, the most important year of our campaign so far, for reasons both good and bad, was waiting for us just around the corner.

Chapter 13

✿

It wasn't at all obvious at the time, but 2016 was the year everything started to change, albeit very slowly.

2016 was, if you remember, the year that witnessed way more than the average number of celebrity icons passing, including Prince, one of my all-time heroes, as well as David Bowie, Gene Wilder, Muhammed Ali, Gary Shandling, George Michael, and Carrie Fisher – alongside whom I'd had the enormous pleasure of protesting against the dog meat trade, together with her French Bulldog Gary Fisher, outside the Chinese Embassy in London, only six months beforehand. It wasn't just the celebrities dropping like flies which affected the national mood; political earthquakes and divisive results both here and in the US ushered in challenging times. Shock outcomes made the unpredictable appear normal, and placed huge pressures on society, relationships, friendships, even families.

Following on from 2015's disappointments, the future of dog welfare in the UK was looking just as uncertain.

As campaigners, Linda, Sue, Julia, Philippa, Mark and I were still fighting hard for the dogs. We'd copy everyone into emails 20-30 times a day, maybe more, sharing thoughts, ideas, detailed research documents, the latest from Westminster, and even more evidence; these were intense times and remember, we were all working full-time in our other jobs too. I was now permanently based at one of the best vet practices I'd ever worked at, in a small town just six miles east along the coast from Brighton called Peacehaven. The practice manager, Grant, was sympathetic to my campaign work and allocated Tuesdays as my day off, so I could carry on travelling up to London and keep campaigning in Parliament. It was a strange existence; one minute I'd be checking a pet guinea pig for mites, the next discussing puppy farming and banning third-party dealers with a Government Minister. Or I'd be removing a diseased tooth from a dog, and then speaking at a rally against fox hunting. My work/campaigning balance was very satisfying, and at the time I think the two complimented each other well. One-on-one routine consultations with clients and neutering pets are the bread and butter of veterinary work, but also finding myself in a useful position to in some way help influence laws to protect animals was not something I took lightly. I always felt privileged to share my Tuesdays in the Palace of Westminster alongside parliamentarians from all parties, as well as some of the biggest influencers and respected animal welfare organisations involved with influencing the country's animal welfare legislation.

Westminster was now my second home. Some MPs joked that I was there more than they were! Occasionally I'd need to be there on a Wednesday too, and Grant would kindly allow me an extra day off, so I'd leave for London with spare clothes and stay over at a friend's house or with my parents. It was quite a nomadic life back then, but at least I was there at the coalface, constantly meeting up with parliamentarians to either inform them about the campaign, or just update them with any latest news.

Our message was simple and never wavered. We needed a ban on third-party puppy sellers to take that first major step in ending puppy farm cruelty. I told MPs that puppy farming was enabled and indeed encouraged by the legal framework in place to sell puppies away from their mums so the public never see them or the conditions in which their precious pups are bred. Many MPs were surprised that this totally licensed, third-party network included pet shops, garden centres, private dwellings and dealers, and were gobsmacked at all the welfare issues associated with it (transportation, disease risk, breeders not selling direct to owners, lack of transparency, lack of accountability, institutionalisation of pups, unsold pups, impulse purchasing, and more). I made it clear that there were no 'improvements' to licensing and regulation (e.g. making it more 'robust') that could ever properly address *any* of these welfare concerns, as pups (and their mums) were already damaged *before* they reached the licensed dealer.

Slowly but surely, more and more MPs were starting to accept that the third-party element had to be removed from the chain if there was to be any meaningful any chance of improving canine welfare. The larger charities continued to be against us, yet *still* weren't able to provide any evidence of how pups being sold away from their mums was ever beneficial to the welfare of the pups, their mums, or their new owners. Nor could they provide any examples of how 'robust' licensing of third-party puppy dealers, which some were appearing to continue to push for, would or could be an effective solution in tackling the cruelty of puppy farming, with its lack of transparency and accountability.

Westminster is a fascinating place, especially when you have no background or knowledge in politics, law, or how on earth the place works, but the more I visited, the more I understood. It was a huge learning curve, and things were starting to piece together: simple things like the difference between parliament and government; what role the individual buildings played; why two houses were required. Slowly it all started to make sense. Getting used to the parliamentary jargon was important too, and whilst doing my campaign work at home I would always have BBC Parliament, *Daily Politics*, or *Question Time* on in the background, even replay old debates, just so I was subconsciously drip-fed the language used – very important when writing emails to MPs or meeting them in person. I was also always drawn to the painting of the two elegant Borzois (my favourite dog breed), standing with Elizabeth I and Sir Walter Raleigh in St Stephen's Hall leading to Central Lobby. This picture became my focal point on every visit to the Palace of Westminster and, walking past, I would always give the Borzois a nod as if to say, 'I'm still fighting for you guys and will never give up!'

I was meeting so many politicians, arranging back-to-back coffees, attending events and receptions, with most seemingly receptive to our campaign; but I was always prepared to argue my point, to fight for those dogs incarcerated in puppy farms, just like little Lucy. I took with me evidence, literature, and always had with me my trusty black notepad. Every meeting saw pages of bullet points crossed off and discussed, and slowly but surely tiny, incremental amounts of progress were being made. I realised a lot of campaigning is about relationship-building, and the more I was seen around in Westminster the more I was becoming accepted in what to me seemed a strange, alien, but now much less unfamiliar environment. Most of my meetings took place in Portcullis House, either in the atrium or individual MP offices. Unless meeting with a Minister or inside No.10, I'd always wear smart jeans, jacket, and untuck my shirt. It was kind of a homage to my dad and his more relaxed dress code when he worked in advertising; I was a campaigner, so dressing a bit rebelliously felt right and in a weird way a statement that made me more mentally prepared to fight for what was right for the animals. In bigger meetings I'd also choose to sit on a table at the side of the room rather than a chair, again feeling and behaving a bit differently from the rest of the crowd, perhaps another way of manifesting the rebel campaigner in me.

After my e-petition debate calling on Government to 'Ban the sale of young puppies & kittens without their mothers being present' was rejected a couple of years before, I was also now keen to support and learn from other animal welfare campaigns and attend their subsequent e-petition debates too. Unsurprisingly there are many different *types* of debate, some voting outcomes more important than others, and like a sponge I kept soaking it all up. Another advantage of debates, whether the result goes your way or not, is the content that's always provided: from the briefing documents, supportive or not, sent in by organisations trying desperately for their words to be included in MPs' speeches, to the speeches themselves, and the resulting Hansard records. These records are a goldmine of information, not only in finding out what was said and by whom, but using those statements for social media purposes, tagging influential parliamentarians, and applying more pressure. Some of the most painstaking and effective campaigning meant taking hours to go through speeches, meticulously word by word, and then tweeting an individual MP's statement, accompanied by the screen shot of them saying it in that actual debate.

Mother's Day 2016 saw Pup Aid launch an awareness campaign using a professional black-and-white photograph of a heavily pregnant woman in a cage, to represent the imprisoned breeding dogs, and 'Where's Mum?' message, all organised by our celebrity liaison officer Laura Critchley.

The picture went viral, shared thousands of times around the world, including by huge celebrities from Ricky Gervais to US pop megastar P!nk.

In March 2016 a meeting took place between some of our campaigning team and representatives of some of the larger charities, a final attempt to find common ground on which to end puppy farming. These meetings were always stressful. We campaigners would have to take a day off work, travel into London, and spend hours reasoning with organisations to help support our proposed ban.

We could reach no common ground, compromise, or consensus. The days were getting darker and we were all starting to wonder what on earth we could do to stem the tide.

If you think things couldn't get any worse, you'd be wrong. Campaigning matters were overshadowed in April 2016 when my family and I were devastated by the loss of my dad to cancer. He'd only had a cough for a few weeks, and had never smoked a cigarette or drunk a single unit of alcohol his whole life. He'd always taken regular exercise and eaten well, and now he was gone. My mentor, my hero, my role model, my inspiration was no longer with us, and my life would never be the same again. But instead of taking my foot off the pedal, the passing of my dad made me even more determined to fight on. He'd taught me to never give up in something I believed in, the importance of always looking out for the underdog, the most vulnerable, and my campaigning proved the best distraction from the reality, shock, feeling of loss, and debilitating grief. And as luck would have it, and maybe it was a sign sent down from Dad, looking back April 2016 was the month when our campaign started to change course for the better, to make some actual progress in Westminster. But we wouldn't actually be aware of just how influential April would eventually prove to our campaign for a good few months to come.

Back in Parliament there was a planned Select Committee Inquiry going on, which I soon learned meant an officially recognised panel of cross-party MPs, who set out to scrutinise existing legislation, with the aim of hearing evidence from a range of experts, then suggesting improvements and recommendations to the government department responsible for that particular legislation. As luck would have it this particular committee was the Environment, Food and Rural Affairs (EFRA) Committee, and they were putting the Animal Welfare Act 2006 under the microscope on its 10th anniversary. The Committee would meet every Tuesday, usually in one of the beautiful rooms in the Palace of Westminster, and these sessions were open to the public to attend. Evidence was first submitted online months before the inquiry started, and then over the next few weeks individuals, experts, representatives of relevant organisations, government bodies, and finally the Minister would be asked questions in front of the panel of MPs. Their answers were recorded and subsequent recommendations were then made to the government. This inquiry was the biggest gift campaigners could have hoped for. Not only was the EFRA Committee chaired by Neil Parish MP, whom I knew well and had my first-ever meeting in Westminster with, but I had already built good relationships with most of the other MPs on my multiple visits over the years too.

Since all these evidence sessions took place on Tuesdays, my day off, I was able to attend all of them. I'd always sit in the same place, mobile phone plugged into the wall, in jeans and smart jacket, shirt untucked, and just observe. After one session I hung around for a few minutes to meet the only MP on the panel I hadn't met yet, Carmarthen West and South Pembrokeshire Conservative MP Simon Hart. Simon won't mind me saying this, but he had a reputation for being quite intimidating, and had previously been Chief Executive of the Countryside Alliance, a national campaigning organisation that supports fox hunting and other so-called 'bloodsports'. But in order to try and influence the *whole* committee I had to arrange a meeting with Mr Hart, so we swapped emails and arranged to meet in Portcullis House the following week. Amongst all the doom and gloom of being a campaigner, where it's not uncommon to experience high levels of loneliness, depression, and despair, when something positive finally happens, it not only lifts your spirits, but also gives you a great deal of hope. My meeting with Simon Hart was one of the most enjoyable and memorable of all my meetings in Westminster, and played a hugely significant part in changing the course of the whole campaign, in more ways than one.

Simon and I both knew we had very different viewpoints on certain issues. In fact, people walking past our table that day did a few double-takes. Why would an animal welfare campaigning vet be chatting with a well-known fox-hunting-supporting MP? However this became a lesson in putting differences aside and just getting on with the job. Not only was Simon a huge dog-lover, but within his constituency of Carmarthen West and South Pembrokeshire was the location of a particularly important licensed puppy farm: the one from which Halo – now Lucy – had been rescued. We chatted for well over an hour, unusually long for an MP meeting in Westminster, and Simon was very interested in our campaign to ban third-party puppy sellers. He told me that if I ever did win the battle, it would be down to sheer 'attrition', and I never forgot that.

When it came to the actual Inquiry, the charities appeared unprepared for the questions they were asked about banning third party sales. It was one of the defining moments of the campaign: somehow the campaigners had influenced an official inquiry. Sitting in my usual seat, I watched open-mouthed; in just those few minutes I felt the power shift in favour of our voluntary campaigners.

It didn't take long for the first newspaper to get in touch, *Our Dogs*, for whom I used to write. They'd been watching the session live online and were horrified at the performance by the charities in the inquiry, so asked me if I'd like to provide a quote. 'Even better than that,' I answered, 'Let me write the whole article!' They agreed and I wrote the front page and page three comparing the answers they'd just given to the statements they'd made two years previously when they supported a ban. The resulting 'Charities Fail to Give Evidence' front page and article was like a bomb going off in the pet and animal welfare sector. When I went to Birmingham that evening to give a talk on the use of social media to help rehome rescue pets, a talk hosted by one of the big charities, it was no surprise that I was met by a few glum-faced representatives.

It was getting messy, but our small group of campaigners was slowly starting to gain traction in Westminster, and, after the last few years of hard campaigning there with little to no results, I won't lie, it felt good, really good. Other highlights of this Inquiry included one of our campaigning team, Julia Carr, giving compelling, evidence-based testimony on behalf of our coalition: no assumptions or speculations, just facts. We were all so proud of her session, and Julia received excellent feedback and high praise from MPs immediately afterwards, a testament to the hard work that goes into being a campaigner with no vested interests apart from improving dog welfare.

The Committee planned to visit to a few licensed puppy farms in Wales. Unsurprisingly, despite giving the establishments over two months notice of their intended visit, one of them refused to let the MPs on their property under any circumstances. This in itself told them a lot, as did their visit to another puppy farm that did allow them inside. Even after the same notice, with plenty of time to clean things up and make significant improvements and renovations, what the MPs saw on their visit was more than sufficient to convince them a ban was necessary.

While the EFRA Select Committee Inquiry continued gathering evidence from its final weekly sessions, our team organised a drop-in event for MPs hosted by the then SNP MP Dr Paul Monaghan, himself a member of that Select Committee. Paul was always a supporter of our campaign and one of the first MPs to call for a ban in a parliamentary debate. Drop-in sessions are a very useful campaigning tool for both campaigners and MPs alike. Just like the 'Where's Mum?' drop-in before our Commons debate, MPs arrive and typically have their pictures taken with a placard, collect literature, and basically show support for that campaign. These sessions can be a bit hit and miss, depending on what else is going on in Westminster during their usual allotted time of one or two hours. This particular drop-in session was aimed at publicising two brand new research papers, compiled by our coalition of Julia (Canine Action UK), Linda and Sue (C.A.R.I.A.D.), Jenny (Naturewatch), Philippa (Karlton Index), Mark (Hidden Insight), and me (Pup Aid). The reports were called 'The Great British Puppy Survey' and 'Licensed Third-Party Puppy Vending in Great Britain', and contained vital evidence into behaviour patterns of prospective dog owners buying puppies from third-party dealers, including of course associated welfare problems. The drop-in was so well attended by cross-party MPs that at one point there was a queue of them coming in the door, which all helped pile on pressure for a ban. That drop-in event was also the first time I had a proper chat with the SNP's Dr Lisa Cameron MP. As well as all this excitement in Westminster at that time, BBC *Panorama* screened a hard-hitting documentary called *Britain's Puppy Dealers Exposed*. Linda, Sue, Julia, and I were all involved in its planning, and thanks to the show's brave investigator Sam Poling, I was honoured to be interviewed at my vet practice and appeared on the actual show, the perfect opportunity to confirm, once again, why a third-party ban was so necessary.

2016 also saw a very successful rally outside Westminster, organised by another anti-puppy farm campaign group, our good friends Boycott Dogs4Us. As the name suggests, this campaign group was specifically set up to protest outside the Manchester and Leeds puppy supermarkets called Dogs4Us who sold puppies brought in from elsewhere. These were exactly the kind of legal licensed third-party commercial puppy dealers that we were trying to stop. Rallies are one of the most basic but effective grassroots campaigning tools, and this one took place on Parliament Square, and was very well attended by campaigners, representatives of small-mid size charities Mayhew, All Dogs Matter, and Raystede, and celebrity supporters Jodie Marsh and Meg Mathews. Cross-party MPs attended and all spoke, including Rob Flello, Paul Monaghan, David Amess, and Margaret Ferrier. In amongst the crowd were Lisa and Lucy too, who later joined Jodie and me for a live interview about the rally and the third-party ban, broadcast live on BBC *Daily Politics*.

Meanwhile, behind the scenes, we were all nervously waiting for the results of the EFRA Inquiry: What would the Committee recommend to the government after hearing all that evidence and, in some cases, even seeing it with their own eyes on their fact-finding trip to visit licensed, legal puppy farms in Wales?

As Parliament reconvened after its summer recess, everyone was on tenterhooks regarding the results of the inquiry and when they would be published. During this time I attended the launch of the brilliant 'Suzy Puppy' campaign in Westminster. The brainchild of excellent charity International Fund for Animal Welfare (IFAW), Suzy Puppy was a cuddly, pretend children's toy, dog complete with bulging bloodshot eye and parasites, in a pink presentation box bearing slogans like 'I've travelled hundreds of miles in a cage', 'Only six weeks to live!' 'Now with worms and conjunctivitis', 'My mum has lived her life in a cage', 'I've had no vaccinations', 'Parvovirus & Diarrhoea', and 'Taken from my mum too early'. On the back were instructions on how to choose a puppy, including 'Make sure you see mum and her pups together', and there was also an accompanying YouTube video as a mock TV advert, which was premiered at the event. A Suzy Puppy was given to every one of the 650 MPs, either in person at the event or distributed to their offices afterwards. The Suzy Puppy campaign is still one of the most impressive, well thought out campaigns I've ever seen, and what's more IFAW had worked with advertising agency JWT to make it happen, the same agency that my dad worked for when he entered advertising. Dad's passing a few months earlier was obviously still raw, so I tearfully thanked the JWT reps present. What with Suzy having been the name of my first ever pet it felt like a few things had just come full circle. What made the Suzy Puppy launch *even* more special was that host of the event, Henry Smith MP, known for his unbridled support of animal welfare, praised the work I was doing, and called for a ban on third-party puppy dealers.

Autumn arrived and we were *still* waiting for the EFRA Inquiry result. Things were tense all round as whatever the 10 cross-party MPs would recommend to the Government, either a ban on third-party dealers or more licensing, would most likely determine the future of puppy farming in the UK and beyond. In between vetting I was invited to the States and received another prestigious Vet of the Year award from Philadelphia-based charity Finding Shelter Animal Rescue who specialise in rescuing and rehabilitating dogs from puppy farms. I stayed to help judge their fun dog show, Sproutfest, named after Finding Shelter's amazing founders Grace and Steve's first rescue chihuahua Sprout; I accompanied Grace on some puppy mill rescue missions; and I was invited to New York to discuss my campaigning with some of the biggest animal charities and campaigning organisations in the US. To be honoured for my campaigning in another country felt incredibly special and solidified the fact that puppy farming is a global issue which should bring charities, organisations, and campaigning individuals from all nations together. This feeling was only strengthened by invitations to lecture on puppy farming in Dublin and meetings at the SNP Annual Conference in Glasgow.

Finally, after anxious months of waiting, the much anticipated final report from the EFRA Inquiry was published, and lo and behold, it was good news. Incredible news in fact. The Select Committee came to the correct conclusion that 'responsible breeders would never sell through a pet shop licence holder. The process of selling through a third-party seller has an unavoidable negative impact upon the welfare of puppies. It also distances the purchaser from the environment in which their puppy was bred. Banning third-party sales so that the public bought directly from breeders would bring public scrutiny to bear on breeders, thereby improving the welfare conditions of puppies.' All good so far. And then came their suggestion to Government, right there in black and white: that the Government should therefore 'ban third-party sale of dogs. Dogs should only be available from licensed, regulated breeders or approved rehoming organisations.' This was a huge milestone for dog welfare: an official evidence-based conclusion which took all the facts into account. One MP who went on the puppy farm visit, Chris Davies, described the dogs he witnessed as so psychologically damaged that they were 'unable to be dogs'. Surely we'd done it? The Committee seemed to recommend exactly what us campaigners and smaller to mid-size rescues and charities were calling for – a total ban on third-party commercial puppy dealers. If Government agreed to abide by EFRA's recommendations, we were just one decision away from the most significant and positive law change in the fight against puppy farming in UK history.

The weeks of waiting for the Government to respond to the EFRA recommendations felt even more uneasy than the months waiting for the EFRA report itself. This was potentially it, the final decision. If DEFRA listened, took onboard, and acted on the recommendation from EFRA's official inquiry, we'd have a ban on third-party puppy dealers, and prospective dog owners would only be able to purchase their puppy direct from the breeder and see him or her interacting with its mum in the place it was born, or adopt from a rescue centre instead. We were so close. Years of stressful meetings, petitions, rallies, MP drop-ins, attending events, and thousands upon thousands of emails were all leading to this one final, big decision. We knew we couldn't do any more. What was becoming even more worrying was that it was still the big charities' voices that the Government was appearing to listen to over any other small-mid size charities or campaigners. While we waited we conducted a quick online poll just to check we weren't going mad. Reassuringly it confirmed that over 99.5% of the public wanted to see the selling of puppies by third parties (i.e. pet shops, dealers) banned ASAP.

We crossed everything in the hope that the Government would come back with a positive response to EFRA and agree to a ban. The days became weeks, and weeks became months. To say they weren't very forthcoming was an understatement. As we waited I kept up the vetting full-time, but also continued supporting charity events in London, appearing on Sky News and *This Morning*, and attending events in Westminster. Representatives of the big charities would be at these events too, and would tell me there was no appetite in Government for a ban. It's fair to say tensions were at an all-time high.

The delay by Government was becoming unbearable. We just needed to know one way or the other what they were going to decide: total ban or more licensing? So I had an idea. Lord Gardiner, DEFRA's Under-Secretary of State at the time, was the official in charge of this decision, and just like Simon Hart MP, had also worked for Countryside Alliance, had been there at exactly the same time as Simon, and so they *must* be old colleagues. I contacted Simon and asked if he would set a meeting up as soon as possible, in DEFRA, to find out once and for all whether the government were planning to agree with EFRA's recommendation for a ban, or were going to reject it. Simon kindly arranged the meeting, and the following week Julia, Simon, and I headed to DEFRA to get our answer. It wasn't long into our 20 minutes allocated time that we learned of their fateful decision.

The Government had decided that it *wasn't* going to ban third-party puppy dealers, rejecting EFRA's recommendation, and referred to lack of clarity over enforcement, stating it supported 'robust licensing' as an alternative solution instead. However, the government reiterated the importance of prospective buyers seeing puppies interacting with their mother in the place they were born, which of course directly conflicted with continuing to permit commercial third-party dealers to sell puppies where the mother is not present, and away from the breeding premises. During this tense meeting it became increasingly obvious that the government was prepared to legitimise an activity which clearly did not match its own best practice recommendations – but why? It was devastating news. Worse still, Lord Gardiner said it would be *at least* another five years until this subject could be looked at again. Simon, Julia, and I tried in vain to argue with the Under-Secretary, but sadly to no avail. We all looked at each other in stunned silence. We'd lost. The poor breeding dogs and puppies had lost. The campaign was dead.

But there was still one key detail that I just had to find out. Who was behind this decision? With overwhelming public support for something so obvious, there had to be someone or something pretty powerful persuading the government not to ban puppy dealers and help end puppy farming. The red mist descended and I lost my cool. It had taken six years to get to this point and I wasn't going to give up without a fight. As the three of us got up to leave, hearts pounding, racked with grief at the Government's decision, I turned to Lord Gardiner, looked him straight in the eyes, and said, 'No one's leaving this room until we find out who's responsible!' 'I'm not allowed to tell you,' he replied, 'It's confidential.' I wasn't done yet. 'OK then,' I continued 'Let's play a game. I'll say who I think it was and you can say yes or no.' Don't forget this was me talking straight to a Minister, a Lord even, in DEFRA headquarters. Before he had a chance to accept the invite to my game, I listed the organisations I suspected were involved. 'Yes,' he said, 'it was them.'

At that moment Julia, Simon and I knew exactly who had effectively blocked a ban on puppy dealers. It was now just a question of what we did with that information. The bigger picture was that we had lost, the Government had decided not to ban, and there was no going back. Julia and I headed to the underground and then to St Pancras where she was getting her train back to Kent. We were shell shocked. As we grabbed coffee together, I could see Julia was crying, and I wasn't far off either. All those years of hard work by our coalition, the reports, the Pup Aid dog shows, visits to Westminster, evidence, drop-ins, years at the heartbreaking coalface of evidence gathering by C.A.R.I.A.D., and for what? For someone to undermine our efforts? Not to mention my own personal struggle in the last few months of dealing with my dad's passing. I never needed him more.

This was by far the darkest day of the whole campaign so far. But unbelievably it was about to get even darker still.

Chapter 14

❖

It was autumn 2016, around Halloween time, so naturally Lisa and Lucy were invited along to the now legendary annual All Dogs Matter Halloween Fancy Dress Show, held at the very dog-friendly Spaniards Inn in Hampstead, North London.

Little Lucy, on trend as always, wore a smart pumpkin-themed hat and, unsurprisingly, was again the star of the show, surrounded by a group of four-legged witches and ghouls, all patiently queuing up with their excited owners to have their pictures taken with this bona fide social media superstar.

Now some dogs are just naturals when it comes to the camera, and Lucy was a pro at posing for pics and selfies, so obviously she took it all in her stride. She was very much a canine celebrity in her own right and after all her fans – both two- and four-legged – had all taken their photos, it was time for Lucy to relax and have a well-earned sleep. Trips to London from the West Midlands were always an adventure for Lisa and Lucy, and this time was no different. That night they had been invited to stay for free in one of the extravagant hotel suites at the world-famous Hotel St Pancras Renaissance and review their special 'Pooch Package' for dog owners, complete with doggie giftbox on arrival containing a pink fluffy flamingo toy to keep, as well as also providing luxury dog accessories including dog bed, bowl, and blanket to make her stay as comfy and perfect as possible. There was also the offer of a one-to-one session with an expert dog trainer if required.

As you can well imagine, Lucy was less needy of the help and advice of a dog trainer compared to the more urgent need to explore tasty treats in her very own bespoke giftbox, in her own extravagant London hotel suite! What a life she was living, star of the Halloween dog show one minute, guest of honour in a luxury hotel the next. Does it ever get better than this for a little dog who started out born into a life of misery and exploitation in cramped conditions in a dismal shed, in deepest, darkest Wales? Lucy thoroughly enjoyed her stay, proceeded to demolish her Lincolnshire sausage breakfast the next morning, and gave the whole 'Pooch Package' experience a glowing paws-up. After all, now having accumulated over 70,000 followers on her 'Lucy the Rescue Cavalier' Facebook page, this particular guest reviewer's opinion really mattered. She was now a true canine influencer. Completing her perfect stay at the Hotel St Pancras Renaissance was the opportunity to be a Spice Girl. Yes that's right, a Spice Girl.

You see the hotel Lucy was reviewing was home to that famous staircase, the one featured in the iconic Spice Girls 'Wannabe' video, shot 11 years earlier in 1996, when the world was first introduced to 'Girl Power'. And yet here, sitting patiently on the stairs, was a girl with more power than Ginger, Sporty, Scary, Posh and Baby put together. A girl that had managed to overcome years of pain, suffering and abuse, and was now able to enjoy the high life, being treated like the canine royalty she had become, in this exclusive London hotel, usually frequented by affluent business types, pop superstars, and romantic couples on surprise weekend getaways.

Lucy had never been more popular or more loved. Her updates and pictures on her Facebook page were now regularly reaching *millions* of fans all around the world, and Lisa worked tirelessly, trying her hardest to acknowledge and interact with as many people as possible, not easy with such a huge following! Life was pretty good for little Lucy; Lisa and her Facebook page were generating unbelievable invitations, golden opportunities, and unique experiences even human celebrities could only dream of.

It was mid-morning on Sunday 4 December 2016 when I got the call. I remember it like it was yesterday because like most traumatic events, even though you know they're going to happen one day, you always try and block it out of your mind until you really have to deal with it. These are the days that stay with you forever.

I was walking along the Undercliff Walk between Brighton and the next coastal village of Ovingdean with some friends, when I saw Lisa's number flash up on my phone. I answered immediately and automatically feared the worst. After all,

Lisa and I only really chatted via text on Messenger rather than phone chats, so something very good or very bad must've just happened to elevate our choice of communication to a proper phonecall.

'Lucy's not well,' said Lisa anxiously. I could hear she was trying to remain calm, but knowing Lisa well I could hear the stress in her voice, and as a result felt a lump in my throat and knot in my stomach. 'I really need your advice and reassurance – I'm taking her to the vet but can I send you a video of her breathing for you to have a look at?' she asked. 'Sure!' I said, 'Of course, send it now!' The short clip Lisa sent was of a dog in respiratory distress. Not respiratory failure or dying. Just distress. The type of laboured breathing that a dog suffering from pneumonia may display, for example, or perhaps a bad heart – after all, Lucy was a Cavalier, so cardiac problems are common in that breed, and often treatable. Lucy's difficulty breathing had come completely out of the blue. Lucy's appetite was always good, especially when it came to cake, and she had experienced no obvious problems with her breathing previously, in fact her heart was actually quite strong considering her breed and background. If there was ever a time I wished I lived closer to the West Midlands, so I could meet Lisa and examine Lucy myself, then this was it.

Breathing difficulties in dogs, and cats for that matter, can happen for many reasons. From infections, to something internal like heart failure, or from parasites like lungworm, or incidents like road accidents causing hernias requiring surgery.

Chapter 14

With such a wide range of causes, some of them more easily dealt with than others, Lisa was doing the right thing by making an emergency appointment to see her vet as soon as possible. But it was a Sunday, and Lisa's regular vet practice was closed, so I texted her some questions to ask whichever new vet she saw, and asked her to call me back as soon as Lucy had been checked-over. Later that day I managed to speak with the duty vet too. After all, I'd only been hanging out with Lucy a few weeks back and she was fairly active, even enjoying a walk in amongst the fallen leaves of a wintry Regent's Park, before the three of us attended the Hearing Dogs for the Deaf Awards. It was the event at which she snored loudly right through Princess Anne's speech, much to the amusement of all around her. Lisa rang her usual vet's number and it gave her the number of the emergency vet to ring. It was about 10.30am on the Sunday morning, and the emergency vet was already at the practice seeing other patients. So Lisa made her way down to the practice with Lucy, to find out what was wrong with her, and more importantly decide what they could do to hopefully put her right again.

Lisa calmly pulled into the vet surgery's driveway and got out of the car, desperately clutching a poorly Lucy. Lisa's sister Sarah met them there a bit later as she was worried about them both. Lisa had to wait in the waiting room for Lucy to be seen but one of the staff could see she was struggling to breathe, so took Lucy through to the back. When Lisa saw the first vet with Lucy, obviously she was very concerned, and they put Lucy straight into an oxygen tent and carried out various tests. It was all incredibly distressing as you can imagine. Lisa felt as though the vet was comparing Lucy to a totally 'well' dog, when in reality they had never seen her previously; so although there was clearly something seriously wrong, she was actually sat up and quite alert. It was during those initial few hours of Lucy being there with that particular vet that she suggested putting Lucy to sleep might have to be a consideration. But as the vet had never met Lucy before, so didn't know what Lucy's 'normal' was, Lisa felt that she was better placed to make that call, like most owners of a vulnerable dog would feel. Lisa felt that as it started to get later in the day, the suggestion of putting Lucy to sleep was clearly their professional opinion. However, it was one Lisa didn't agree with as Lucy seemed far too alert, she was still sat upright, and Lisa was still able to hand-feed her using a spoon; plus after all she had been through in her life, surely she deserved a chance. Lisa posted on Facebook letting Lucy's followers know that she was poorly not long after she'd taken Lucy to the vet's.

Lucy remained stable in her oxygen tent all afternoon. I had a chat with the vet too so I could find out in veterinary terms what was going on with regard to Lucy's condition and treatment plan, and then explain anything extra to Lisa that potentially needed clarifying. As Sunday 4 December 2016 dragged on, deep down Lisa and Sarah felt there was definitely still a glimmer of hope, but the vet wasn't so optimistic, appearing to give the impression that it would, in fact, be better to put Lucy to sleep. Lisa felt she was being repeatedly pushed for this to happen at least two or three times. Even if this wasn't the case, it's the all-important vibe that's given off by the vet, and it's that whole experience that remains in peoples' minds for the rest of their lives. Besides, Lisa thought, this vet had never even met Lucy before. She didn't seem to appreciate that Lucy wasn't a well dog beforehand, so clearly had nothing to compare today's downturn with. Either way this scenario of never seeing an animal before is all quite normal for an emergency vet, but it's the attitude and impression given by the professional on duty, whether they're the vet, nurse, or even receptionist, that can often influence treatment options, and therefore outcomes.

The initial emergency vet that Lucy first saw that morning eventually went home around 7pm, with the nurse leaving slightly later. The plan was for Lucy to be given initial emergency treatment and then be left alone once her breathing was stable, in her oxygen tent, with no supervision. This was not a plan that Lisa or sister Sarah were particularly happy about, especially after everything Lucy had had to overcome in her remarkable life. Concerned about Lucy being left in a strange environment, either under the vet's care or on her own, Lisa asked if she could stay by Lucy's side, but for health and safety reasons they told her that wasn't possible. Lisa had already asked about transferring her to the nearby specialist vet, but they said they had no portable oxygen, so she would most likely get into difficulties on that journey, and possibly not even make it.

This was when Lisa had to look at the only other option of asking another vet in to come in and look after Lucy overnight – another lady who, once again, was also unfamiliar with what 'normal' Lucy looked like. When this emergency vet arrived at the practice, she was very keen to let Lisa know all the costs, and that payment must be made upfront, there and then. This vet wouldn't just be popping in to check on Lucy, she was intending to stay with Lucy, so Lisa asked this new vet to send regular text updates throughout the night. Already there were two GoFundMe pages set up online, very kindly organised by two amazing followers of Lucy that first night she was poorly, to help Lisa with costs; one contained the majority of donations, the other about £1,000. These fundraising pages, as well as some PayPal donations too, would help pay for the overnight vet, as well as any remaining daytime fees, and ongoing treatment at the next vets too. However these donations weren't available to draw immediately, so in the interim Lisa had to borrow the money to pay the vet.

The night vet arrived and insisted the whole estimated amount of £1,300, just for the overnight supervision, was paid upfront. In my opinion, as a previous out-of-hours vet with years of experience working nights and weekends in an emergency clinic environment, it's always the outward caring attitude of the veterinary professional to the worried owner's beloved pet that matters most. Pushing for full payment for Lucy's overnight stay beforehand only makes owners more anxious, if that's even possible. I mean, who has access to thousands of pounds on the spot? Even if an owner has pet insurance it's still an amount most people would struggle to find if asked to pay up front, right there and then. With emergency work it's not uncommon for people to take days or even weeks to raise that sort of cash, sometimes having to borrow off friends and family, or even order a new credit card.

In what sounded like a very unnecessary heated debate at the vet clinic, when all energies really should've been focused on prioritising Lucy's welfare, Lisa borrowed the money to pay the sum requested. The resulting amount for the initial emergency treatment from the first vet came to over £600 so around £2,000 for the initial 24 hours of treatment. Of course, it's not uncommon for vet bills in these situations to rack up into the thousands very quickly, especially when emergency treatment's involved.

As dawn broke the next morning Lucy was still rallying in her oxygen tent. The practice owner had arrived and called Lisa to come down to the practice and collect Lucy. Hoping to see the overnight vet that had been paid for, Lisa arrived at the practice on the Monday morning, and was disappointed that that vet had already disappeared, gone home without waiting to speak to Lisa in person, rather than just via text. To be safely transferred to another vet clinic with dedicated 24-hour emergency on-site staff, Lisa had to find some portable oxygen to administer to Lucy en route, and give her the best chance of making it the 20 or so miles to the next vets alive.

So, she frantically posted an urgent message on Lucy's Facebook page, desperate to locate some portable oxygen, as well as calling every local business likely to have access to a cylinder, including the fire brigade. Finally a friendly company got in touch with Lisa and arranged to meet her at the vet's where Lucy was still being kept. Lisa paid the remainder of her bill, and the practice kindly let Lisa borrow their oxygen tent, with portable oxygen cylinder now attached, and off they drove to the next vet clinic.

After a nervous half-hour journey which seemed a lot longer, whilst desperately trying to keep Lucy stable with the portable oxygen, they finally arrived at the referral vets. Here they had so many specialists, from cardiologists to neurologists, internal medicine experts to a purpose-built hospital complete with its own intensive care ward. On arrival, although Lisa knew full well that Lucy's condition was still very serious, she immediately felt a positive attitude from the kind staff, which reassured her that Lucy was in good hands. Lisa was told they would continue with her emergency treatment, tweaking where appropriate, observing her closely, and giving Lucy the very best hope of recovering. Lisa found their compassion very reassuring, and within minutes of arriving she felt happier.

As our brave little Lucy was admitted on Monday 5 December 2016, instead of an oxygen tent, she was now connected to a piped nasal oxygen supply, directly into her nostrils through special plastic tubes, to give her even more of a chance of recovery. Furthermore, Lucy's breathing pattern, respiratory and heart rates, and ECG were all now being closely monitored by a high-tech machine too, beeping away in line with all the activity going on in her chest.

But Lucy's breathing was still laboured, even with the nasal oxygen, and when the vets took initial conscious (no sedation or anaesthetic) chest X-rays, they detected a lot of white opacity, most likely fluid in the lungs, where black air should have been instead. But even though the outlook for Lucy was grim, the vets told Lisa not to give up hope just yet as they'd enjoyed success a few weeks previously with a similar case, albeit a previously 'well' dog, that arrived having trouble breathing. The staff asked Lisa to be patient. They weren't talking about putting Lucy to sleep; on the contrary they were clearly determined to give her their best shot and explained that as Lucy wasn't a well dog to start with, it might just take her longer to recover. Lisa was so impressed with the positive 'can-do' attitude shown by these vets, that she tagged them on Lucy's Facebook page, praising them for their kindness, positivity, and understanding. You can only imagine how many posts of support were now starting to roll in. Messages of love, prayers, poems, pictures, and thoughts were being sent in from all over the world. Lucy remained stable on nasal oxygen, monitored around the clock by friendly staff, state-of-the-art equipment, and expert veterinary care.

That first week in December 2016 Lisa and Lucy were actually meant to be joining me in attending London-based animal charity Mayhew's annual Christmas 'Tinsel and Tails' fundraiser, held at the Grand Connaught Rooms, London, for an evening of glitz, glamour, and generosity. But instead Lucy was poorly 100 miles away in hospital, doing her very best to stay alive, and because Lisa had posted on her page about her being poorly, she was clearly on everyone's mind at the event.

One of the Mayhew's prizes, the chance to win a live portrait painting of your dog right there in the room, donated by longtime Mayhew supporter and artist Claire Thorogood, was just one of the prizes up for grabs that night, as well as a generous raffle, which this year I was honoured to have been asked to compère. Artist Claire had met Lucy a few months beforehand at Pup Aid, and had already painted a beautiful portrait of her since the Primrose Hill dog show, keen to show Lisa for the first time when she arrived. On my way to the stage, to read out the lucky raffle winners, I asked Claire if I could borrow her portrait of Lucy for a few minutes, to which she kindly agreed.

It was the evening of Tuesday 6 December, and I was sad to be there without Lisa and Lucy. The three of us had been so looking forward to attending together. Lisa had been planning her dress for months, and which of Lucy's colourful harnesses to wear for even longer before that. Typically Lisa and Lucy would arrive looking all glamorous, gracing the red carpet, and then Lucy would meet everyone, fall asleep, and snore away in her carry bag. Just like at the Halloween event a few weeks back, people would form an orderly queue to say hello to Lucy, and if they were lucky, maybe get a selfie. Not this year though. Lisa and Lucy were still up in the West Midlands, well away from any ballgowns or tuxedos, bubbles or festive red ribbons. Just before I started revealing the raffle prize winners, I asked everyone for silence, and held Lucy's portrait aloft for the whole room to see.

As Lisa, Lucy, and I were all so close, I was always kept informed up to the minute of Lucy's condition, and so felt, as most people there who already knew Lucy was ill were all asking, that I would inform everyone attending of the latest news. In a very emotional little speech I let everyone know Lucy was still in intensive care, and that the veterinary staff were doing all they could for her. I asked everyone to please think of Lucy, and send their positive energy and vibes in Lucy and Lisa's direction. My voice choked. Relaying information like this when you care so much about a dog and their owner is never easy, and the room fell even more silent; not an easy gig. I continued with my raffle duties, but it was obvious everyone in the room was preoccupied with the seriousness of Lucy's condition, there were hugs and tears between guests on many tables, including mine, where Linda and Sue from C.A.R.I.A.D. were sitting, trying desperately to keep it together. I was proud to have represented 'Team Lucy' that evening, acting as official spokesperson to many of her closest friends, fans, and followers.

Believe it or not, everyone's thoughts and positive energy that Tuesday night must've worked, as well as the empathy, compassion, kindness, and expert veterinary care given by the referral vets. Lucy picked up on the Wednesday. She was starting to breathe better for the first time since being admitted into hospital three days earlier. Another Lisa, from Daisy's Dog Deli, actually sent Lucy a liver cake in the hope it would encourage her to eat, and also shared a recipe for chicken broth which Lisa made, but uncharacteristically Lucy wouldn't try any. She wasn't eating but whatever the drugs she was being given, they appeared to be working. Lisa was busy updating Lucy's page as soon as she knew the latest about Lucy's health status. As you can imagine, thousands and thousands of well-wishing messages were now filling comment box after comment box, populating Lucy's Facebook page's wall, and overwhelming her private inbox too.

We all knew that Lucy was a much-loved little dog, but this was unprecedented. With every get-well-soon message it was becoming clearer that not one of her followers could ever imagine a day of their lives without Lucy's cheeky face popping up on their computer screen, or wearing a cute outfit, or even a video of her being caught doing something mischievous, or one of those classic photos of her being tightly held in another celebrity's arms. Some of her adoring fans had literally no sleep, nervously waiting for Lisa's next update, and practically holding their breath with anxiety about their dearly loved social media friend.

But alas, it just wasn't to be. Although Lucy appeared to rally and perk up on the Wednesday in response to her treatment, on Thursday Lucy's tiny body – ravaged by years of abuse in that dreadful puppy farm – was failing, and her condition started to quickly deteriorate once again. This time, it seemed, for the final time.

The vets were now so overly concerned about her state that they told Lisa they were going to see how she responded to a few more hours of intensive care, oxygen tent, drip, intravenous treatments, and nasal tubes piping fresh concentrated oxygen straight down into her respiratory system. The beeps and readings on the heart monitor were now noticeably slower. Lisa knew this was the last chance for her brave little soldier.

Lucy had battled to stay alive since the moment she was born in that puppy farm a total of two lifetimes ago: one horrifically cruel life and one that was entirely magical. Years of exploitation kept cooped up in the dark in that cramped space; giving birth to litter after litter and then cruelly separated from the pups nature intended her to bond with, and them to their mother – litter after litter brutally torn away and transported hundreds of miles away by greedy, heartless puppy dealers. The debilitating epilepsy, the arthritis, the dry-eye, the anxiety in all its many forms; Lucy's body was shutting down, quickly now, her frail organs just too tired to carry on anymore. Lisa and Sarah were given an appointment just after 3pm, and were told that if she hadn't improved, they'd have to look at their options. Lucy was now preparing to take her last oxygen-rich breaths and snorts. She was deteriorating fast. It wasn't long before Lisa and Sarah arrived in the waiting room. Amazingly, she'd hung on until they were all in the same building.

The two sisters were taken through to see the specialist, who advised that he thought it was now time to let Lucy go. Lisa was heartbroken, totally devastated, but accepted Lucy had been given the very best chance and it was now time to say goodbye. Lisa and Sarah had been in his consulting room barely five or ten minutes when he got the alert that Lucy was crashing. He rushed out to attend to her. And as the vets and vet nurses tried desperately to save Lucy, there was nothing more that the specialist or anyone could do to help her. The heart of one of the bravest dogs this world has ever known had stopped beating forever. The lines on the monitors measuring her cardiac and breathing rates and rhythms had all flattened. There were no more beeps, just silence. She was gone.

After disconnecting Lucy from her drip, machines, and nasal oxygen, they brought her through to a distraught Lisa, who held Lucy's lifeless body tightly to her chest, telling her again and again and again how much she loved her, that she'd always love her, and that she'd never ever be forgotten. Not just by Lisa and her family, but by her other dogs, and of course all her fans right around the world. How on earth was Lisa going to break the awful news? So many dogs and humans depended on Lucy. They needed her in their lives, and they'd wake up expecting to see her latest picture. It's one thing regularly updating a post multiple times a day reporting on the failing health of one of the most popular dogs on the planet, but it's quite another dealing with the tragic and predicted response after she'd passed; especially when her condition had defied all the odds and improved markedly the day before.

First Lisa herself had to try and deal personally with what had happened, the passing of her very special sidekick, her best friend, her soulmate. She was utterly heartbroken, but Lisa also felt a strong sense of duty to inform Lucy's followers straight away, writing the Facebook post on her way home. It was, and still is, one of the most heart-wrenching posts I think I've ever read. A post that people are still commenting on years later. Lisa shared one of her favourite portraits of Lucy, wearing her pink jumper with a pink headband made of pink roses, accompanied by these words: *'I'm totally devastated to tell you that Lucy has passed away. My heart is broken beyond repair. I'm going to take a little time out to try & get my head round what's happened xx I will love you forever Lucy x please keep raising awareness in her honour until we are strong enough x #teamlucy #iwillloveyouforever'.*

The outpouring of grief for Lucy's passing was extraordinary, people from around the world paying their respects to this incredibly brave dog who was very much part of their lives too. Lucy's page was filled with thousands of messages of love and sadness, and Lisa definitely found some comfort in this.

Lisa arranged for Lucy to be cremated, choosing to receive her ashes back, of which a small sample were funneled into a special silver pet memorial bereavement ring that, unsurprisingly, remains Lisa's most prized possession to this day. It's even designed as a pair of tiny angel wings – how appropriate, since Lucy's original name was Halo. Lisa kept the rest of Lucy's ashes and some of her fur too. As the unrelenting sorrow and heartache felt by literally thousands of Lucy's fans continued to stream onto her Facebook page relentlessly, for the first time Lisa couldn't even attempt to respond to the comments as she'd always done in the past; it was far too hard a task to even contemplate. Not just overwhelming due to the sheer numbers, but as you can imagine, the immense struggle it would be trying to read them all through endless tears as well.

In the days that passed Lisa, although still traumatised by what had happened, noticed that the two GoFundMe online fundraisers to help pay for all the specialist veterinary treatment and care Lucy had received, had now smashed the £10,000 target in the first few days since she went downhill just days before, such was the emotion and pain felt by her fans. From the UK to Europe, North America to Brazil, Asia to Africa, the resulting wave of generosity displayed by her followers made sure that at least Lisa had no outstanding vet bills, with the leftover money donated to help other dogs in need. People were only too happy to donate, to give something, anything they could afford. Lucy had thousands of friends all around the globe, and as they all slowly learned the tragic, devastating news, Lucy's page soon became a shrine – a special place where everyone was welcome to pay their respects, share their fondest memories of Lucy, and even post their favourite pictures. To this day Lisa remains forever grateful for everyone who helped with, supported, donated to, and shared those GoFundMe pages.

As well as the countless online messages and comments, plus sympathy cards and bouquets of flowers, such was the love for Lucy that some of her followers even purchased and named actual stars in the sky after Lucy. Lisa's other dogs, Cavaliers Annabelle and Lady, still had each other, and just seemed to get on with life as animals often do. But Lisa's heart was well and truly shattered, broken into a million tiny pieces. Her little shadow, from the first day she came to live with her as tiny Halo with her arched back, wasn't there shuffling around her ankles anymore. There was no more snoring at night, and slices of doggy cake remained untouched. The world had just become a much sadder place. One of its brightest lights of hope, educating the public about the plight of puppy farm breeding dogs and rescue pet adoption, a light that had brought so much joy and happiness to so many, had been extinguished *far* too soon.

But, just as an early evening sky will host a breath-taking, unforgettable sunset followed by an unexpected and unimaginably beautiful afterglow, so little Lucy's impact on the world after her passing was to prove equally, if not even more dramatic.

Chapter 15

❖

It was early 2017, and we were all at our lowest ebb, really at rock bottom. Lucy had passed away, as had my dad and now Philippa's Mum too. Our campaign had been blocked and we'd been told by Government officials that it would be *at least* five years until this subject could even be discussed again. It was an extremely tough time for all of us trying desperately to fight this fight.

It was the perfect moment to take a step back, assess the situation, and try to come up with yet another new strategy. It would've been so easy to give up at that point, but quitting was never on the cards, not with all the stresses of the last few years of campaigning we'd all suffered already, and more importantly not with the fate of potentially millions of the UK's dogs still at stake.

When I played chess growing up, I was more than accustomed to finding myself in tricky situations where all the odds were stacked against me, but I never conceded defeat, instead always trying and often succeeding in eventually finding a way out, forming an escape plan and, more often than not, even winning the game. Stubbornness and unwillingness to compromise when the most vulnerable will suffer as a result are definitely traits picked up from my dad, but my determination to never give up was also most definitely passed down from my grandma Judy.

Let me tell you a bit more about her. It was a seemingly ordinary day in 1938 when 17-year-old Judy returned home in Meissen, a small town in Saxony, Eastern Germany. As soon as she arrived, she knew something was very wrong: the front door was wide open, and her parents and sister were gone. A neighbour hurriedly told her that the Gestapo had taken her family away, and that they would soon come back for her. Judy took just a few minutes to pack a small case, grab her papers and some money, and head off to the nearby city of Dresden, where she knew there was a synagogue. The staff there told her that a Kindertransport train was leaving that night from Leipzig, and advised her to try and muscle her way onto it. Judy had no ticket for the train, and none of the official 'movement' paperwork that the children travelled under either. However, as this was her best chance of escaping the Nazis, she knew she had to take it.

When Judy arrived at Leipzig station, the train platform was teeming with distraught mothers saying goodbye to their screaming children. One lady thrust her tiny youngster at Judy, begging her to look after the child on the long journey ahead, but a terrified Judy said no. It was at that moment she came up with her daring plan. Judy hurriedly left the station and ran as fast as she could to a nearby 'party shop', where she knew they sold fancy-dress outfits. She selected a white apron and a white hat with a red cross on it, and found somewhere to quickly change into this makeshift nurse's uniform. She returned to the train station and began taking charge of some children, with the intention of passing herself off as their nursemaid. Judy was banking on the idea that the German SS soldiers would automatically respect her uniform and let her through; as luck would have it, she was right. It was a nerve-racking journey through Germany and Holland, but she successfully made it through each checkpoint and arrived safely via the Port of Harwich, into Liverpool Street Station, London. During the war Judy got a job sewing uniforms for British soldiers, needle skills that would also come in handy years later when she knitted blankets to keep people warm living in poorer communities in Eastern Europe. Quick thinking, resourcefulness and creativity saved my grandma Judy's life, and ultimately meant that, two generations later, I had a chance at life too.

The odds were against us, but with a role model like Grandma Judy, my coalition of campaigners and I were even more determined not to be beaten. We just needed to rely on that same quick thinking, resourcefulness and creativity. My thinking cap was most definitely on. I did a live interview with James Whale on talkRADIO. James was a big fan of Pup Aid fun dog show, always bringing along his two Bichons Daisy and Shaggy, and he would call me up for comment whenever there was a pet-related story he wanted my thoughts on. This time he wanted to discuss puppy farming and the correct way to get a puppy, but couldn't understand why breeding dogs, often of small fluffy breeds like Bichons, were still being kept in atrocious conditions.

James was quizzing me in his own inimitable way, live on his afternoon radio show, when he asked if I knew why puppy farming continued to be practised. I was very open about what I thought about the ban on puppy dealers. James was clearly horrified and couldn't believe his ears. Surely it's in everyone's interests to help *stop* welfare problems and protect the health and happiness of the UK's dogs. The show's producers then asked the other parties for comment. I was using my position again as fall-guy, provoking a response. So I called my buddy Rob Flello MP.

Rob and I chatted about possible options, and then an idea came to him that would elevate our campaign to the next level. Don't forget that at that time the campaigners were seen as troublemakers: we'd challenged the Government, we were hated by the pet industry, and now we were suggesting we had proof that some of the biggest and most publicly trusted outfits in the UK were standing in our way to ban puppy farming and third-party dealing. We were hardly on any person of authority's Christmas card list, and we were feeling very alone, all while sitting on vital information. Rob's genius idea was to set up what's known as an All-Party Parliamentary Group (APPG) for dog welfare. APPGs are informal cross-party groups within Parliament that are run by, and for, Members of the Commons and Lords, though many choose to involve individuals and organisations from outside Parliament in their administration and activities. APPGs often discuss topics, sometimes contentious, with a view to reaching consensus, making progress on these issues, and sometimes even positively influencing legislation.

The mainstream media were now starting to pick up on what has been going on, starting with a shockingly revealing Independent article entitled 'Move to ban sale of puppies in UK pet shops derailed following opposition from leading dog charities'. What was becoming clear was that every argument or reason wheeled out time and time again to justify opposing a ban (ranging from risking restricting the supply of pups to the suggestion that sales would go underground) were all largely unsupported claims and speculations. When the APDAWG meeting came around, the room in Westminster filled with campaigners, charities, and journalists in anticipation of these larger, more corporate-behaving charities coming in to justify their reasons for persuading Government to block the ban.

Out of all my meetings in Westminster up to that point, this inaugural APDAWG meeting, chaired by Rob and me, was easily the tensest, but also the most exciting. As attendees filed in, we were informed that some of the charities could not attend, but had instead sent statements to be read out to the room. One organisation had sent a representative though, and the stage was set in order to try and establish the facts.

Statements were read out. As I gazed around the room, all eyes were on this person, mostly in disbelief that an organisation that had previously supported us was now backpedalling.

I took the opportunity as co-chair to firstly thank them for coming, especially as some of the other charities refused, and secondly to ask why they had sent a briefing to the Government to block our campaign. The air in the room thickened, like breathing was now an effort. 'Emailing a briefing isn't lobbying,' they replied nervously. 'Can I just stop you there,' I interrupted, sensing we were now right on the verge of a rather large reveal in the world of animal welfare campaigning. Everyone in the audience was now staring at me, wondering what I was going to do next. 'Who here thinks emailing a briefing is the same as lobbying?' I asked the room. Everyone's hand shot up. Unanimous agreement. It was obvious to everyone there that this organisation, along with another, had indeed undermined the inquiry and blocked our ban. The news was out there. As you can imagine it didn't take long for articles, tweets, and online petitions to emerge, sharing the depressing news and actively asking animal-lovers to help change their stance. I felt the pressure lift from my shoulders. The first ever APDAWG meeting in Westminster had proved to a target audience what we already knew, and as a result we'd found a way to regain some control. Now we just had to work out our next move.

Once again it all came down to resources. Our tiny coalition of campaigners had nothing but the evidence and the positions of those organisations which had now been made public. What could we do next with the minimal tools at our disposal to try and reverse this desperate situation and change the law?

It was my dad who taught me that any message you're trying to communicate to the public, e.g. a brand's slogan, strapline, or catchphrase, is most effective when kept short and sweet. Our campaign was calling for a law to immediately ban commercial (for profit) third-party sales of puppies and kittens, which I think everyone would agree was a bit of a mouthful, and possibly hard for the public to quickly grasp from that description alone. Lucy's sad passing granted us a unique opportunity. I clearly remember that this time the idea didn't come to me in the bath or even on a plane, but during the removal of an infected womb (pyometra) from a Siberian Husky in my operating theatre. We already had an army: over 70,000 of Lucy's followers who were all upset, mourning, and angry at the injustice of puppy farming and the third-party puppy dealing that caused thousands of dogs like Lucy to suffer. Surely by personalising our campaign, and naming it after Lucy in her honour, we could harness that emotion and move forward. Plus, like a gift from the branding gods, 'Lucy's Law' was an alliteration too, making it catchy, easy to remember, share, and hopefully much harder to ignore. As I closed the wound and my patient recovered from her anaesthetic feeling a lot better, I couldn't wait to tell Linda, my sounding board for *everything* confidential and campaign-related.

On my drive back to Brighton that evening I called her as I did every night – I can't emphasise enough the importance of having someone like Linda to share innermost campaign thoughts with – and told her that I had an epiphany about our campaign whilst operating and thought I might've cracked it. 'Go on?' she replied, sounding more excited than she had done lately during the last few dark months. 'I think we should call the campaign "Lucy's Law"!' I said those two words out loud for the first time, and it felt even better than it had going around and around my head for the last few hours since placing that last suture in that Husky's wound. Linda also loved Lucy deeply and had also recently lost one of her own beautiful ex-puppy-farm rescue dogs to cancer. There was a brief moment of silence and I knew it was because she was fighting back her tears, but she managed to practically scream down the phone 'YES!' followed by, 'Oh my God. Lucy's Law! It's perfect! And what a beautiful tribute to our little friend!' Then the tears started again. It felt like suddenly everything seemed to make sense and almost click into place, and at that moment, whilst driving back along the coast road between Peacehaven and Brighton, and with Linda at home in West Wales, we were the only two people in the whole world who knew about it – about Lucy's Law.

Linda and I were used to sharing secrets; an integral part of campaigning is finding out confidential information and then deciding if, and how, to use it to progress your campaign. One thing was for sure, if we were going to name our campaign Lucy's Law, I had to first seek permission from Lisa. I knew I was going to see her soon at one of the summer fun dog shows, I think it was Mayhew's 'Hounds on the Heath', and I preferred to wait and ask her in person rather than call her.

On arrival I spotted Lisa and we started chatting as usual. I must admit I was a bit nervous. What if she said no? Perhaps it would be too painful a reminder, or it would be too soon to even mention Lucy, let alone make her the poster girl for all the dogs just like her, that our campaign was determined to help. I took a deep breath and just went for it. 'Can I run an idea past you?' I asked apprehensively. 'Sure, what is it?' Lisa replied with a slightly concerned look on her face. 'I'd like to name the campaign "Lucy's Law", in honour of little Lucy, what do you think?' Lisa looked at me and started welling-up, which of course made me very emotional too, igniting raw emotions from my dad's passing the previous year, so I gulped a load of air down and continued, 'If we're successful, your little Lucy will be the dog that changes the world.' And with that we were both crying. Lisa was nodding in approval, too emotional to say the words. I put my arm round her, and in stunned silence at a fun dog show on the middle of Hampstead Heath, we both tried to take on board the enormity of this idea, and, if successful, its potential impact on the future of animal welfare. Now a total of three people knew, and it wasn't long before that became four.

Someone else who will always keep information confidential is actor and animal welfare campaigner Peter Egan. Peter and I are often invited to judge at the same fun dog shows, usually because we're ambassadors of exactly the same rescue charities, and also because we both find it almost impossible to say no. Peter had also met Lucy numerous times and had shared our frustration; he had been there at that game-changing APDAWG meeting in Westminster a few weeks back, so had himself witnessed and heard first-hand all the evidence. I quietly ran the Lucy's Law idea past Peter and he immediately became all teary too. 'Oh, that's marvellous,' he said in his deep, warm, inimitable voice, and then gave a long pause while he processed the information further, his voice now slightly breaking with emotion. 'What a fantastic idea!'

Lucy's Law really was the last throw of the dice. Our group of campaigners was physically, psychologically, and emotionally worn down. It had been years since we'd all started our own individual campaigns, and over four years since we'd met up and began campaigning together as one. We were still up against the 'fortress' of the government and the multi-billion pound pet industry – proper David and Goliath stuff. But we were still very much the poor minnows in a pond full of huge, rich, powerful fish. We all had proper jobs, some of us were grieving loved ones, both two- and four-legged, and were still trying to do all this in our spare time, which invariably meant very little downtime or any decent sleep.

In order for Lucy's Law to garner as much attention as possible we needed to launch it cleverly, strategically, and with significant impact. Lucy's Law was exactly that kind of slogan or catchphrase, that kind of marketing gold the value of which my dad had taught me to appreciate. Its simplicity and alliteration were a gift; it had to be handled with care. We were also more than aware of the reality that Lucy's Law was most likely our last chance to change the law. We knew we might never get another opportunity like this one ever again. But at the same time, we were confident that nothing had ever felt more right.

It was July 2017 when I first discussed Lucy's Law with Linda, Lisa, and Peter. I'd gained all their approvals and positive feedback, so next I called Julia in Folkstone, Sue in Wales, and Philippa in Sheffield, to tell them all about our new top-secret plan one by one. Some things are just far too important, and so much better shared by phone than email. You also get that person's initial reaction which, unsurprisingly, in each case so far, had been very emotional. Everyone loved the idea of Lucy's Law, so I started thinking about how best to proceed. Even though Parliament doesn't sit during the summer months, I was still vetting and, of course, Bex and I were busy organising September's Pup Aid celebrity-judged fun dog show in Primrose Hill, which was now in its ninth year and bigger than ever, which also meant there was a hungrier appetite for change.

But Pup Aid had been suddenly dropped by its main sponsor without warning, for no apparent reason, presumably because of pressure from the pet industry, so I was now also desperately trying to find a replacement sponsor. One Pup Aid fun dog show costs about £20,000 to put on, so it was vital to find some cash, and with the event coming up in just a couple of months, we needed to find it fast. This really wasn't an easy task at all as most pet foods are stocked by big retail park pet superstores, i.e. the very people refusing to support our campaign, so we desperately needed to find a dog food brand that was only sold in independent pet shops that don't sell animals, or ordered online and delivered. After a few unsuccessful meetings with some of the wealthiest pet food companies tied into big corporate pet shop chains, with their predictable 'We'd love to help but we just don't have any budget at the moment' attitudes, I arranged to meet with Nutriment at their headquarters in Surrey, and they kindly and generously agreed to become Pup Aid's main sponsor. Looking back, it's highly unlikely Pup Aid would've happened that year, or ever again, if they hadn't, so I really can't thank them enough for their generosity and support.

When planning the Lucy's Law launch, I knew it had to be in Westminster, but more importantly it needed to be kept top secret. I worried that any hint or leak of Lucy's Law would be open to more blocking. However, we had to have exactly the right people to be in the room at the launch, so how could we achieve that without telling them what they were actually being invited to attend? After many more chats with Linda and my campaigning crew, we realised we already had the perfect carrot with which to attract everyone, without needing to make the big reveal until the day, at the event itself.

Just over a year beforehand we had launched the Great British Puppy Survey to gather data on the public's puppy buying experiences over previous years, research that was used as vital evidence to support our campaigning. With her vast experience of rescuing and rehabilitating ex-puppy-farm breeding dogs, Linda decided it was time for the next phase in information gathering, so created the 'Ex-Breeding Dog Survey' with the help of Julia and Sue, in order to ascertain if their own involvement rescuing and rehabilitating these poor dogs mirrored those of others who had adopted or fostered them. This comprehensive survey, which was most likely the first of its kind in the UK, was launched in autumn 2017. The response was overwhelming; people were only too happy to share their experiences. What could be more appropriate than to reveal the results from the first stage of this survey in Westminster? The date we set was hugely significant and symbolic too, as that week in December marked the first anniversary of Lucy's passing.

Meanwhile, I was trying to nail down a media partner for the Lucy's Law launch and subsequent campaign. With Andrew Penman's previous extraordinary commitment to our work, he was always going to be the first journalist I approached. After a series of peppermint-tea-fuelled meetings in the Carluccio's below his *Mirror* headquarters in Canary Wharf, one of which included convincing the head of the whole organisation that owns the *Mirror* that this was a good idea, and had a slim chance of being successful, Andrew and his boss agreed: the *Mirror* would be the Lucy's Law campaign's official media partner, and we started to plan our combined activity.

Our first mission was to design the Lucy's Law campaign logo, the brand if you like, which I sketched once, showed

Andrew, and which his *Mirror*'s graphic design colleagues very kindly turned into reality. My first attempt was the one we used; I must've been channelling my dad's expert branding powers that day. The components were obvious: a picture of Lucy that Lisa had approved; Lucy's favourite colour pink; and the all-important #LucysLaw hashtag. With the logo agreed, the *Mirror* continued to generously prepare for the launch, designing literature, pledge cards, impressive banners, and picture boards featuring pictures of Lucy in the arms of numerous celebrities for the December Westminster launch event. I took myself off to Gozo near Malta for 10 days of scuba-diving in the day, and intense campaign work every night, planning the next few months in my head, going through every outcome, as well as confidentially priming MPs and everyone associated with hopefully making our next battle in Westminster our last.

That autumn was filled with equal measures of excitement, anticipation, and anxiety. What if Lucy's Law was unsuccessful? Then what would we do?

In the autumn of 2017 my friend and lawyer Paula Sparks, Chair of the UK Centre for Animal Law, introduced me to licensing barrister Sarah Clover from the Institute of Licensing, another special relationship that would eventually help change the course of animal welfare history. I also travelled to Philadelphia with Peter Egan and rescued some puppy mill breeding dogs with my friends from Finding Shelter Animal Rescue and celebrity dog trainer Victoria

Stilwell. Amongst the few dogs we rescued was a very poorly shut-down German Shepherd, later named 'Victoria'. A few of us also spoke at the very well attended 'United Against Puppy Farming' rally outside Parliament, coordinated by numerous campaign groups in England and Wales, all calling for a ban on third-party puppy dealers. This was perfectly timed to coincide with a 'Sale of Puppies' debate in Westminster, in which the Minister concluded that 'We do not believe that a ban on third-party sellers is necessary, and that view is shared by many stakeholders'; those 'many' stakeholders were later revealed in a Parliamentary Question to DEFRA by a friendly MP.

Off the back of that rally I heard a rumour that there would soon be another puppy-related debate in Westminster Hall, this time focused on smuggling. It's pretty obvious that puppy smuggling relies 100% on puppies being sold away from their mothers by third parties: exactly what Lucy's Law would help tackle. There are many components to ending this illegal trade, but surely removing the market for smuggled pups and the legal third-party framework that enables this illegal activity *must* be a priority?

After doing some digging, I discovered that the MP bringing the puppy-smuggling debate to the House of Commons didn't have an obvious track record in publicly discussing or promoting animal welfare − first alarm bell. Secondly this MP's constituency was where a rehoming centre belonging to one of the charities that were still appearing to oppose our campaign was located – second alarm bell. Had that particular charity requested this debate to make themselves look relevant, perhaps try and gain back some control, or use the debate as a vehicle to oppose and frustrate our campaign even more? With the puppy-smuggling debate scheduled for Westminster Hall in two days' time, and after repeatedly requesting to urgently meet with the MP and being consistently refused, his office finally conceded, and I was allowed five minutes with him in Portcullis House the following morning. I'll be honest, it wasn't one of the most relaxed meetings I've ever had in that place, but all I was asking for was the inclusion of one line, for the MP to mention a ban on third-party dealers in his opening speech, as just a part of the multi-pronged solution to ending puppy smuggling. With the launch of the highly confidential Lucy's Law in a few weeks' time, this was potentially a golden opportunity for MPs to voice their support for a ban, but it had to be brought up first.

After I'd explained why a ban was so important to tackle puppy smuggling, the MP said he'd consider mentioning it, which he later confirmed after meeting that day with a representative from our friends and fellow third-party ban supporters International Fund for Animal Welfare (IFAW), the charity responsible for the brilliantly clever 'Suzy Puppy' cuddly toy campaign launched in Westminster months earlier.

I was working back at the practice on debate day, so as usual when there was something going on in Westminster that I needed to watch live, Grant would generously rearrange my appointments and surgical procedures so I could observe Parliamentary proceedings on my laptop on my consulting room table. As the debate unfolded, I watched with bated breath. Would the MP keep his word and mention the ban? It wouldn't be in the interest of the big charity – but if he did, I hoped it would provide the hook for other MPs to also mention it, and hopefully express their support too. In the end, not only did the MP mention the ban at the end of his opening speech as agreed, but the majority of attending cross-party MPs then all spoke in favour of it too! We'd controlled the debate, but that wasn't the end of it. That evening I took screenshots of each MP verbally supporting the ban, then tweeted the image with their exact words (taken from Hansard), tagging in the then Secretary of State, Mr Michael Gove. It's the most primitive form of campaigning when you have no other resources, and it takes hours to do properly, but amazingly Mr Gove not only shared two of my tweets, but also some encouraging comments as well. We'd not only successfully orchestrated the outcome of this Westminster debate in our campaign's favour, but also enjoyed some positive responses from one of the chief decision-makers himself: the perfect result and set-up for what was to come next.

December arrived. After months of careful planning, meetings, constructing and analysing the ex-breeding dogs survey, more meetings, and some rather unique finishing touches if I say so myself, we were ready to launch Lucy's

Law in Westminster. Philippa was unable to join us for this next chapter of our campaign – she just wasn't well enough to attend. Our campaigning family was saddened, but equally we were determined to put a brave face on it and make this a huge success in honour of Lucy and the UK's dogs.

As well as inviting journalists, MPs, fellow campaigners, representatives of charities supporting the ban, and of course Lucy's owner Lisa, I'd also asked singer-songwriter Lucy Spraggan, *X-Factor* star and owner of Boston terrier Steve, to come along and play a few songs on her guitar. Adding a sprinkling of celebrity dust to campaigning events always makes them more memorable, as Pup Aid had shown, and, as you can imagine, having a famous, dog-loving, hugely popular and talented Lucy present, with hundreds of thousands of followers on social media, was a lovely tribute to our own Lucy, who had passed away exactly a year ago that week. As our guests arrived to witness the reveal of our ex-breeding dog survey, all the Lucy's Law banners and placards were either covered up or turned to face the wall. At that moment only about six people on the planet knew what was just about to happen.

As the vegan canapés and vegan wine were passed around (you'd be amazed at how many animal welfare events in Westminster promoting animal welfare aren't vegan or vegetarian-catered), I prepared to give the first speech, and for the first time, let everyone in on our big secret. I was able to get most of my words out OK, but knew my voice would crack when describing little Lucy, the significance of the date, and how much she was missed. On announcing Lucy's Law and instructing all the banners and picture boards to be revealed and displayed as rehearsed, that second I felt a unique energy in the room that I'd never experienced before: an energy of hope, positivity, and of a kinder future for animals.

As well as my words, there were also speeches from my campaigning sister and confidante Linda from C.A.R.I.A.D., who delivered the main findings of the research report on ex-breeding dogs; Andrew Penman from the *Mirror*; barrister Sarah Clover; and a beautiful tribute to Lucy from actor and campaigner Peter Egan. MP-wise, we heard from Lisa Cameron, now Chair of APDAWG after Rob Flello lost his seat in the 2017 election, while Labour's Sue Hayman and the Conservatives' Zac Goldsmith, Giles Watling, and Chris Davies made up the cross-party support. Lucy's Law was *specifically* the 'immediate' ban on puppies sold by commercial third-party puppy dealers such as pet shops; immediate so as to not give any individual or organisation the opportunity of saying they agreed to the principle of Lucy's Law but weren't prepared to support it *yet*.

Our Lucy's Law launch in Westminster was one of the most incredible and emotional experiences of my life. After almost eight years of campaigning for a ban, our little group of campaigners had just revealed a campaign with so much potential that MPs, fellow campaigners, and the majority of charities were only too proud to get behind it. That evening, as Lucy Spraggan belted out three of her hits on the terrace of the Commons, in this beautiful venue overlooking the Thames, we knew something had shifted. And remember that urban myth about Cavaliers not actually allowed in Parliament – well here was Lucy's beautiful and vulnerable face staring out from her own logo on every carefully designed poster and banner around that room. Little Lucy had brought fresh hope to the campaign to ban cruel puppy dealers – a hope that felt like it could in fact change the world forever.

As news of Lucy's Law spread, first on social media, followed by the *Mirror*, then in the doggy publications *Dogs Today* and *Our Dogs* who also attended the launch, animal welfare organisations the length and breadth of the country started publicly voicing their full support for Lucy's Law. These included RSPCA, Kennel Club, International Fund for Animal Welfare (IFAW), Dog Breeding Reform Group, and Conservative Animal Welfare Federation, as well as many small-midsize charities including Mayhew, All Dogs Matter, Edinburgh Dog and Cat Home, Raystede, Celia Hammond, and many many more. We knew Government was still appearing to ignore all these well-respected organisations as well as the public, but renaming and personalising the campaign after one of the bravest, funniest, and most vulnerable dogs we'd ever known had more of an impact than any of us could have ever imagined.

As December 2017 drew to a close there was definitely a new energy in the animal welfare world. To coincide with the launch of Lucy's Law, Lisa Cameron MP had also launched the Lucy's Law Early Day Motion (a type of official Parliamentary online petition which only MPs can sign, and which quickly gained around 100 cross-party supporters). The APDAWG group held its 'Unsung Heroes' event in Westminster to celebrate and showcase campaigners and smaller charities doing good work for dog welfare with minimal resources, a meeting that was attended by PC Dave Wardell and his brave dog Finn, who would of course be ultimately responsible for Finn's Law passing into legislation. It finally felt like the mould had been broken. Campaigners and smaller organisations were being listened to; our views, expertise, and most importantly evidence were now being considered, making an impact, and most importantly taken into account by the actual decision-makers in Westminster.

As the year drew to a close Lucy's Law was mentioned twice in a Westminster Hall debate thanks to Lisa Cameron and Zac Goldsmith, then in the Main Chamber of the Commons by Lisa again in another debate, as well being highlighted in the Scottish Parliament too. That Christmas Day I made my annual appearance on Sky News with Kay Burley, this time inviting onto the sofa with me Eileen Jones from Friends of Animals Wales. We discussed puppy farming and making your New Year's Resolution to adopt a rescue pet and of course support Lucy's Law. Eileen had brought with her two very special rescued ex-puppy-farm breeding dogs, a Westie called Wendy and a Bichon called Ursula – both absolute heartbreakers. When asked by Kay, I told viewers what they could do in 2018 to help animal welfare and make Lucy's Law a reality. These included uploading a picture of their pet to social media platforms and adding hashtag #LucysLaw inviting their MPs to sign the Lucy's Law Early Day Motion (EDM) 695 calling on the Government to 'immediately ban the sale of puppies by pet shops and other third-party commercial dealers', visit the *Mirror*'s new and dedicated Lucy's Law microsite, and even consider swapping their profile pic for the Lucy's Law logo.

2017 was finally over. It had started with those dark days of the Minister telling us there would be no ban, and that the situation wouldn't change for at least another five years. In less than 12 months, and undeniably still burdened with grieving the loss of close family members, we'd restrategised and in the strictest confidence rebranded, created, and launched our campaign, Lucy's Law, and now the whole world knew about it.

We were more hopeful than ever that change was coming in 2018. The poor breeding dogs in the UK and beyond, still being exploited for their pups, had never needed Lucy's Law more. After the Westminster launch, on my way out of Westminster Palace that night, I remember walking through Central Lobby, and then past my favourite picture of the Borzois in St Stephen's Hall. I gave them a nod as I always did, but this time it felt very different, and the next few months would prove to be some of the most exciting, and mind-blowing, our tiny coalition of campaigners would ever experience.

Chapter 16

❧

When campaigning with little to no resources, you need to dig deep. Larger organisations have their own dedicated PR teams and impressive marketing budgets, specifically set aside to pay individuals, often celebrities, to endorse their products or campaigns and spread the word, but in cases like ours, with no financial reward on offer, it's often the cause itself, or, perhaps more importantly, the relationship with the actual campaigners, that will attract a well-known public figure or figures on board, hopefully leading to greater awareness-raising, and important messages, even petition links, shared on their hugely popular social media channels.

Furthermore, nowadays the actual word 'celebrity' is an interesting one. To me, growing up in the 80s, celebrities were usually only famous movie stars, TV personalities, musicians, inventors, explorers, sportsmen and sportswomen, high-profile politicians, and members of the Royal Family. Celebrity status back then was usually confirmed if you had achieved something monumental, had your own *Spitting Image* puppet, or a waxwork at Madame Tussauds; all three, and you were most likely more than qualified to enjoy celebrity status.

Dad had often worked with celebrities who would endorse products in his advertising campaigns. He always enjoyed meeting new people, and especially people he admired on telly or elsewhere. I remember one morning waking up to a signed photo, an autograph, with my name and everything, from Lenny Henry who he'd worked with on a photoshoot in London. As you can imagine, being a huge fan of *Tiswas* and *Three of a Kind* growing up, this was incredibly exciting. Go forward a generation and the autographed pictures of the 80s are now the selfies of today, literally snapshots of time personalised by a celebrity.

What qualifies someone to be a celebrity these days appears to be very different. Reality TV shows, 24-hour news channels, and of course social media, have widened the scope for well-known personalities. Degrees of achievement and influence all contribute to someone's status as a potential celebrity. Campaigns involving celebrities now have a different focus. It makes sense that in order to spread your message as far and wide as possible, it helps having someone, a human brand if you like, with a much bigger reach, and preferably one that's both well respected, popular, and relevant too.

But without the enormous budgets to entice celebrities, or even access to their contact details, how does one go about recruiting these well known personalities, or 'influencers', as they're often referred to these days? Most influencers will have agents whose contact details can be found online if you search for their management agency websites. In Pup Aid's early days, while I was working in various vet practices around London, I spent every spare minute of my lunch hours, gaps in consulting, and free evenings, frantically emailing hundreds of celebrity agents and managers asking for their clients' support. My nurses thought I was mad. That was in the days before Twitter had really taken off, so emailing was pretty much the only way to make contact. Sadly, trying to persuade celebrities, most of whom owned pets and lived in London, to attend a brand new puppy farming awareness dog show down in Sussex, on a weekend, was pretty soul-destroying, especially when you knew as animal-lovers they'd most probably enjoy it – not to mention feel proud to play a small part in changing the future for dogs. My philosophy was that the more emails I sent out, the more likely I was to get a bite. Rejection, or just no reply, was by far the norm, but I didn't mind as I knew my spare time was filled with trying, and I'd rather try than not do anything at all – campaigning in a nutshell.

Another way to get in touch with celebrity influencers was to attempt to meet them. Not finding out where they live and hanging around outside their homes waiting to ambush them; but rather attending fun dog shows organised by animal welfare organisations, to which ambassadors, patrons, and celebrity supporters are often invited. Between Mayhew's excellent 'Hounds on the Heath' and All Dogs Matter's wonderful 'Great British Bark Off' fun dog shows, I'd met a fair few celebrities, who were all quite happy to have a chat and share either their own or their manager's contact details. This second way of enlisting celebrity support is much easier than emailing blindly, but does of course involve the effort of finding out where and when these dog shows take place, and the expense and time taken out of a weekend to travel there and back. It always helps to be a fan of these celebrities, do your homework, and follow their social media accounts too, as you'll often know of any upcoming events they may be planning to attend, and have something to talk about when you eventually meet them. Sometimes you'll come home with no results, but the above campaigning mantra still applies: better to try than to not try at all. Nowadays with Twitter, Facebook, Instagram, and personal blogs on their websites, most celebrities can often be messaged directly, either on the public timeline or privately, depending on their settings or if they follow you back, or via their website. If these are your chosen routes please always be polite, respectful, and very patient.

One of the first, and most exciting, experiences I ever had inviting a celebrity to be involved in the early years of the Pup Aid campaign was as part of my 'guitar' project. It was Christmas 2009, and I was on holiday over 6,000 miles away with my mum, sister, and her two boys Nathan and Jordan, who had all booked into an all-expenses-paid five-star resort holiday on the western coast of Mauritius. The resort they'd chosen was far too expensive for me, but I'd just completed a few weeks vetting so had just enough to pay for a cheap flight and £20-per-night shared guest-house perched on a clifftop about an hour and a half's walk down the pristine white beach that encircled this tropical island paradise. I was there to scuba dive twice a day every day and, after completing my dives, I'd walk up the beach to find the others. Now my mum likes to talk, to everyone, male or female, old or young, canine or feline, and especially on holiday, so it was no surprise that after a few days she knew everyone around the pool: what their names were, what they did for a living, and whether they owned a dog, cat, or both.

One day, Mum introduced me to a nice lady from Royal Leamington Spa called Tracy. Tracy was holidaying with her parents, and her father was a driver for the world famous Gibson guitar brand, based in Fitzrovia, Central London. After a few poolside cocktails whilst explaining my embryonic Pup Aid campaign – we'd only just had the one initial fun dog show in Brighton at that point – Tracy suggested it would be worth me asking Gibson to donate one of their fancy guitars for me to get signed by a dog-loving rock legend to endorse the campaign and help raise awareness. That's all it takes sometimes, a random conversation with a stranger, and a tiny glimmer of opportunity.

After a meeting at Gibson headquarters in Rathbone Street, London, on my return, surrounded by some of the most beautiful guitars I'd ever seen, it was confirmed that they would donate one of their classic Epiphone Casino guitars, the iconic instrument played by none other than the Beatles'

John Lennon, if I found someone worthy enough to sign it. I only really had the one contact in the music industry who could help me; I emailed Pup Aid's newly appointed patron Meg Mathews, asking whether she thought perhaps one of the Gallagher brothers from Oasis would do the honours. It wasn't long before Meg replied with the good news: Liam had agreed to sign the guitar, and, as a massive Oasis fan, I was totally made-up.

On signing day Milton, Stuart and I travelled up to London and waited anxiously for Liam to arrive, all wondering if he'd behave like his on-stage 'don't give a f*ck' persona. At 1pm on the dot, as promised, a black cab pulled up, delivering not only lead singer of Oasis Liam Gallagher, but also his partner at the time, All Saints singer-songwriter Nicole Appleton, *and* their black and tan, smooth miniature dachshund Ruby Tuesday too! Liam was classic Liam outside, complete with Lennon-esque sunglasses and characteristic swagger, but once inside with sunglasses removed, and shoulders more relaxed, he was one of the funniest, most charming celebrities I've ever met. We were only allowed the one photo, but we only needed one; the picture featured in most mainstream tabloid newspapers and websites (favourite headline: 'Champagne Super Rover!') the next day. I thanked Liam and Nicole for their support and offered the only thing I could in return: a visit to their son Gene's school to talk about caring for animals, which I honoured every year for the next few years. Bumping into Liam at the school gates and chatting about the latest football news was always a major, albeit surreal, highlight. Thanks to Liam, Pup Aid's campaign messages of puppy farm awareness, always seeing pups with mums, and adopting from rescue were reaching a whole new audience of potential dog owners, including lots of music fans.

After Liam signed the guitar, I remember looking down at all that extra space left on that beautiful Epiphone Casino and deciding to invite some more rock legends to add their signatures too. Surely it would create even more PR, puppy farming awareness, potentially encourage even more people to choose a dog responsibly, and then eventually I could auction off the guitar, with all proceeds going to a couple of my favourite rescue dog charities. Suddenly I had a brand-new mission.

My best mate Russell and I had tickets for V Festival that year, so I strategically chose a week's locum work in Essex, close by the festival site, so we were only a short taxi ride from a proper roof to sleep under instead of in a soggy tent. Looking at the line-up I noticed rock legend Paul Weller was playing the main stage on Saturday afternoon. I was determined to get his signature next if I could, so I grabbed the guitar, and off we went. We made it just in time. Mr Weller was still on stage, so imagine a scenario when you're at the back of a field full of tens of thousands of drunken festival goers, knowing that you've got to get that person currently performing to sign a guitar, without *any* planning whatsoever. Nothing like a challenge, eh? Russell and I headed in the direction of backstage, and at every barrier the security guards would ask who we were, what we were up to, and where we thought we were going. Every time we were quizzed, I'd just unlock and gently lift the lid of the guitar case. Every single security guard's reaction was like that bit in *Pulp Fiction* when they open the suitcase and that golden light shines out, mesmerising everyone. Through one layer of tight security, easily through the next, and the next. All of a sudden, we found ourselves right outside an artist's portacabin with a handwritten 'Paul Weller' sign sellotaped to the door, holding a guitar case. Understandably his management were a bit nervous, but after explaining why we were there, and showing Paul the photo of Liam signing which I had on my phone, he was more than happy to sign, and we shook hands. The guitar now had two rock legends' signatures.

For the next few months I carried on inviting more rock legends to sign. Next up I arranged to meet another one of Meg's contacts, lead guitarist from The Clash, Mick Jones, at his house in Notting Hill, who immediately played me 'Should I Stay or Should I Go' right there! Next up were Brighton-based David Gilmour from Pink Floyd, Brian May from Queen, Led Zeppelin founder and guitarist Jimmy Page, The Who's founder and lead singer Roger Daltrey, and the legendary singer-songwriter and guitarist Gary Moore, just weeks before he tragically passed away. The final two signatories were guitarist, singer, and songwriter Eric Clapton, and co-founder and guitarist of the Rolling Stones, Keith Richards. What a list of rock legends, with all their autographs on one guitar. Mission completed, my next task was to find an auction house, and indeed a specialist sale appropriate for this particular piece of rock memorabilia, in order to give it its best chance of raising funds to help rescue dogs. After some research, I found the perfect opportunity at world-famous auction house, Bonhams in Knightsbridge, London. I nervously attended the auction, and in amongst the original Beatles lyrics, as well as other signed instruments, I was proud to witness the signed Pup Aid Gibson guitar sell to a collector bidding online for a few thousand pounds, which also raised even more awareness of puppy farming.

This whole exercise showed how a single innocent comment, made months before during a conversation thousands of miles away on a remote desert island, had led to a guitar signed by 10 rock legends raising thousands of pounds for dog charities. Campaigning was about being resourceful, sensing an opportunity, imagination, then following it up in your spare time, achieving positive results for animal welfare using creativity, ambition, and relationship building, rather than always depending on heavily branded, corporate in-house PR departments with bottomless budgets.

The Pup Aid guitar project did more than help raise awareness about puppy farming, the importance of seeing a pup with mum, and of course rescue pet adoption. As well as being auctioned off to raise much-needed funds to help dogs in smaller, rescue shelters, that guitar boasted one signature which sparked the beginning of a very special friendship with legendary Queen guitarist and cat-owner, Dr Brian May.

Like most people born in the 70s, I was a massive fan of Queen, and even managed to get a ticket right at the back of the 37,000-capacity Estadio Municipal in Marbella, Spain for their It's a Kind of Magic tour in August 1986. Obviously due to my unbelievably geeky priorities of collecting a chemistry prize, I'd missed seeing them at Live Aid the summer before, but still to this day remember the sea of outstretched clapping hands on that balmy Mediterranean evening, as 'Radio Ga Ga' engulfed and energised the excited crowd. So when I first came face to face with Brian himself, over 20 years later, at his wildlife sanctuary in Surrey, guitarcase in hand ready for him to sign, the only thing I could manage to say to the great man was 'the last time I saw you, you were this big!' holding up a tiny invisible peanut. Brian smiled and gave me a big hug. That's Brian all over: charming, friendly, and a very good hugger. As well as signing the guitar he also took time to introduce me to the injured badgers and orphaned foxes he was helping to rehabilitate.

Over the next few years Brian would attend Pup Aid in Primrose Hill, share my petition posts on social media, and invite me to march and speak alongside him at numerous wildlife rallies outside Parliament too. We'd email each other sharing our deepest campaigning thoughts and pressures, often in the middle of the night. You see, whether you're a world-famous rock legend fighting for badgers, foxes, hedgehogs, and other wildlife, or a passionate small-animal vet desperately trying to end puppy farming, being so heavily invested in campaigning can often make you feel lonely, exposed, depressed, and vulnerable. But one thing I've learned over the years is that it doesn't matter who you are: when you're connecting with another animal welfare campaigner either in person, by phone, or on email at 3 o'clock in the morning, it becomes like a weird type of counselling. No arguments, no confrontation, no feeling of someone trying to trip you up or make you explain the obvious; just mutual respect, huge admiration, sharing thoughts, and calmness. Over the years Brian and I became very close friends, and I even created a special file just for his emails named 'Brimance' – but he doesn't know that, so please don't *ever* tell him.

Another huge celebrity supporter of the Lucy's Law campaign was TV presenter and mathematician Rachel Riley, known mainly for her appearances on Channel 4's daily *Countdown* show, and more recently the late night comedy version *8 Out Of 10 Cats Does Countdown*. I'd always been a fan of Rachel, but had no idea she was an animal-lover until an appearance in July 2014 on the first episode of an internet-based topical quiz show *Virtually Famous* on E4, described then as a 'hilarious new panel show that discovers all the weird and wonderful characters we find online'. Rachel was teamed up with another good mate of mine, comedian Romesh Ranganathan, and in one round a remote-control stuffed cat called Orville, constructed by Dutch artist Bart

Jansen, complete with propellers attached to its paws, was flown directly over them both. Rachel's reaction said it all, and by the fond way she then talked about her own Ragdoll cats, I knew she was not only an animal-lover, but would be a perfect ambassador for the campaign. But how do you make contact with such high profile celebrities, let alone invite them to be involved with your campaign? With Rachel I was in luck, as about 20 accounts which already followed me on Twitter were also being followed by her. I privately messaged them all, asking them to please ask her to follow me back. And one of the only accounts that actually asked Rachel was none other than Brian May himself – talk about teamwork! Rachel, who was based in West London, followed me back, and we arranged to meet for breakfast after I'd appeared on an episode of *The Wright Stuff*, filmed on the top floor of Whiteleys Shopping Centre in Bayswater, near where she lived.

Rachel and I became good friends, and she and her *Strictly Come Dancing* partner Pasha Kovalev attended Pup Aid in London multiple times, where they enjoyed meeting little Lucy too. Rachel Riley's contribution to the Lucy's Law campaign was nothing short of enormous, and for the last few years, on the eve of Pup Aid she'd even mention our fun dog show with *Countdown* host Nick Hewer on Channel 4, encouraging animal-lovers to come along to Primrose Hill the next day. I would regularly meet up with Rachel to update her on the campaign's progress, and one day she invited me up to Manchester to be a guest in the audience of *8 Out Of 10 Cats*

Does Countdown. After the warm-up guy had done his bit, on came the presenters followed by the comedian panellists, all of course to a rapturous TV-audience applause. As soon as Rachel and her partner in crime, Dictionary Corner's Susie Dent, arrived on stage, they surrounded host Jimmy Carr and began whispering in his ears and pointing up at me… 'You're the puppy guy!' Jimmy shouted in front of the whole audience, before seconds later making a joke about needing puppy farms to make puppy fur coats! He finally conceded that I was doing a good job and he, as a dog owner himself, was also giving me his full support.

Sitting in the audience that night as a comedy fan, I felt a mixture of incredible pride that Jimmy Carr, a comedian I respected and had admired for years, had an appreciation for my work too. Furthermore, as well as her numerous mentions of Pup Aid on *Countdown*, as well as attending our annual Primrose Hill dog show multiple times with Pasha, Rachel's support on Twitter was also incredible, culminating in a tweet she posted on 13 March 2018 that simply said 'I'm after a favour…' followed by the hashtag #LucysLaw, petition link, and a short video of Rachel talking into her phone, saying: *'This is a message for animal-lovers, asking – if you haven't already signed the petition for Lucy's Law – please take 10 seconds and do it now. If you don't know what it is, it's a campaign by a vet called Marc Abraham, who was sick and tired of treating animals who'd come in with the same diseases – families had unwittingly got them from puppy farms and they came in and it cost a lot of money, a lot of distress, and a lot of pain for the animals, and we want it to stop. There's 87,000 people who have already signed this petition in the last two weeks, we need to get to 100,000 and then Government debates it in parliament. They are keen to do so, they are keen to get the law in, they just need to see the public supports it, so please, take 10 seconds for Lucy's Law. Thank you very much.'* And with that, a few hours later we'd smashed the 100,000 target and were planning our debate in Parliament, but more on that later. I'll never forget the phenomenal impact Rachel made on the whole campaign, and how valuable her individual input was in helping it get over the line.

Ricky Gervais was another person who generously gave us his support to ban third-party puppy dealers and finally get Lucy's Law passed. Weirdly it wasn't at a dog show when I first properly met Ricky. My friend Julie-Ann, the Brighton-based artist, invited me to the private view of a charity exhibition she'd organised at the intimate Catto Gallery in Hampstead, as I'd been asked, amongst many other 'media personalities', to submit a painting to be auctioned online. The night before I'd stayed at my folks' house in Stanmore, and before setting off, I was watching *This Morning*, which not only had a litter of cute Golden Retriever puppies running around the studio, but also special guest and comedy legend Ricky Gervais.

Seeing puppies on such a popular show always makes my stomach churn, as I imagine everyone watching immediately googling 'puppies', 'cute pups', 'Golden Retriever pups', and so on, with puppy farmers up and down the country now rubbing their grubby little hands with glee. I left before the end of the show, frustrated that there had been no mention of rescue dog adoption, and was also annoyingly missing Ricky's interview too. On arrival at the gallery there were already a few high-profile guest artists present, including Arsenal and England striker turned TV pundit Ian Wright. A few minutes later, in walked Ricky, straight from *This Morning*, accompanied by his partner, best-selling author Jane Fallon. After a while I plucked up enough courage and asked to have my picture taken with Ricky, both holding our respective canvasses: mine of the Brighton starlings, and Ricky's of one of his weird and wonderful Flanimals creations. I don't often get starstruck, but meeting a comedy hero will do that to me, and Ricky and I chatted briefly in a quiet corner amongst the canvases. 'I was watching you on the telly earlier,' I said, 'What a shame they didn't mention rescue dogs.' 'Don't worry,' Ricky replied, 'I did!' From that brief exchange and observing his obvious respect for rescue pets, I knew right at that moment that meeting Ricky Gervais was the start of something special for the future of animal welfare. As Ricky and Jane left the gallery, I seized the opportunity and asked Jane if I could contact her in the next few days with a few campaigning ideas. She very gracefully said yes. Later that day Jane followed me back on Twitter, privately messaged me her email address, and one of the biggest windows of animal welfare campaigning opportunity had just been opened.

Over the next few years Ricky helped spread the work of the campaign with his millions of followers, including our all-important petition links. He attended the first and last Pup Aid fun dog shows in Primrose Hill, and shared literally hundreds of Pup Aid's social media posts promoting rescue pet adoption. As the years went on, unsurprisingly we bumped into each other at more and more dog-related events, supporting the same charities, as well as at the Animal Hero Awards when we both received one, and we became good friends. For me, the culmination of our campaigning partnership was when I arranged to meet Ricky backstage at one of his first SuperNature warm-up gigs in Finchley, North London in May 2018. Ricky agreed to hold the placard saying 'I'm helping to end puppy farm cruelty by supporting #LucysLaw', which proved to become one of the most game-changing photos in all the 10 years of the campaign to ban cruel puppy dealers. To this day I can't thank Ricky and Jane enough, as well as Ricky's assistant Jonathan, for always generously supporting all my campaign work and helping change the world for animals.

Last, and by no means least, another major celebrity influencer to help with the success of Pup Aid and Lucy's Law is actor Peter Egan. Those of you who are on Twitter and Facebook will know only too well that Peter is unique: not just a huge British acting talent, having starred in countless stage, television, and movie productions, including playing Shrimpy in the hugely acclaimed ITV series *Downton Abbey*, appearing in *Chariots of Fire*, and most famously playing Paul Ryman in one of the greatest British sitcoms of all time in the 80s, *Ever Decreasing Circles*. But Peter, or 'Sir Peter' as he deserves to be called, is so much more than 'just' a great actor. Owner of a few rescue dogs himself, and patron and ambassador of many animal welfare organisations, including his beloved Animals Asia, Peter is one of the bravest, most determined animal welfare campaigners there is. He just doesn't stop fighting for the animals and throwing his weight behind so many campaigns to protect the most vulnerable, but will also go above and beyond, supporting campaigns on social media, attending dog shows and events, as well as travelling to China, Romania, Indonesia, or wherever his voice is needed to fight animal cruelty. We were so lucky that over the years Peter came along to every single Pup Aid fun dog show, even the ones down in Brighton, attended many a charity event, march, rally, and gathering with me in Westminster, and we even flew all the way to the States once to support charity Finding Shelter Animal Rescue, where we visited some puppy mills, and helped rescue an ex-breeding German Shepherd later named Victoria. What's more, and this is pretty crazy as coincidences go, Peter even worked with my dad back in the 80s, doing a voiceover for one of his commercials! Peter met Lucy many times and became a great friend of Lisa's too. Like everyone that's ever met him, or just been fortunate enough to be in his company, I have nothing but full admiration, utmost respect, and a great deal of love for my buddy Peter Egan, another great hugger, and I always look forward to sharing our new father-son type relationship whenever and wherever we hang out.

Chapter 17

January 2018 started very calmly, with the annual sponsored walk at my favourite spot in Sussex, the Cuckmere Haven, in aid of my favourite local rescue centre Raystede, a shelter within a wildlife sanctuary that always supported my campaign to ban third-party puppy dealers, way before it was renamed Lucy's Law. As well as doing my day job vetting in nearby Peacehaven, January also saw me back in Westminster on my days off as usual. We'd found out that the government was planning to introduce new animal welfare regulations in October 2018 but, alas, Lucy's Law was not in those plans. But Michael Gove was now Secretary of State for the Environment, chief decision-maker for all things animal welfare, and had brought with him a refreshing 'can-do-will-do' change of attitude to the Department. Enthusiastic and energetic, Mr Gove immediately started to make positive changes to government policies aimed at protecting the environment. Mr Gove's new role was to prove crucial to what would happen next with our campaign. The end of 2017 had been extremely eventful campaign-wise, what with the launch of Lucy's Law in Westminster after almost 10 years of fighting to end puppy farming. The event was a huge success and now, as hoped, news of the campaign was going viral. The beautiful and brave Lucy had passed away over one year ago now, but her picture and energy were still being shared through the Lucy's Law logo across the UK and beyond, mainly thanks to *Mirror* journalist Andrew Penman's weekly column. After almost a decade of campaigning, we had now exposed the opposition, and it was time to try and navigate around them, especially with the government discussing new animal welfare laws; this was potentially the perfect legislative window to bring in Lucy's Law. 2018 was also the Chinese Year of the Dog, and we and many other animal welfare campaigners and charities already supporting Lucy's Law were determined to honour that.

If only it were that simple. The apparently impenetrable 'fortress' of some of the UK's richest animal welfare organisations was still refusing to support Lucy's Law in favour of keeping puppy dealing legal and licensed, while representatives of the pet industry and Government officials working in the department responsible for animal welfare were all blatantly ignoring the almighty fanfare of the Lucy's Law launch in December 2017. We had some serious work to do; it was time to take a different approach. After years of trying to go through the 'correct' channels (i.e. the Government department), but being blocked every time, I had no choice but to attempt to bypass the lot of them, and reach out to the main decision-makers in Number 10. Over the last five years of visiting Westminster I had made some amazing and useful contacts, some of whom were now working behind that famous black Downing Street door. I was offered a meeting with one of the Prime Minister's closest special advisors which I gratefully accepted. This was to be the first of a number of private meetings in Number 10 with various members of the Prime Minister's Office directly responsible for the country's legislation. I was also allowed to take in with me members of my campaigning team, notably the two experts on the minutiae of puppy buying and selling legislation, Julia Carr and licensing barrister Sarah Clover. It now felt as if we were really making progress. Our evidence and, importantly, solutions were now being respectfully listened to, challenged in a fair and constructive way, and carefully worked through. We were more than happy for Number 10 to play devil's advocate, because we had all the answers. We knew despite what other people thought that there were no downsides to Lucy's Law, or 'unintended consequences' as they called them; the tide was now being allowed to turn. Unsurprisingly we kept all these meetings top secret.

Getting the right information to the most influential people is one thing, but having it listened to and positively entertained is another. This is parliamentary campaigning in a nutshell. We desperately needed a solution which provided transparency and traceability for the puppy buyer, and ensured accountability of the breeder. Lucy's Law was this solution. So why, with so much support from MPs, the public, and hundreds of animal welfare organisations across the UK, was there still a small group acknowledging all this, yet trying to stall any progress? There were a few main reasons given, all very easily debunked, some of which are even still used today by the same organisations to criticise the campaign.

At that time the government department was still being influenced by these seemingly disingenuous organisations, and to be fair, why shouldn't they? One of their arguments against Lucy's Law was that it would drive the trade underground, just like drugs and guns. This was one of the easiest pushbacks to refute, because of course if puppy selling was completely undetectable by the public, it would be impossible to sell them! Commercial puppy dealers rely on being visible to make their sales and are totally dependent upon advertising 'overground' to attract prospective buyers, which in turn makes them visible and traceable to enforcement agencies. Furthermore, puppy buyers have no need, or desire, to deliberately seek out a black-market puppy on the dark web. What makes the 'underground' argument even more silly is that they also support a ban on dog fighting, an activity which only happens underground. As I'm sure you'll have noticed, 'What's the point of banning puppy dealers if they'll only find a way around it?' is another way of saying 'What's the point of having any laws at all for anything?' It would be hilarious if it wasn't so serious.

Another popular reason for not supporting Lucy's Law was the 'fake mum' argument: 'They'll just bring out a false mother,' they said. But not only are fake mums, or 'stooge dogs', easy to spot because they don't interact with puppies in the way their real mum would (in fact they're often scared of the actual mum turning up and returning to her pups) but it'd also be unlikely for the fake mum to be suckling, or indeed have any milk either. Furthermore, with Lucy's Law taking away the middleman, by default the sellers automatically become the breeders, meaning that any problems such as sick puppies can now easily be traced back to the seller (accountability) and investigations into fake mums carried out using DNA tests. With this sudden seller/breeder accountability it's just not in their interest to sell faulty goods with dodgy parents when the new owners know who they are. The fake mum argument is therefore hard to defend.

The third most common reason for refusing to support Lucy's Law was over concerns about how such a ban would be enforced, bleating out that local authorities don't have the resources for *even more* legislation, and that a ban would therefore be impossible to police. What they didn't seem to understand is that not only was this ban *replacing* complicated licensing conditions that had failed the dogs until now, but it would also be policed by the public, much like smoking in pubs and restaurants. A ban works differently from a licence. An example of an outright ban is in relation to smoking. Smoking indoors was banned in places like pubs, hotels, and workplaces in 2007. It was, and still is, very noticeable and very easy to enforce, because no one is allowed to do it, so if smoking is observed it is a clear infringement of the law and can be dealt with accordingly. Such a visual law means that anyone selling a puppy without its mum, or in the presence of a suspected fake mum, can be easily investigated by the authorities after they have been alerted by a whistleblower, such as a concerned prospective puppy-buyer. A ban on third-party puppy sales would be similarly identifiable, known as 'policing by consent', and entirely enforceable. This would not only be more effective than licensing, but would also mean using fewer local authority resources, and being a lot cheaper to enforce; yet another myth debunked, confirmed and supported by the Institute of Licensing (IOL) too, after an excellent coffee with Sarah Clover, IOL Chair, and Dan Davies, owner of rescue Bichon Archie; strategic too, as we presumed the organisations refusing to support us would next turn to IOL, which some did, but it was too late as IOL had already given Lucy's Law their full backing. Time and time again we heard that the opposition favoured more 'robust licensing' over a ban, in spite of them admitting there were insufficient resources to pay for existing, let alone more robust, more complicated enforcement. More importantly, they kept ignoring the fact that the licensing of third-party dealers legitimises them in the eyes of the public. We all know it's *impossible* to protect the welfare of puppies by licensing because the harm is ingrained in the process of third-party selling, i.e. puppy farm conditions, travelling to the sellers, puppy smuggling, etc. It's unsurprising that in all 10 years campaigning, these organisations were never able to provide even one example of 'robust licensing' of a third-party puppy dealer that would ever protect the puppy or its mum, or that wouldn't negatively impact on their health or welfare. That's because these licenses don't, and actually can't, exist in the first place.

After the first few baseless excuses were easily dismantled, the next wave arrived. We were told that very few high street pet shops even sold puppies nowadays, so what was the point of banning third-party dealers? Well, firstly, if there aren't that many high street pet shops selling pups, then banning puppies from high street pet shops presumably wouldn't be missed or be a big deal if banned. Plus it's essential to remember that legislatively speaking, a 'pet shop' is *anyone* operating a business of selling animals as pets, even if they are selling from home, a farm, their garage, riding stables, or premises other than a traditional high street 'shop'. The number of puppies traded by licensed, i.e. legal, commercial third-party dealers in 2018 was significant; potentially around 80,000 puppies per year were being sold through this route, not to mention that this legal motherless selling provides the framework for illegal motherless selling activity, virtually indistinguishable by the puppy buyer. It was no surprise that the next reason, and in many ways one of the most disturbing, was presented.

There are those who were – and still are – concerned about the supply of puppies being reduced and unable to fulfil public demand. This is the argument which I, as an animal-lover, found hardest to stomach. Third party dealers don't actually produce puppies but merely distribute them, so Lucy's Law would force prospective buyers directly to the breeders, making mums and breeding environments visible, thus driving up welfare standards by making all breeding establishments open to public scrutiny. Importantly, it's the buyers that would be doing the travelling, as opposed to third-party sellers delivering, meeting at service stations, using pet shops, etc. Lucy's Law would help remove irresponsibly bred, sick, impulse-purchase puppies from the system. It seemed like their main priority was ensuring a high demand of puppies was met by a high supply of puppies, no matter where they came from, which was very worrying indeed.

Removing the market for cheaper, poorly bred puppies can only create demand for responsibly bred puppies or consideration of adopting from rescue, maybe even their own shelters, as an alternative. There is no evidence to support the belief that there are not enough responsibly bred puppies to meet the demand. A market saturated with cheap, readily available puppies will most likely have reduced the demand for more responsibly bred puppies in the first place. Besides, none of the responsible puppy buyers I've ever met in my consulting room have ever complained about driving hours to visit a decent breeder, and often seem prouder the greater the distance they'd travelled!

As the days and weeks went on in early 2018, we continued successfully answering each and every attack on Lucy's Law. The difference now, however, was that policy makers in Number 10 were listening to the campaigners, and most importantly, agreeing with all our evidence-based, common-sense explanations. Lucy's Law's increasing popularity online, on social media, among celebrities and the public, as well as with all the other animal welfare organisations and charities meant that pressure on the government to ban third-party puppy dealers was growing fast.

I was confused and disappointed about the general stance from some organisations on this particular issue. I've always proudly supported the work done for rescue dogs, whether judging fun dog shows or attending glitzy events, and have the deepest respect for all involved in the world of animal welfare. But this was purely about policy and PR, very separate issues from caring for and rehoming dogs.

One of the last 'unintended consequences', or 'loopholes', was the suggestion that third-party dealers would just set themselves up as rescue centres; yet again in my opinion another ridiculous myth, as not only could they already do this before Lucy's Law (so technically unrelated), but local authorities would just have to perform a simple business test to confirm they were a for-profit third-party dealer and not a non-profit shelter. The fact was that there were clearly no excuses for not implementing an immediate ban on third-party puppy sales. Furthermore, a ban had to be brought in as soon as possible, because any breeding dog like Lucy spending even another second imprisoned on a puppy farm, kept behind closed doors away from public view, was a second too long.

Lucy's Law answered a simple moral question with a simple moral solution. While all these falsehoods circled around the campaign and spread around Westminster, it was becoming obvious that the main decision-makers fully understood and accepted all our counterarguments against their Government department. What happened next entirely proved that, and was actually the tipping point, so strap in folks, as it all starts to get crazy from here on in.

I remember it so clearly. I'd just returned to the practice after one of my local school visits to talk to pupils about caring for animals when my mobile rang. Reading the name on the screen made me immediately nervous. Being a campaigner hardwires you to increased stress levels and paranoia, and means you're always prepared for bad news whenever anyone in a position of authority calls. But unlike the 99.9% of calls informing me that something bad's happened again, this was one of the best calls I'd ever received in my life. The policy and legislation team at Number 10, after consulting with Michael Gove, had now considered all our evidence, and comparing it to all the speculation and lack of evidence presented to the Government department by other parties opposing Lucy's Law, had now decided to take a huge major step forward. The Government were planning to launch what's known as a 'Call for Evidence', a three-month consultation where members of the public, campaigners, welfare organisations, and charities in the UK are all invited to submit their views on whether to ban third-party sales of puppies or not. In a nutshell, my tiny team of campaigners had just taken control. To even achieve this hugely significant milestone was already a victory for Linda, Sue, Julia, Philippa, Sarah, and me; we'd just rerouted the previous legislative process that had ignored Lucy's Law's existence to one that was now positively considering it! What's more, the Conservatives' PR team asked whether I'd like to prerecord a short video outside Number 10 explaining the reasons for this Call for Evidence to use for the government's own PR and social media channels! Not only had all our meetings behind that well-known black door been successful, I'd been selected to tell the world by the actual decision-makers themselves, which I obviously agreed to do!

A week later this caterpillar-collecting nerd was now, once again, standing outside the most famous front door in the world, prerecording an announcement that my team of campaigners and I had fought tirelessly for, for almost a decade. I wore my dad's dark grey suit, his belt, his watch, and his cufflinks, and my special Gresham Blake pink dog tie. I stared straight down the camera lens and, totally unrehearsed, in one take said:

'Hi, I'm Marc Abraham. I'm a vet and I'm also from Pup Aid, the anti-puppy farming campaign group. Myself and my fellow campaigners have been campaigning for a ban on third-party puppy sales for nearly 10 years. So obviously the news from Number 10 today is very well received. Puppies should only be bought direct from the breeder — that makes the breeders transparent, responsible, accountable, or better still

adopted from a rescue shelter. So this call for evidence from Number 10 is a huge step forward for dog welfare. Puppies should only be bought from a breeder, seen interacting with their mum in the place they were born. And this is in line with Number 10, the Government's own advice. So please, with this call for evidence for a third-party ban – and there is plenty of scientific evidence to back it up – please submit evidence, back the third-party ban, it's called Lucy's Law, check it out online – hashtag #LucysLaw – and be part of change for dogs. This is a massive step forward and thank you to Number 10 for announcing this call for evidence for a third-party ban.'

When it went live two days later it took everyone by surprise. And I mean *everyone*. Until now we'd been locked out of all official discussions involving the Government department, big charities and pet industry, and no one had thought we'd been busy meeting Number 10 representatives and providing them with all the necessary evidence to prove the campaigners were right all along. That morning, in fact for the next few days and weeks, social media was flooded with excitement as the public, campaigners, small to mid-size animal charities, and celebrities all learned the good news. It was so popular that *Good Morning Britain* prerecorded an interview with me to go out on Thursday's show. Even Prime Minister Theresa May's Twitter account tweeted: 'We're cracking down on unscrupulous puppy breeders to further raise the bar on animal welfare standards – and we need your help to find evidence so we can ban third-party puppy sales.' The words 'so we can ban' highlighted Number 10's intention to ban third-party puppy sales at last. This was huge.

8 February 2018: *everything* had changed. Number 10, the Prime Minister's Office, appeared to now be well on the side of the campaigners. It felt amazing. Our recently launched Lucy's Law Early Day Motion 695, that official Parliamentary statement to which only MPs can add their names, was also building momentum within Westminster, with around 100 cross-party MPs also now calling for Lucy's Law. With mainstream media widely reporting the news, as well as countless celebrities giving their full support on social media too, pressure for Lucy's Law to happen was quickly escalating both inside and outside Parliament. Back in Brighton I discovered the practice I was happy working at had been sold to a corporate chain, so I quit immediately and started working for another independent practice in Brighton which was owned by my friend Shaun who was too ill to work. In other sad news, the last few months had not only claimed my father, Philippa's mother, and of course Lucy, but now Sue's mother and Julia's father had also passed, and Linda's mother's health was rapidly deteriorating as well. It felt like our tiny group of campaigners were being unfairly punished, but luckily we were always there for each other like our own little family, and campaigning for Lucy's Law provided the best distraction. All this progress and personal heartache made us even more determined not to give up, to keep fighting for the dogs.

In March 2018, and with support for Lucy's Law appearing to grow everywhere by the hour, it was now time to pull the trigger on one of Parliamentary campaigning's golden guns and submit another Government e-petition in order to show them just how popular Lucy's Law was nationwide. Our first had of course been rejected by Government in 2014 after being debated in the Main Chamber of the House of Commons, but now the political climate and appetite for Lucy's Law was now very different indeed. We know these debates rarely decide one way or the other if a law will be passed, but they are a brilliantly useful way of getting a feel for where Government stands on the issue, as well as raising awareness of a campaign, seeing which MPs and organisations are supportive, and of course – and often of more use – identifying the ones refusing and their briefings revealing their reasons. So on 1 March we launched the Lucy's Law Government e-petition to ban third-party sales, and none of us could've ever anticipated its popularity and how fast this would explode. The groundwork done over the last few months and years was certainly paying off. From the thousands of members of public to high-profile celebrities like Ricky Gervais and Sue Perkins, from cross-party parliamentarians to hugely respected animal welfare campaigners, charities, and organisations, the Lucy's Law petition was being signed and shared by tens of thousands of animal-lovers in just its first few days.

Mother's Day conveniently fell on the following Sunday, the Sunday of Crufts no less, so there could be no better opportunity to make even more of an impact. The only question was how?

Once again, a bit of creativity in campaigning was required. I decided to design a giant three-metre high Mother's Day card with Lucy's face in the middle with some text arching over her portrait saying 'Happy Mother's Day??' – referring to all the breeding mothers still imprisoned on puppy farms. What's more we ordered 1,000 bright 'Lucy's Law pink' rosettes and gave them out free to members of the public, accompanied by cheaply printed leaflets of the Mother's Day card design containing the petition link encouraging them to sign and share. We set up on Pup Aid main sponsors Nutriment's stand in Hall 1, hoping our combination of giant card, bright-pink rosettes, and flyers would attract attention – and attract it did!

I've always had a good relationship with the Kennel Club (who run Crufts), and had already given them the heads-up as to what I was planning; as supporters of Lucy's Law they were keen to cover our publicity stunt. Not only that but when they arrived on the Nutriment stand, the giant Mother's Day card towering over them, they brought with them the Channel 4 crew, filmed an interview with one of the TV presenters and me, and unbelievably it went out to the masses just before Best In Show that evening, i.e. primetime for millions of dog-loving viewers, with main presenter Clare Balding urging viewers to sign and share our Lucy's Law petition! We watched the petition website in disbelief as we collected around 20,000 new signatures in an hour, taking us to about 80,000 in just over a week. With the final huge push over the line from Rachel Riley's video on Twitter a couple of days later, the Lucy's Law petition smashed 100,000 in just 13 days, making it one of the fastest animal welfare, or otherwise, Government e-petitions of all time. As well as continued support from Andrew Penman at the *Mirror*, the *Sun* also featured the petition success in a centre-page spread, and Lucy's Law was also now being mentioned over in the Welsh Parliament too; hugely significant because animal welfare laws are devolved in the UK with legislation separate from Westminster, so it would be up to every individual country to potentially introduce Lucy's Law themselves.

April arrived, and with a definite spring in everyone's step, our Lucy's Law campaign was now in full swing. The Government's 'Call for Evidence' public consultation was two months into its three-month window, around 100 MPs had now given their support for the Lucy's Law Early Day Motion, and our petition had now collected over 120,000 signatures, so a debate was most likely on the cards. Numerous dog-loving celebrities and major news outlets from the *Mirror* to the BBC's *Watchdog* were all talking about Lucy's Law and/or the dangers of third-party puppy sellers. Back in Brighton I was vetting at my friend Shaun's independent practice, every day tinged with even more sadness as his health deteriorated fast. My days off were, as always for the last six or so years, spent in Westminster, attending meetings all over the Parliamentary estate, from the Commons to the Lords, Portcullis House to Number 10. Everything was about Lucy's Law, inspired by that little Cavalier and a determination to put an end to the conditions into which she was born, and in which she had been cruelly abused and exploited for years. The Petitions Committee informed us that the Lucy's Law e-petition was to be debated on 21 May, shortly after Number 10's Consultation had closed and at the point when decision-makers would be sifting through responses, collating results, and preparing to make their decision, Lucy's Law or no Lucy's Law? It was important to keep the pressure up.

I got some Lucy's Law placards made and arranged a drop-in for MPs in Westminster. It was very well attended by various cross-party MPs, and, thanks to the *Dogs Today* magazine staff who kindly assisted me that day, I was able to give them each an official Lucy's Law pink rosette, debate briefing paper, and have their all-important pictures taken too. Before one of Ricky Gervais' early work-in-progress SuperNature gigs in Finchley, North London, I arranged to meet him beforehand and grab a picture of him holding the Lucy's Law placard. I had Parliament, Number 10, and now one of the most influential people in the world on my side too, all kindly lending their support to Lucy's Law. The pressure continued to increase, as Lucy's Law was mentioned on BBC One's popular primetime *The One Show* – publicly endorsed by sofa guests, comedian Jon Richardson and a representative of the RSPCA. Over on the UK's other major TV channel, our campaign was being promoted on ITV's *This Morning*, when hosts, owners of rescue dog Maggie, and committed Lucy's Law campaign supporters Eamonn Holmes and Ruth

Langsford interviewed Beverley Cuddy, editor of *Dogs Today* magazine. Support for Lucy's Law on some of the biggest shows on mainstream TV, radio, and online was growing ahead of May's much-anticipated Westminster Hall debate.

The weekend before the debate I was invited on my mate Luke's stag do to Lisbon, Portugal. But I still had to help with two MPs' speeches and email debate briefings to about 200 MPs! On arrival at our Airbnb, close to the city centre, I explained to the boys that I would have to work from 10am-6pm every day, then come find them for drinks and food in the evening. Meanwhile, back in England, Beverley Cuddy was working tirelessly to ensure that every MP was sent an envelope containing a bright-pink Lucy's Law rosette, hard copy of the debate briefing, and covering letter reminding them of the debate thanking them for their support. Talk about coordination and teamwork! As I landed back from Lisbon, after one of the strangest work/boozing weekends ever, it was straight to Downing Street to hand in our petition, which contained exactly the same message as our 2014 one had: 'ban puppies sold without their mums i.e. third-party dealers'. After just two and a half months it had collected over 143,000 signatures, the extra 43,000 with no extra effort whatsoever, such was the campaign's unprecedented popularity. The Lucy's Law debate in Westminster Hall was that afternoon.

Our little group of campaigners sat in the public gallery in Westminster Hall and watched in awe as one of the greatest debates we'd ever witnessed began to unfold. Not only did it start with some MPs proudly wearing their Lucy's Law rosettes in the chamber, which is strictly forbidden so they were told off and had to remove them, but every single MP save one called for Lucy's Law. This support included, for the first time ever, a positive summing-up by Government Minister George Eustice, who even gave me a cheeky thumbs-up as he left the Chamber; it was the complete opposite of our 2014 debate which had been rejected our motion to ban cruel puppy dealers point-blank, as had every puppy-related debate since. To add to all the social media pressure, social media giants UNILAD produced an online documentary about puppy farming and Lucy's Law featuring interviews with most of our campaigning team, a film to which I was very proud to contribute to, and one that reached, educated, and raised awareness for a whole new demographic. I was also invited to appear as a guest on Channel 5's *The Wright Stuff*, now the *Jeremy Vine Show*, talking about animal welfare, Lucy's Law, and reviewing the day's newspapers too!

But away from all the excitement up in Westminster, June started on an extremely sad note as my good friend and fellow vet, Shaun, passed away from cancer. Shaun was always one of the good guys of vetting, fiercely anti-corporate, kind, charming, funny, compassionate, and always putting his patients first. Shaun was a hero of mine and did loads for charity both in the UK and abroad. He would always treat injured wildlife brought in, and all the pets and pet-loving community of Brighton and Hove loved and respected him.

I left the practice shortly after Shaun's passing, as the place would never be the same again.

With the Government's three-month public consultation on Lucy's Law now well and truly closed, the campaign was out of our hands, and we were all now nervously waiting for the thousands of responses to be examined by Number 10, and the *biggest* decision to ever potentially affect millions of dogs to be made. In Westminster, as well as more meetings on Lucy's Law, I also met with Lord Gardiner, the Minister who had told me 18 months earlier that it would be five years before the law would be looked at again. Not only was Lord Gardiner more upbeat and positive this time round, but he also agreed to be photographed wearing a Lucy's Law rosette too – what a turnaround! Finally, in June, I was honoured to be invited to the beautiful city of Tallinn in Estonia to give a talk on Lucy's Law to the Federation of Companion Animal Veterinary Associations (FECAVA), a hugely respected professional organisation representing more than 25,000 companion animal vets in 40 European countries. I gave my presentation to all the heads of the European veterinary associations, seated in a giant horseshoe around me, and was grilled by a few of them, challenging me on those same old imaginary loophole arguments: underground, enforcement, supply, and fake mums, etc. Back home there were even more mentions of Lucy's Law in the mainstream media including on BBC, ITV News, Channel 5 News, and in popular women's magazine *Closer* too. Lucy's little face was everywhere!

In July 2018, after my friend Luke's wedding in Italy (remember the stag do in Lisbon) I extended my trip and headed to the Colosseum in Rome, somewhere I'd always wanted to visit. Standing in the arena and looking up at where the Emperor and baying crowds would have sat deciding the gladiators' fate, I felt completely overwhelmed about the fight our coalition of campaigners and I had been on over the last decade, as well as the all-important decision that was currently being made in Westminster, and just how close we were to winning the battle for the dogs. With minimal resources, opposition from the most unlikely of organisations, and losing loved ones, we couldn't have done any more; this really was it.

Back home, as the 2018 heatwave gripped the nation, I was invited to give another talk on Lucy's Law at a big dog show in Peterborough, and then attend a very special event in Cardiff; a unique Lucy's Law rally had been organised by Linda and Sue from C.A.R.I.A.D., and Eileen Jones from Friends of Animals Wales, and hosted by Welsh Assembly Members (AMs − Welsh equivalent of Westminster MPs) Eluned Morgan and Vikki Howells. The gloriously sunny day began with numerous AMs on the steps of the Senedd building, all proudly wearing their Lucy's Law rosettes, and having their pictures taken holding Lucy's Law placards or cuddling brave puppy farm survivor ex-breeding dogs. I remember feeling a bit overwhelmed seeing the bright pink Lucy's Law banners that had now also been translated into Welsh. We all went inside, where specially baked vegan Lucy's Law cupcakes awaited us, and I gave a speech in the Parliament about Lucy's Law and all the progress we'd made in England. Other speakers included Linda, Eluned, Vikki, and Welsh Minister Lesley Griffiths, herself responsible should Wales choose to adopt Lucy's Law. It's always an honour and a personal highlight to be invited to speak in any country's Parliament, and this event was even more poignant as Wales' reputation had been tarnished for years by the scourge of puppy farming in some of its south-western counties like Carmarthenshire, where little Lucy was born. Minister Lesley Griffiths said she'd make announcement soon, and we were due to hear the result of Number 10's call for evidence imminently. And then on Tuesday 14 August 2018 it arrived by email, and at that minute, at precisely 4.13pm, I knew that the world of animal welfare would change forever.

Chapter 18

When you lead a campaign you're also automatically that campaign's spokesperson, and therefore often the first to know any big news, good or bad. So when you're waiting for something to happen, and receive an email from a Government department official saying 'I am writing from DEFRA press office about a potential announcement next week on third-party puppy and kitten sales', I'll be honest, your heart rate does increase a little. The email continued, asking very politely if I'd be 'happy to provide a supportive quote for a press notice for national media'. Regarding tone of email, when you're asked for a quote like this, it's usually good news. But this wasn't good news. It wasn't even very good news. It was the *best* news I'd received in the last decade, possibly in my whole life to this point. Of course I agreed to provide a quote, and then the second email arrived with the strictly embargoed draft press release. It read:

Ban on third-party sales of puppies and kittens announced by Michael Gove

A ban on third-party puppy and kitten sales in England will be introduced to help drive up animal welfare standards, the Environment Secretary Michael Gove announced today.

Confirming the government's support for the prominent Lucy's Law campaign, DEFRA has published a consultation on an outright ban that will mean anyone looking to buy or adopt a puppy or kitten must either deal directly with the breeder or with one of the nation's many animal rehoming centres.

The aim is to bring an end to the grisly conditions found in puppy farming and to tackle a range of existing animal welfare issues. These include the early separation of puppies and kittens from their mothers, their introduction to new and unfamiliar environments and the increased likelihood of multiple journeys the puppies or kittens have to undertake. All of these can contribute to a chaotic start in life and lead to serious health problems and lack of socialisation.

Environment Secretary, Michael Gove, said:

'A ban on third-party sales will ensure the nation's much-loved pets get the right start in life. I pay tribute to the Lucy's Law campaign who have fought tirelessly for this step.

'People who have a complete disregard for pet welfare will no longer be able to profit from this miserable trade.'

The proposed ban on third-party sales is part of a series of reforms on pet welfare including banning the sale of underage puppies and kittens and tackling the breeding of dogs with severe genetic disorders. New laws come into force on 1 October this year banning licensed sellers from dealing in puppies and kittens under the age of eight weeks and tightening the compulsory licensing of anyone in the business of breeding and selling dogs.

We'd done it.

We'd *actually* done it. The expression 'No words' is carelessly bandied around these days when describing something monumental, but this was so much more than that. The sense of achievement and disbelief wasn't really about our victory; it was about the dogs – and cats too – that were now guaranteed a brighter, healthier, and happier future. To have the best start in life is everything, not just for all the puppies and kittens, but for their mums too, often the hidden, forgotten victims. This was about them, breeding dogs like Lucy, who would now be seen by the public, treated with respect, and not bred to death and tortured in puppy farms. What made Environment Secretary Michael Gove's quote even more poignant, was that he paid 'tribute to the Lucy's Law campaign who have fought tirelessly for this step', i.e. everyone associated with the campaign. I'd never felt so proud in all my life. After speaking to the Government Official who sent the email I learnt that the call for evidence on Lucy's Law had generated a consultation response of over 70% in favour of the ban, with the remaining 30% a mixture of not just those against, but also those who supported the ban in theory but were unsure how it would be implemented.

I gathered my thoughts and called Linda, my number one confidante, my voice breaking with the news.

August is typically one of the quietest months in the parliamentary calendar, with MPs and Ministers away on holiday, so even though we knew the Lucy's Law consultation was closed, we didn't expect any response from Government until everyone was back in Westminster, September at the earliest. After the last few months of incredibly tough campaigning for Lucy's Law, unprecedented media exposure, and incredible support from cross-party parliamentarians, these emails confirmed what we'd dreamt of for years: the ban on third-party puppy dealers known as Lucy's Law was *actually* going to happen. But that wasn't all of it. Oh no. The official public announcement was to be made a week later, and Number 10 Downing Street would honour the campaigners with a special garden party in their back garden to celebrate! Furthermore, as campaign leader, I was allowed to invite who I wanted – it's true – I had the guest list to the coolest party in town! Not bad for a geeky kid who grew up never being invited to anything and in any case turned down to receive a chemistry prize on the one occasion he was. And here I was being asked to put together a list of names and share their emails with Downing Street staff so they'd be sent official invitations. The plan was to announce the success of the Lucy's Law campaign at the garden party, laid on especially for the people who helped make it happen!

With only a few days' notice I frantically started compiling my list. It was important to represent everyone who'd contributed to this success, so I started with my coalition of campaigners: Linda, Sue, Julia, Philippa, Sarah Clover, and of course Lucy's owner Lisa. Bex and Stuart who helped with Pup Aid came too. Among the 100+ invitees, all proudly wearing their bright pink Lucy's Law rosettes, I also invited other animal welfare activists, representatives and CEOs of smaller-mid size charities, as well as campaign groups that had all supported Lucy's Law, as well as a sprinkling of celebrities, and of course my family, including my mum and grandma. As you can imagine it was most people's first visit to Downing Street. Once again I wore my dad's suit, and as I walked in through the front door with my best mate Russell, and as all the other guests arrived at Number 10, we were all shown into the impressive hallway, past Winston Churchill's favourite chair, past the Henry Moore sculpture on the left, past the Cabinet Room, and down the rear staircase into the back garden. The next two hours were surreal to say the least. Eamonn Holmes, Peter Egan, and Brian May were chatting with campaigners; Michael Gove was chatting with my grandma; Tony Lewis (the first ever vet I saw practice as a schoolboy) was chatting with roadside protesters who – in the face of legal action – had still turned up every weekend for the last few years to demonstrate outside a notorious puppy-selling pet shop in Maidenhead (which has since closed down, attributed to to these protesters and Lucy's Law); and to top it all off, my favourite thing about the whole garden party experience, we'd also been allowed to invite rescued puppy farm breeding dogs along; as well as making vegan canapés for the human guests, the Number 10 kitchen staff had even baked special bone- and paw-shaped treats for the dogs too! It was like the final episode of a box set, where characters from each episode of every season are all gathered together. And only very few of us knew exactly what this special occasion was in aid of; most guests had no idea there was about to be an announcement by Environment Secretary Michael Gove. About an hour into the event Mr Gove approached the microphone, the crowd of excited guests shuffled into place, forming a semi-circle around him in silent anticipation, everyone ready for the big reveal…

'Ladies and gentlemen, I'd just like to welcome you here to the beautiful garden in 10 Downing Street, just in order to say thank you.

My name is Michael Gove. I am the Environment Secretary. Today we are making a significant announcement in the history of animal welfare and the protection of companion animals and pets.

From tomorrow we will absolutely confirm that we will be consulting on how we implement Lucy's Law.

We will be making sure that the third-party sale of pets, of kittens and of puppies, ends.

You are all here because you have been part of that campaign. You are all here because you have made sure the public are aware of the horrors of puppy farming and that government has been compelled. I am delighted that we have been compelled to act. Because we all know if you bring an animal into your life, and into your home, the transformative effect that it can have is wonderful.

But if you are going to look after a pet, if you are going to take a puppy or a kitten into your home, then you have an obligation to make sure that that animal has been brought up in circumstances free of trauma and in a way that ensures that it can lead a fulfilling life.

Far too many of the pets that people, with the best will in the world, bring into their homes we know have been brought up in squalid circumstances. In circumstances of pain and suffering and misery which should never be inflicted on any living thing.

That's why, by making it absolutely clear that if you're going to buy a puppy or kitten in the future, that you need to be absolutely certain that you can buy it from an ethical, regulated breeder. Who can show you the parent of that puppy or kitten.

We will eliminate puppy farming and ensure that animal welfare is safeguarded in this country as it always should have been.

Now these changes only come about as the result of campaigning. One person who deserves to be singled out is Marc Abraham from Pup Aid. Marc's pioneering work as a vet, as someone who puts animal welfare at the heart of everything that he does, has been inspirational. And there are people here who have seen Marc in action on the media and in person, and know that he's a force of nature.

There are other people here who I just want to say thank you to. People like Brian May and Meg Matthews who have done so much to help raise the salience of this issue in so many ways.

Parliamentary colleagues of mine, like Alex Chalk, the MP for Cheltenham, and of course the chairman of the EFRA select committee Neil Parish, whose work in this area has helped make the case for change. And people from other political parties as well like Lisa Cameron, the Scottish Nationalist MP who has played such a prominent role in making sure that this is a UK-wide campaign as well.

And in politics of course you get used to the fact that not every decision you make is always going to be popular, but to my mind it's a rare privilege when you are in a position to make a change, which I know reflects what the British public want and what they've asked for and what they've demanded.

And in some respects, I imagine the only question that some people will be asking is why has it taken so long. Well, my view is we're now at a point where we can make the change that all of us believe is necessary in order to safeguard the future of pets for every family in this country.

And speaking for myself, as the proud owner of two rescue dogs, conscious of the fact that they lived their lives in the very first few weeks and months in circumstances from which they needed to be rescued, knowing that we will do as a government and you all as individual citizens and campaigners will be responsible for having made this change – well, that is a cause for celebration. So I hope all of you will now raise a glass, and raise a glass of course to Lucy's Law, and to a better future for pets everywhere. Lucy's Law! Thank you.'

Everyone whooped and applauded, and I genuinely don't think I've ever been prouder. The only thing that tinged the whole day with sadness was that my dad wasn't there to experience it all. He'd taught me the importance of always fighting for the underdog, to never give up on something you believe in. I was pretty sure that all those games of chess he'd played with me, my first ever experiences of strategy, patience, and being prepared to play the long game had definitely had a decisive effect on me standing in the back garden of 10 Downing Street after winning this 10-year campaign. Dad would've loved that garden party; he would've had fun chatting with Michael Gove, meeting all the dogs, hanging out with Brian, Eamonn, and of course his old mate Peter, and would have been so incredibly proud of what all our tiny bunch of campaigners had achieved. Saying that, it was amazing to have my grandma Judy there, with her memories of escaping the Holocaust, and whose inspiring story of survival had taught me that against all the odds *anything* is possible, which proved to be a very useful lesson indeed for a campaigning vet like me. The other 'person' missing was of course little Lucy – she would've loved all the attention, meeting her celebrity friends, and of course trying all the specially cooked doggy treats! I really can't thank every member of Number 10 staff enough for organising what was the most perfect celebration of Lucy's Law anyone of us could have ever imagined.

After two hours of one of the greatest and most special experiences of my life, the garden party was over. We all shuffled out, reluctant to leave one of the most famous addresses in the world; I was the last to exit Number 10, and standing beside Lisa, who was holding her ex-puppy-farm dog Plum Pudding, and cradling Lisa's sister's dog, ex-puppy-farm breeding rescue dog Minnie, in my arms, I looked up and noticed everyone shouting 'Speech, speech!' So, not wanting to disappoint a jubilant Downing Street crowd packed with friends, family, celebrities, dogs, and of course fellow campaigners, I suddenly began an impromptu victory speech from the steps of Number 10 – another life highlight! Overwhelmed by the whole occasion, I said:

'I can't thank everyone enough. Everyone here has played a part in getting to here, and being in earshot of that [Michael Gove's] incredible speech we just heard. And Lucy's Law… huge credit to Lisa, must've been incredibly tough to have her little best friend's name mentioned god knows how many times on social media for the last 18 months, so a massive round of applause for Lisa. From everyone, from charities, to campaigners, to celebrities, to members of the public, to everyone that's been involved with the campaign, thank you. From Linda, from Julia, from Sue, all our gang, including Philippa who couldn't make it today. Everyone, this shows that campaigners can do it. It shows that if you get blocked there's a way around it. If you get blocked again there's a way around that as well, and it shows that if you have the minimal resources, and you're doing it in your spare time, you can still get here [pointing to No. 10] and actually get a positive result. So let's make this campaign inspiring not just for animal welfare, but across all sectors, and prove that if you're a campaigner, do not be put off by the big organisations. You can do it! You can do it! And do you know what? We've all done it! We've all done it today. So enjoy it, you're all responsible, and I personally can't thank you enough. Thank you very much.'

That night we all stayed in London: Lisa, her Mum, Lisa's dog Plum Pudding, and Lisa's sister's dog Minnie, in a hotel kindly organised by ITV. We were already booked to appear on the following morning's *Good Morning Britain* and *This Morning*, incredibly rare for both shows to share the same guests on the same day, but Eamonn Holmes was keen to get Lisa and me on the sofa. All around those studio interviews we were busy giving quotes, as well as live and prerecorded interviews for many different TV, radio, print, and online outlets. The front page of the *Mirror* led with the headline 'THE END OF PUPPY FARMING' with a picture of Lucy. From Sky to BBC, Channel 4 to LBC, regional to national, everyone wanted to talk about Lucy's Law and find out about what this new legislation meant, as well as discussing puppy farming, rescue pet adoption, and, most importantly, find out about little Lucy herself. The media frenzy went on for weeks, with foreign media picking up the story too. Just like when we launched Lucy's Law eight months previously, Lucy's face was everywhere again!

It was late August, and while the world's media was discussing Lucy's Law, Bex and I had our 10th fun dog show to organise – Pup Aid in Primrose Hill was only days away. With the incredible news that the Government was confirming Lucy's Law was going to happen, this made 2018 one of the most special Pup Aids yet, if not *the* most. Our fun dog show had always been part of the main campaign to ban third-party puppy dealers, which had now been successful in helping change the law. Bex and I knew this was to be the last Pup Aid, and the theme was to be a big celebration of Lucy's Law. We ordered another batch of bright pink rosettes, and when the day arrived, it couldn't have been more perfect. The sun shone, there were 85 trade stands, vegan food stalls, have-a-go agility, as well as live music, and of course the parade of rescued ex-puppy-farm breeding dogs, the same formula as the World's Biggest Puppy Party exactly 10 years earlier. There were our usual host of celebrities, from Ricky Gervais, Peter Egan, Jane Fallon, Meg Mathews, Rachel Riley, Pasha Kovalev, Gail Porter, Victoria Stilwell, Hannah Waddingham from *Game of Thrones*, as well as stars of reality TV shows like *Love Island* too; the paparazzi and reporters were spoilt for choice. Even our friends Grace and Steve from Finding Shelter Animal Rescue came over from Philadelphia to help us celebrate. After a decade of campaigning and giving my 10th and final annual speech to inform everyone of our progress, the feeling of standing in the middle of Primrose Hill telling everyone we'd actually done it – they'd done it – was just incredible; a moment I'd dreamt of for years.

There were so many pink Lucy's Law rosettes on show that day, pinned to owners as well as their dogs' leads and collars, as they proudly paraded their pooches around Primrose Hill; thousands of dog-lovers over the last 10 years had helped create this unique atmosphere of people linked simply by being a part of positive change for animal welfare. What a way for Pup Aid's fun dog show to bow out in style, with the most incredible victory for the dogs. That incredibly special day couldn't have been possible without Bex, or our main sponsors Nutriment, as well as Specsavers, Leivars Design, PetsPyjamas, Leucillin, Brewdog, our incredible pro bono PR team Borne Media, Belle PR, celebrity liaison Laura Critchley, brilliant compère Simon Happily, Halo Dogs, displays from Hearing Dogs for Deaf People and *Britain's Got Talent*'s amazing Lucy and Trip Hazard, all the stall holders and exhibitors, our loyal official photographer Julia Claxton who'd taken pictures at every single Pup Aid, and of course everyone else involved in making it one of the best days of the last decade for animal-lovers! I'd also like to thank first aiders, litter pickers, volunteers, white wicker fence guys, Phil Cowan and Jo from iLovePrimroseHill for informing the community, putting up Pup Aid posters, and helping me put the banners up around the park. Last but not least Nick Biddle and his Royal Parks team for trusting us from the beginning, and allowing Pup Aid to happen in one of the most exclusive open spaces in the whole country.

The momentum continued. All of a sudden Lucy's Law was named 'Top [Campaign] of the Month' in the very well-respected *PR Week* magazine; the journalist who interviewed me seemed particularly impressed by the fact that Lucy's Law was only eight months old when the Government agreed to it, that the Westminster campaign relied on no PR company or any press releases, and that we had minimal financial resources either – a proper grassroots campaign run by a handful of volunteers in our spare time. The accolades continued to pour in only a couple of weeks later, with Lucy's Law winning a prestigious Animal Hero Awards Special Award – an award both Lisa and I had won at this event previously on separate occasions! This was a complete surprise to us both; we only found out when it was announced on the night. Lisa and I went up to collect our award from TV presenters Nicky Campbell, Victoria Stilwell, and Amanda Holden, followed by me giving an emotional seven minute off-the-cuff speech, proudly dedicating our latest award to little Lucy, and my dad.

Meanwhile over in Wales, not only were our friends Linda and Sue from C.A.R.I.A.D. launching their own e-petition calling on the Welsh Government to adopt Lucy's Law, but, thanks to some incredible campaigning from Linda, various Assembly Members, and local councillors, some of Wales' 22 individual councils had already voted, and passed motions for Lucy's Law, or as we called it, 'turned pink' for Lucy's Law. Astonishingly, some of the first councils to turn pink were three of the most notorious puppy farming regions in West Wales: Ceredigionshire, Pembrokeshire, and even Carmarthenshire, the very place Lucy was born! Over the next few weeks and months, Wales slowly turned even more pink, with more councils confirming their full support for Lucy's Law, not only representing amazing progress and incredible work being done behind the scenes, but also putting mounting pressure on the Welsh Government to make Lucy's Law happen there too.

With so much Lucy's Law activity going on in both England and Wales, news of our success had now reached the USA, and I was invited to address Senators in Pennsylvania's Capitol Building in Harrisburg, their State Parliament! I spoke for about 10 minutes, giving a brief overview of the

Lucy's Law campaign story, and ended by holding my pink Lucy's Law rosette up high and declaring 'If we can do it – so can you!' which was met by rapturous applause and cheering *Jerry Springer*-style – another proud moment, albeit another very surreal one. While I was in the States, I was also invited to give a talk on Lucy's Law to a bootcamp on puppy farming campaigning hosted by Humane Society of the United States. Little Lucy was really influencing thoughts and minds thousands of miles from the dark Welsh shed she was born into years before. Yet another sign of the 'Lucy effect' was a new campaign started by our friends Grace and Steve from Finding Shelter Animal Rescue. One of the ex-breeding dogs rescued a year beforehand when Peter Egan, Victoria Stilwell, and I were visiting Philadelphia, a German Shepherd named Victoria, had also followed in Lucy's pawsteps and, in the face of a very guarded prognosis, shown abnormal strengths in healing, bravery, and resilience against all the odds, now being honoured as poster girl for the 'Victoria's Law' campaign, which calls for a ban on retail sales of puppies, kittens, and rabbits. My trip concluded by once again judging the Sproutfest fun dog show, where I enjoyed the opportunity to inform and update every dog-lover attending about the progress and success Lucy's Law was enjoying back in the UK.

While I was over in the States, I got some incredibly tragic news: our dear friend and fellow campaigner Philippa Robinson had lost her battle with cancer. Philippa was not only so much fun to be around, but she was totally committed to improving the lives of the UK's dog population, and solely responsible for setting up the phenomenal resource the Karlton Index in March 2011. Philippa was a major player in the world of canine welfare, well respected by all sides of the debate, and her huge personality, sheer grit and determination to help dogs will be much missed by all who had the privilege of knowing her. Philippa had played a major part in the original coalition team determined to ban third-party puppy sales, at that inaugural Twickenham meeting way back in 2014, years before our campaign was renamed Lucy's Law, and Linda visited Philippa shortly before she passed to let her know about Lucy's Law's success, which made her smile. Philippa will always be remembered at the annual APDAWG Unsung Heroes event in Westminster, when we award an individual for their exceptional work and outstanding contribution to dog welfare with a trophy in her honour.

As one of the most eventful years in animal welfare came to a close, there was really no let-up in the world of campaigning. I was invited to give a talk on Lucy's Law at the Institute of Licensing's Annual Conference in Stratford-upon-Avon, and then it was up to the Scottish Parliament accompanied by Sarah Clover to discuss Lucy's Law with Scottish Environmental Minister Mairi Gougeon MSP, almost exactly two years since I'd made the same journey with Julia, and had sadly witnessed no progress since. November finished on another high as the Lucy's Law campaign picked up yet another prestigious award, this time the prestigious PRCA Public Affairs 'Voluntary Sector Campaign of the Year' Award at a glittering ceremony in London, and I'd like to thank Newington Comms (previously Bellenden Ltd) for their support and help with the submission. As December 2018 arrived, our now multi-award-winning Lucy's Law campaign was still making progress and more headlines. In Cardiff a fascinating debate took place in the Welsh Parliament, and after a phenomenal speech by Andrew RT Davies AM, the Welsh Minister Lesley Griffiths summed up by announcing that she would launch the Welsh Government's Lucy's Law consultation in spring 2019. Our end of year APDAWG 'Unsung Heroes' meeting invited the small volunteer-run charity Friends of Animals Wales CEO Eileen Jones to give a presentation, in which she revealed that a number of puppy farmers knew that the game was nearly up, and had now started to abandon their breeding dogs into her rescue centre. This was proof that Lucy's Law had begun to work well before its implementation. At the same meeting Owen and Haatchi were awarded the inaugural Philippa Robinson Dog Welfare Award.

With Christmas upon us, another fantastic and much-anticipated embargoed press release asking for a quote arrived in my inbox. The Government was ready to announce the results of its second Lucy's Law consultation, the one on its implementation announced at the Garden Party back in August. Unbelievably no fewer than 96% of the responses were in favour of Lucy's Law. The only next step was for the Government to set a date for Lucy's Law to actually enter English legislation and become law. Once again, Lucy's story and the multi-award winning campaign she inspired was picked up by the world's press and went viral, reaching all parts of the world from the US to Brazil, Spain to Israel, showing that there's hope globally for an end to irresponsible dog and cat breeding, selling, and everything in between. I was invited back into the Sky News studio, accompanied by rescue greyhound Ava, to share the good news. On New Year's Eve the Welsh Lucy's Law petition ended by smashing 11,000 signatures, and Lucy's Law was listed as one of 2018's top animal welfare wins in the world in the *Independent* – the perfect ending to a phenomenal year. With Lucy's Law now confirmed in England, and making a difference over in the States too, campaigners, charities, and the dog-loving public all wondered how long it would take for the devolved parliaments of Wales and Scotland to follow suit. Luckily, with a bit of extra campaigning, we'd know the answer in just a few months' time. After all, puppy farming was a nationwide problem, so the aim was always to ban third-party puppy dealers from the whole of the UK, and not give them any places to keep operating.

Chapter 19

The start of 2019 was easily the most exciting start to a year in the last 10.

But we weren't done yet. Not by a long way. Simply banning third-party dealers in England wouldn't solve the puppy farming or puppy smuggling issues in Wales, Ireland, Scotland, and Eastern Europe. Of these other nations, Wales had shown the most interest in Lucy's Law, especially after our rally and event at the Senedd the summer before. Scotland appeared to be showing the least ambition for banning puppy dealers as, even after two visits to present evidence to Members of the Scottish Parliament in 2016 and 2018, we were still, depressingly, being completely ignored. Additionally, the messaging regarding the puppy trade seemed only concerned with the illegal trade, not the legal trade as we'd pointed out years before. By only targeting the illegal trade it would there-fore remain totally acceptable, even endorsed by the Scottish Government, to allow a puppy born on a legal, licensed puppy farm in, say, Ireland, to be transported to Scotland by a legal, licensed third-party dealer. The chain was still legal and Scottish laws were by default appearing to protect this common route to market; particularly worrying as many pups bred on puppy farms in Ireland, both legally and illegally, were entering Scotland through the port of Stranraer.

Though Wales was in our eyes closer to making progress, when the Welsh Minister's promise of a Lucy's Law consultation still hadn't materialised by February, I decided in true grassroots campaigning style to apply some gentle pressure. This was to be another publicity stunt at Crufts in March, in the same vein as the giant Lucy's Law Mother's Day card the year before. One thing about Crufts is that there are always opportunities to create awareness, and with the aim of encouraging Welsh Minister Lesley Griffiths to announce her Lucy's Law consultation, this year was no different. So what would we do? Well, what both Crufts and Wales share is a few Welsh pedigree dog breeds, large groups of which would be attending to be judged. I met with the Kennel Club in January, discussed my idea, and they gave me their approval. After looking at the numbers of entries for each Welsh breed and their physical descriptions, I decided the Welsh Springer Spaniel would be perfect for this stunt. It had red and white markings, so would look good against the green flooring of the show rings, and also the Welsh Springer was the first dog owned by Lucy's owner Lisa, before her attention more turned towards Cavaliers; it was meant to be. My vision was to give every Welsh Springer handler a Welsh flag bandana and pink Lucy's Law rosette, and, when the judges were ready, for all the 150 show dogs to suddenly enter the showring at a specific time, flashmob style, for a big group photo. The press release, with headline 'Welsh Springers Call on Welsh Government to Spring into Action for Lucy's Law!' was already written; it was just a case of making that photo happen. We now needed permission from the Welsh Springer handlers themselves, so Adam from *Our Dogs* shared with me the breed club contact details and I asked them. They were already big fans of Lucy's Law, like most – if not all – responsible breeders, so they too gave me their blessing, and began informing the owners and handlers planning to attend Crufts. Finally, the Welsh Kennel Club Chairs, Ann and Graham Hill, who had taken me under their wing at their championship show in mid-Wales over 10 years before, were also keen to supply a quote as they'd been following my campaigning the past decade. The day came around and it was decided to do the Welsh Springer flashmob in between the judging of the male dogs and bitches. That gave me and my fellow volunteers just enough time to go around all the benches in the morning handing out Welsh flag bandanas and Lucy's Law rosettes. Everyone was so excited about their dogs being part of changing laws to end puppy farming, so they all proudly attached their white, green, and red Welsh flag bandanas around their dogs' necks, and bright pink rosettes to their collars, and waited for my signal.

Organising doggy flashmobs isn't really the done thing at big championship dog shows like Crufts, so this was a bit of a first. But already having the Kennel Club, Welsh Kennel Club, and Welsh Springer Spaniel breed clubs onboard made things a lot easier, caused minimal disruption or delay to the actual judging, and most importantly we got our picture: 150 Welsh Springers all wearing Welsh flag bandanas and Lucy's Law rosettes. The photos and press release were sent out that day, and just four days later, Welsh Minister Lesley Griffiths announced her government's Lucy's Law public consultation – job done. What I loved about this PR stunt was its simplicity, use of resources to hand, and relative immediacy of its intended result. Campaign-wise it really did tick all the boxes and was definitely one of the most fun and successful dog-related, awareness-raising PR projects I've thought up, organised, and executed. After all, Lucy's Law in Wales was also crucial to getting Scotland engaged, since the devolved powers often compete with each other to be the first to do something. If Wales adopted Lucy's Law, like the majority of its individual councils had by now, Scotland would be the only place to deal puppies legally, as well as continue to generously provide the template for illegal dealing and smuggling too, so going forward it would most likely be easier to apply pressure north of the border. And apply we did, to both governments, relentlessly tagging their respective Ministers in tweets and Facebook posts every single day so they were constantly notified. Unsurprisingly they never responded, but I knew this constant bombardment of invisible activism would be having some effect.

In spring came the other news we'd all been anxiously waiting for. There was another announcement from (the) government informing us that the 'Statutory Instrument', the name given to secondary legislation that has the power to alter existing laws without Parliament having to pass a brand new Act, was being created for Lucy's Law – or, to give it its posh name, the Animal Welfare (Licensing of Activities Involving Animals) (England) (Amendment) Regulations 2019. Before making it onto the 'Statute Book', an expression describing formal laws that have already been passed, it had to be debated in the Houses of Commons and Lords; just a formality, I was told, but I still feared the worst. What if it was rejected? Or opposed? What if the last 10 years had been a complete waste of time, and that after these debates we'd be back to square one, and dogs like Lucy would continue to exist on legal licensed puppy farms, in legal, licensed, unseen squalor, with their pups sold on by legal, licensed third-party dealers? What if we'd have to restart the campaign and do the whole thing all over again?

One of the friendly opposition MPs' staff shared with me an email containing debate briefing statements: one last attempt to block! They listed all their imaginary loopholes, providing MPs with reasons and excuses not to support today's historic change in the law. Luckily, I was able to 'put these fires out' immediately, sharing important information with opposition MPs just minutes before the actual debate. It was to be the last time I'd worry about a Lucy's Law debate in England, my final test, before MPs entered the Main Chamber and took their place. Luckily, I needn't have worried.

On 5 June 2019, almost five years since our first ever petition was rejected, I sat up in the same Commons Public Gallery with Linda, Peter Egan, and my mum, listening to speech after speech from cross-party MPs, all in rare agreement (especially as Brexit was currently top of their agenda), paying personal tributes to little Lucy, praising our coalition of campaigners, and once again mentioning their own pets. Lisa Cameron MP even mentioned my mum in her speech; she was so happy to be in Hansard! Minister David Rutley summed up with an excellent speech, and when it was put to the vote, the Lucy's Law Statutory Instrument passed unanimously and that was it – we'd changed the law! Unless something catastrophic happened in its final reading in the Lords a few days later – we'd done it! Lucy's Law was now enshrined in English law. As we left the Public Gallery elated and emotional, completely opposite feelings to five years beforehand, and each clutching the actual paper Statutory Instrument of Lucy's Law in our hands! It didn't feel real. We met Lisa Cameron downstairs at my favourite place in the Palace of Westminster, by the picture of Elizabeth I, Sir Walter Raleigh, and the two Borzois in St Stephen's Hall. Lucy's Law was an *actual* law on paper now, to be enforceable from 6 April 2020, in order for businesses to prepare and the government to form an awareness campaign which I'd been invited to help them with. That evening I had to fly to Jersey to give a talk the following day on Lucy's Law, to a Women's Institute-type group in a smart hotel, which was the first time I could end my presentation proudly waving the actual new piece of legislation in the air.

A few weeks later it was more good news. After their three-month consultation, the Welsh Government announced that they were also going to introduce Lucy's Law. I was in London, and Linda had just arrived into Paddington from Wales, so we met up at the hotel in the station and shared some celebratory bubbles, and a few tears too. Wales' victory was Linda's, accompanied by her C.A.R.I.A.D. campaigning sister Sue, and Eileen from Friends of Animals Wales. Welsh Minister Eluned Morgan AM, who'd been so supportive of Linda's work, also came to say well done on her way to Wales from Westminster. Lucy had now changed the law in two countries, England and Wales. With all eyes now on Scotland I began working out my next move. I'd visited the Scottish Parliament twice in the last few years and attended two Scottish National Party Conferences as well, but up to that point all my campaigning had been ignored. It was going to need something clever, simple, powerful, shareable, and very media-friendly.

The Welsh Springer publicity stunt had been a huge success but doing another flashmob would have been unoriginal. But it was the Scottish Kennel Club's Championship Show in late August so, just like Crufts, all the breeds would be there; I decided to organise a picture of the five iconic Scottish terrier breeds: Cairn, Scottie, Westie, Skye, and Dandie Dinmont, all lined up wearing bright pink Lucy's Law rosettes, in front of the Scottish flag with blue and white St Andrew's cross, or 'saltire' as it's also known. After sending all the necessary emails, helped again by the Kennel Club, *Our Dogs*, and this time the Scottish Kennel Club, we arranged the picture to be taken in a gap in the judging. The following evening the picture of the terriers accompanied my 'Scottish Breeds Call on Scottish Government to Announce Lucy's Law!' press release, and it was widely picked up by the Scottish press – generating lots of links to share on social media, tagging Scottish Ministers and Government officials in each post. Two weeks later I was invited up to Edinburgh by Government Officials for a big announcement. I took Julia up with me, and met both Linda and Sarah at Edinburgh airport, where we'd also arranged to meet Scott Blair, a barrister from the Scottish branch of the Institute of Licensing. Also present were representatives of the Scottish SPCA and Edinburgh Dog and Cat Home of which I'm a proud ambassador. The first two minutes were the most memorable of the whole two hour meeting, as Government officials immediately confirmed Lucy's Law would happen in Scotland, and we spent the remainder answering questions clarifying any confusion in the new law, as well as reassuring them by explaining and debunking all of the potential 'loopholes' that actually never existed in the first place.

Lucy had now changed the law in a third country – Scotland – and so the UK mainland would eventually be free of cruel puppy dealers, thus making it impossible to sell pups bred on Irish puppy farms, whether legal or illegal (so helping end puppy farming in Ireland by simply removing the market), and obviously much harder to sell smuggled puppies too. What a result! After a big group photo with everyone at the meeting all wearing their bright pink Lucy's Law rosettes, we jumped in a cab and visited Lucy's Law supporters from the beginning, Edinburgh Dog and Cat Home, and then went to pay our respects to the beautiful, iconic statue of Greyfriars Bobby, the famous terrier who became known in 19th-century Edinburgh for spending 14 years guarding the grave of his owner until he died himself. We took a group selfie still wearing our pink rosettes and I've never seen four people smile so widely – we'd come to Scotland and finally been successful. Julia and I were particularly overcome with emotion. We'd shared the most horrific, confrontational experiences in meetings during the last decade, and we also both missed our Dads and wished we could tell them about it all. I was also overwhelmed as I'd studied to be a vet in Edinburgh and now, 24 years later, I'd led the campaign to change the law to protect animals there.

The final Lucy's Law victory story of 2019 is possibly my favourite one of all. It was definitely the most surreal, and couldn't possibly have made the whole 10-year journey end in any more impressive fashion. It goes something like this.

It was summer, and Prime Minister Boris Johnson and his partner Carrie Symonds had just moved into Downing Street. I'd already had the pleasure of meeting Carrie, who is a phenomenal animal welfare campaigner herself, a few times at various animal welfare events in Westminster, and she'd very generously supported Lucy's Law and always shared our tweets during the campaign. So when I heard a rumour that she and Boris were looking to adopt a rescue dog I wasn't at all surprised – and immediately had an idea to run by her. I privately messaged Carrie and she invited me to Downing Street to discuss my cunning plan: 'Come to No.10 at 4pm tomorrow, I'll come down and collect you from the entrance hall, and take you up to the flat,' she said. The 'flat' being the official residence of the Prime Minister of the United Kingdom. I did as she said and within minutes, we were sipping cups of tea in their front room. All totally normal so far, as I'm sure you'll agree. With the unprecedented exposure and publicity that Downing Street's new dog would no doubt generate, I began to explain how their choice of rescue dog could carry a significant message to the world if she and the Prime Minister took my advice and chose carefully.

As a fellow campaigner, it was no surprise that Carrie understood exactly where I was going with this. We chatted about the prospect of their rescue dog raising global awareness of Lucy's Law, puppy farming, as well as smaller volunteer-run rescues, and rescue centres which only take in sick puppies unlikely to be sold and would otherwise most likely be drowned, or ex-breeding dogs that are infertile so would most likely have been shot and chucked on a bonfire. Furthermore, by adopting a puppy from a rescue centre it would help educate the public that you don't have to visit a breeder to find a pup, or indeed spend a fortune on a pedigree or the latest designer crossbreed. As we carried on chatting, I described the incredible work of Friends of Animals Wales, a charity that ticked every box, run by my friend Eileen Jones, who together with her dedicated network of fosterers takes in these abandoned puppy farm dogs and sick puppies, which is why their outstanding vet's bills are in the tens of thousands of pounds. Many of these dogs require specialised treatments and often expensive surgical corrections, not to mention the rehabilitation of ex-breeders like Lucy; dogs that for these reasons – money and time – some organisations often appear to refuse to take in. Carrie loved the idea of helping an abandoned puppy with an uncertain fate, so I email-introduced her to Eileen, had a cheeky guided tour of their 'flat', said a quick hi to Larry the cat, and came back to Brighton.

About 10 days later I still hadn't heard anything. There was no rush for a decision, but after the positive year the Lucy's Law campaign had already enjoyed, I was excited about the awareness adopting a rescue pup from Eileen's Friends of Animals could potentially generate not just in the UK but worldwide. It was August now and I'd just arrived on holiday in Spain, and had arranged to meet best mate Russell and some friends on the beach at Malaga for lunch. Unsurprisingly beers and red wine flowed, and after a few hours it was time to go back to my hotel, have a little siesta, and get ready to go out that evening.

Chapter 19

As I was dozing off into a Rioja-San-Miguel-enhanced snooze, my mobile rang displaying an unfamiliar British number on its screen. My policy with unrecognisable numbers is to always ignore, let them go to voicemail, then call back if necessary, but this time, in my half-asleep, slightly inebriated state, I answered and waited to hear who was at the other end.

'Hello?' the voice said, 'Is that Marc?' Now there are some voices in the world that are so unmistakable that not even the best impressionists can copy them. This person was very well spoken, in fact *exactly* as he sounded on the telly, and after confirming I was indeed Marc, the mystery voice also revealed his identity. 'It's Boris here,' he continued, 'I'm with Carrie and we've chosen Dilyn.' The Prime Minister was calling me to discuss adopting a rescue dog. Again, all totally normal, right? 'Are you abroad?' he asked, presumably because of the ringtone. 'Yes,' I replied, 'I'm in Spain.' 'I'm terribly sorry for interrupting your holiday, Marc,' he apologised. 'That's OK, Prime Minister – you can call me anytime you like!' As we chatted, I wondered if I was actually mid-siesta, perhaps still under the influence of wine, beer, and maybe even a bit of sunstroke? But no, it was definitely the Prime Minister, and they had selected their new dog, a nine-week-old Jack Russell cross listed on Eileen's website as Dilyn, meaning 'follow' in Welsh. We chatted for about 10 minutes, discussing logistics, dates, and how I could 'help make this happen.' Eileen had already visited Number 10 for last year's Lucy's Law celebratory garden party, so had technically done a house visit, which meant it was just a case of coordinating diaries and, just like the Prime Minister said, making it happen.

Dilyn had been born onto a Welsh puppy farm and abandoned by the farmer because of an undershot jaw, meaning he was unlikely to be sold. After further correspondence with the Prime Minister and Carrie, mainly comprising cute pics and videos of Dilyn, it was agreed that Eileen, Debbie and another fosterer, Kerri, all from Friends of Animals Wales, would bring Dilyn from Wales to Downing Street. We agreed on the handover date, Monday 2 September, and were all very excited about this high-profile pet adoption. I remember when Barack Obama bought his Portuguese Water Dog pups and thinking, with my animal welfare campaigner hat on, 'What a missed opportunity!' And now here I was masterminding the adoption of the UK Prime Minister's pooch, which would hopefully raise awareness of rescue dogs, puppies in rescue, puppy farming, third-party dealers, smaller non-corporate volunteer-run rescues, and of course Lucy's Law.

The weekend before the handover, excitement levels were peaking. Team Dilyn was ready to make this little abandoned pup the star of the political show. The *Mail on Sunday* and *Telegraph* had already both covered the story, so it was no surprise that when I carried Dilyn in in his red pet carrier, and turned the corner into Downing Street accompanied by Eileen, Debbie, and Kerri all in their scarlet Friends of Animals Wales t-shirts, there was a bank of photographers representing the world's press, all poised, ready and waiting to get that first snap of the newest four-legged resident of Downing Street. As I approached the famous black door, the photographers were all shouting 'Turn around!' at me, which I did very slowly, and Dilyn, like the tiny legend that he is, was staring straight back at them through the fine mesh of his carrier. We entered Number 10, handed our phones in as is protocol, and went up to the 'flat'. We unzipped his carrier and out leapt an enthusiastic Dilyn. Within seconds he was running around his new home, sniffing the skirting boards and wagging his tail with excitement. I could tell from Carrie's expression she was already smitten, and when the Prime Minister joined us, he immediately picked up Dilyn, gave him a big hug and a kiss, and I could see that he was too.

We all went down into the garden, the same garden where exactly 53 weeks beforehand we'd been celebrating Lucy's Law, and the Number 10 official photographer got pictures of Dilyn, Boris, Carrie, and Eileen, Kerri, Debbie, and me too. I'd also brought a bag of bright pink Lucy's Law rosettes with me and everyone took one. 'Would you mind putting your rosette on for a photo?' I asked the Prime Minister. 'I'd be honoured to!' he replied. In that moment it all hit home the enormity of what we'd achieved. Grassroots campaigners had taken their campaign to the top, been successful, and now the Prime Minister was wearing our rosette and playing with his and his partner's new puppy farm rescue pup. As we walked out of Number 10 and turned our mobiles back on, we were inundated with notifications from Twitter, Facebook, texts,

Messenger, WhatsApp messages – it was crazy. None of us had any idea of how many news channels had covered this story, many of them filming live as we walked in. We went to the pub across the road in a state of happy shock, which lasted a good few hours. Dilyn's story was picked up by the world's media; he was – and still is – promoting rescue dog adoption, puppy farm awareness, and of course Lucy's Law, all on a global scale. It was one of the proudest pet adoptions I've ever been involved with: how apt that an abandoned puppy farm dog, now safe and secure in his forever home, was carrying on little Lucy's legacy.

Chapter 20

'If you think you are too small to make a difference, try sleeping with a mosquito.' said the Dalai Lama, and this remains one of my favourite, and to my mind most appropriate, quotes of all time.

I never set out to be a campaigner. Does anybody? After all it's incredibly stressful, depressing, lonely, costs money, and can take years before you make any noticeable progress. All I ever really knew was that I wanted to help animals. Law, politics, campaigning... these were all subjects and activities other people did. I was way too busy memorising flags, drawing birds, or reading *New Scientist* magazine. But I was always brought up looking out for the underdog, being aware of the most vulnerable, and helping out in situations if I was in a position to. As a qualified vet I've assisted in many human emergencies, from in-flight heart attacks, to road traffic accidents, to a drive-by shooting on the Brazil/Argentina border. My point is that if you use what resources you have in a positive way it can only make the world a better place. Ignoring situations where you can genuinely make a difference is far worse, leaving behind feelings of guilt that are potentially much harder to live with.

For me, getting into campaigning happened purely by chance. That fateful night on duty, treating those sick pups at my emergency clinic was the catalyst, igniting my sense of injustice to a point where I felt I just had to do *something* about it. Understanding why and how those puppies got to be so ill, and finding out for myself about the chain of events leading to them being in so much pain from parvovirus, not to mention what state their mums, like little Lucy, would've most likely been in back on the puppy farm, meant I was in a position to do something. Admittedly all I could do back then was raise awareness by getting a cool guitar signed by famous rock stars and inventing a different type of dog show. As fun and useful as those two methods of campaigning were (not that I knew I was actually campaigning – just doing what I could and felt was right), it still wasn't going to change the whole country's behaviour when it came to choosing a dog responsibly. It wasn't going to end puppy farming overnight.

But in its simplest form: that evening in my emergency clinic I witnessed something I didn't like the look of, thought was wrong, felt very uncomfortable about, and used what resources I had to try and change it. Of course, this doesn't always have to be animal welfare-related (though, what with greyhound racing or sea mammals in aquatic parks, it's never been easier to get fired up about some issues), but mistreatment, unfairness, and exploitation of the most vulnerable are usually triggers for most campaigns to start. It's pretty obvious why: if you don't provide their voice, then who will? These days there's really no excuse not to do something to protect others – and there are so many tools available to help us, so many more than even a decade ago when I treated those poorly puppies, and most of them completely free to use. As for what they are and which one you should use first, that depends on the individual campaign, but if it's a law you'd like to change, I'd highly recommend starting with the Government's e-petition system. Furthermore, in our great UK democracy we all have easy and excellent access to our parliamentary representatives, the law-changers and decision-makers, whether Members of Parliament (MPs), Members of the Scottish Parliament (MSPs), or Assembly Members (AMs).

If you don't fancy going down the political route, that's obviously fine – it's not for everyone and you may not always need it if you're just trying to raise awareness. Social media is one of the most effective, least expensive, influential, and potentially most time-consuming ways of campaigning, especially over the last decade as sharing platforms like Twitter have evolved to be game-changers in many ways. Whilst campaigning it's always essential to keep your 'conversation' going, both behind the scenes and in the public eye. If you don't, and your social media accounts or websites remain inactive or even stagnate, your supporters will assume either that your campaign's been successful or that you've lost interest, usually the latter. Lucy's

Law had many thousands of supporters, all invested emotionally, and so it was always crucial to show them that the campaign was very active and that it was working hard. Some of the ways we achieved this, especially in the later years, was by tweeting a picture of the iconic, easily recognisable, Big Ben and House of Commons every time I emerged from Westminster Tube station. Taking a picture of the same subject from the exact same place, on every visit – Exit 2 to be precise – accompanied by exactly the same message, simply 'Here for meetings :)', accompanied by my trusted hashtags (#wheresmum, #adopt, and after December 2017, #LucysLaw), meant that I could provide assurance to our followers, plus that brand continuity which our brains subconsciously crave, even expect. In much the same way, followers of Lucy's Facebook page appreciated consistency of content posted by Lisa, when Lucy was still with us. This all helped reassure Lucy's Law supporters that we were busy trying to change the law, but importantly not give away precisely where or with whom in Westminster I was meeting. This proved essential considering the behaviour of those organisations determined to stop us succeeding. I had to remain in stealth mode without revealing my position. I could have been in the atrium of Portcullis House, treading the red carpets of the House of Lords, inside Number 10, or even grabbing some lunch downstairs at the Red Lion Pub around the corner on Whitehall; all our followers needed to know was that I was somewhere in Westminster trying to make some progress for the dogs.

With so many different social media platforms accessible nowadays, it's important to choose the most appropriate, or the ones best-equipped to assist with your campaign. Everyone's campaign is different and must appeal to its correct demographic. For the Lucy's Law campaign there were only really two social media platforms that were relevant: one that had the potential to engage the public, politicians, media, and key opinion leaders influential in change, i.e. Twitter, and one that Lucy's followers were already engaged with in great numbers i.e. Facebook. Also by having two active accounts with each platform, '@marcthevet' and '@pupaid' on Twitter, and 'Marc the Vet' and 'Pup Aid 'on Facebook, I was also able to share posts from both, to cross-pollinate as they call it, thus helping spread the net even further. Both Twitter and Facebook are excellent for sharing petitions on too, which made a huge difference, especially when engaging with celebrities and utilising their extensive fanbases to help reach their targets. Indeed, in the early years of political campaigning, just before launching our first e-petition I politely asked Ricky Gervais if he'd be happy to share it. 'Yes,' he confirmed, 'Just wait for me to get back from New York in a few days.' So I did, and Ricky was incredibly generous not only sharing the petition links, but also my slightly gushy 'Thank you Ricky' tweets every time he did, which also non-coincidentally contained the petition link, and which he'd then share as well! The incredible power and reach of social media helped both e-petitions reach their 100,000-signature goals to trigger debates, the first unsuccessful in the Commons Main Chamber back in 2014, the second much more successful in Westminster Hall four years later.

Social media also provided the opportunity to share posts displaying our campaign's core values, i.e. kindness, compassion, and empathy. Posts about adopting from rescue, always asking to see mum interacting with pups, and useful links to content like news articles relevant to the campaign all helped build trust and encouraged loyalty with our followers. This means that when you make specific requests of your supporters, perhaps to sign and share a petition, or to contact their MP, known as 'call to actions', then they are much more likely to do so. Another feature of social media useful for campaigning, and there are so many, is tagging pictures on Twitter with accounts so as not to waste any valuable space in the body of the tweet. These accounts can include reliable animal welfare allies with large followings that will be notified and almost always share, as well as politicians, celebrities, and even accounts not engaged with the campaign yet. Sometimes it was fun tagging in accounts whose minds or governments we'd yet to change, and just making them aware of the progress being made elsewhere. Twitter for me is the most useful campaigning tool and for years, as I'm sure those who follow me will be well aware, I spent a lot of time on it – not just posting updates and replying to and sharing fellow campaigners' posts, but sadly also constantly looking out for replies and posts from those individuals and organisations clearly desperate for us to fail, so as to try and predict their next moves. Including images was always important, and never too shocking, just like Lucy's Facebook page. Yes, it's important to educate, but often people check social media in their downtime, so it's often unwise to upset followers or, worse, give them any reason to unfollow you or your campaign. Of course we had our fair share of trolls, unjustified criticism, and needless negativity over the years, but I find the easiest way to deal with them is by simply ignoring and usually muting. A friend told me once 'the bigger the target you make yourself, the more likely you are to get hit' – amazing advice, and so true. Being 'hit' was always a compliment, we were making a difference, our campaign was working. My theory is that by engaging, even blocking someone, you immediately make them feel relevant, which is usually what they're desperate for in the first place. Finally, when using social media, and relying on other accounts to share our messages, it was important to follow them back and share their messages too, simple Twitter etiquette which also ensured our timelines weren't just 'Me, me, me!' Finally, we always tried to appear approachable. One easy way to do this was for my campaigning account Pup Aid to try and follow *everyone* back. Any prospective follower stumbling on your account and considering supporting your campaign will always press follow on seeing roughly equal numbers of followers and following, so very first impressions of your campaign's inclusive-looking 'brand' online are most likely positive.

Following on nicely from use of social media is the importance of branding: clearly a huge and complex topic that affects all our lives, from the food we buy to the newspapers we read, the organisations we trust to the celebrities we respect. Most successful brands remain consistent in appearance and message, typically making their visibility appear effortless. But trust me, from someone who's grown up watching some of the most successful brands being invented: the easier a brand is to recognise, the more work has gone into its creation. Specific branding, marketing, and advertising agencies are paid fortunes by companies to make their brand more noticeable than their competitors, to really stand out from the crowd, and ultimately give the consumer or supporter the best chance of choosing it, ideally staying loyal to that brand for life. Simplicity of messaging is one of the most important properties of a successful brand too, as well as speed of recognition, understanding that brand's personality, and of course taking onboard the all-important information communicated. Some brands have evolved over generations, successfully keeping their supporters and customers engaged and loyal, by gradually tweaking their eye-catching images, logos, fonts, and nowadays, their vital hashtags. With today's fast-moving lifestyles and ever dwindling attention spans, brands often have to be noticed, understood, and processed in milliseconds.

As well as the thousands of everyday instantly recognisable brands like Specsavers, BMW, and Starbucks, animal welfare organisations and campaigns are also brands too, enjoying their own particular appearance and brand values specific to them. As consumers, our own 'brand' values, or personalities, will often closely mirror those of brands we trust, much like finding a partner. After all, a match is a match, right? Unsurprisingly the more attached we become to that brand, the more we trust it and are likely to remain loyal. Both the Lucy's Law and Pup Aid campaigns are themselves brands, each with their own, albeit very similar, brand values. Using social media and brand visibility, not to mention the annual fun dog show, both brands were able to attract a loyal following, so any subsequent messaging was not only well received, but extensively shared too. What's more, all our celebrity endorsements were never paid for, unlike corporate partnerships, with well-known personalities happy to attend our fun dog shows, sharing our posts online, and even writing their own supportive content. Further endorsements from politicians, fellow campaigns, other respected organisations, even American movie documentaries, were also welcomed, helping once again to increase our brand visibility – handy when you have a very limited budget. Our instantly recognisable, now iconic Lucy's Law logo and brand, using Lucy's favourite colour of bright pink, that also formed the basis for the bright pink campaign rosettes, was helped greatly by the *Mirror* newspaper with whom I worked closely to turn my initial sketch and vision into law-changing reality.

Talking of newspapers, there is still very much a role to be played in campaigning by traditional media i.e. print, TV, and radio. Although it feels like it, not *everyone* is always online these days, and there are people from all demographics who still prefer to start the day by holding an actual newspaper in their hands whilst sitting in their favourite armchair rather than by turning on a computer or checking their phone. Relevant articles and stories describing your campaign's successes, especially those that make the front page, can easily be photographed using your smartphone, and those pictures uploaded to social media. As already mentioned, the tagging option on Twitter, and to a lesser extent, on Facebook too, allows supporters and loyal accounts to be notified, encouraging them to share your posts. In terms of print media, I really can't thank the *Mirror*, *Dogs Today* magazine, and *Our Dogs* newspaper enough for all their support of the Lucy's Law campaign over the years. My relationship with the *Mirror* really started when I worked with one of their investigative journalists, Andrew Penman. Andrew had, and still has, a regular column in Thursday's *Mirror* that often exposes and educates readers about scams and general wrongdoings in society. Back in the day when my fellow campaigners and I were constantly approached by the press, they were only interested in running stories about puppy farms if they could actually get into the farms themselves to take pics or record footage. Sadly it was always the deal-breaker, as we could never guarantee entry, for a number of reasons; so unfortunately many stories being planned by a number of initially hopeful high profile journalists fell by the wayside upon discovering that although it was technically possible, it wasn't that simple getting into these hellholes.

But I remember speaking with Andrew during those full-on campaigning days in late 2015. Back then Mr Penman was 'just' another journalist contacting me, planning a trip to Carmarthenshire in Wales, the capital of licensed commercial dog breeders in the UK, to write an article about puppy farming. I assumed it was just a matter of moments until that familiar conversation, typically starting enthusiastically with the energy of someone about to single handedly end puppy farming with one article, would slowly fizzle out and end with 'Oh, well if I can't get inside the puppy farms there's really no point,' which usually meant no article at all. I gave Andrew my well-rehearsed speech about the practicalities and potential difficulties entering these large-scale commercial breeding facilities. But then I had a thought. Government's advice at that time was for prospective puppy buyers to 'always see the puppy with its mother' and to 'always, if possible, see the puppy in its natural environment' – by far the two most important and useful pieces of advice anyone could give someone looking to buy a puppy. However, the vast majority of these largely legal puppy farms, inspected and licensed by local authorities though they were, typically refused entry to the public. So how could anyone possibly practice the Government's excellent advice, to actually see the puppy interacting with its mum, let alone view the place where it was born? This was the story! And it was a far stronger message: that people weren't actually allowed onto these farms in the first place. With that, Andrew headed off to Wales; he couldn't and didn't lose. The resulting article, entitled 'Puppy farms operating behind firmly closed doors – what have they got to hide?' described Andrew's account of repeatedly being refused entry to these licensed commercial dog breeders' premises, and was one of the biggest game-changers for me and the campaign. In just one piece of writing in which he'd posed as an innocent puppy buyer, Andrew had exposed the crux of the issue: lack of traceability and accountability. By being constantly refused entry to every large-scale commercial licensed dog breeder he approached, it was impossible for him to take a look inside, to see the pups interacting with their mums, and therefore he was repeatedly unable to follow the government's buying advice.

In this absolute milestone article in the *Mirror*, Andrew describes being denied access by one breeder with 53 licensed breeding bitches, another with 88 licensed breeding bitches, with both using pathetic excuses. A third breeder said they'd rather 'remain anonymous because it's such a hotbed, there are so many people against puppy farms.' Another breeder licensed for 80 breeding bitches told Andrew, 'I'm not interested. I've got my thoughts but I'm keeping them to myself. I am doing it correctly, we are above board, but it's very difficult,' and another, 'It's not an advisable thing to do really, we've been told it's easier not to get involved. It's not worth the hassle.' Others simply slammed down the phone without giving a reason why he wasn't allowed to visit. Andrew had proved that this blanket refusal to allow potential buyers onto legal, licensed dog breeding establishments, the exact kind where Lucy was born onto and then abused and exploited for her puppies, made a complete mockery of the Government's advice to hopeful puppy buyers. I took this article with me to Westminster on every single visit from then on, as it also showed Andrew's photos of the puppy farms themselves, albeit from a safe distance obviously. The article became important evidence of how and why the law was failing the dogs and why it desperately needed changing. 'Why does Government recommend that buyers always see the puppy with its mum, and then license establishments that make this totally impossible?' I quizzed MPs, 'They are recommending one thing and legislating for the opposite. It's crazy – and more importantly it's killing dogs.' Andrew's story was a vital piece of the puzzle, as most puppy farms were clearly dependent on third-party dealers to sell their puppies to the public. By banning these third-party dealers that enabled and encouraged puppy farming to exist, well away from prospective puppy buyers, commercial puppy farms would finally be forced to open their doors to the buying public and instantly become transparent and accountable.

Andrew continued to write regular articles about puppy farming and our campaign to ban third-party puppy dealers. He was instrumental in securing the *Mirror* as media partner for the Lucy's Law campaign, arranging a meeting between me, him, and the boss of the whole newspaper group, and never failed to devote his column, both in print and online, to reporting the very latest Lucy's Law news every single week of the campaign and beyond. We used to meet to discuss tactics and strategy over our fresh peppermint teas at Carluccio's, tucked away beneath the space rocket-shaped giant Canada Square skyscraper in Canary Wharf. Andrew's columns, most notably the 'What have they got to hide?' piece, as well as Lucy's Law latest news, an iconic front page, his online content, and his attendance at every relevant event along the campaign trail, gave us grassroots campaigners so much strength. Endorsement by a journalist of Andrew's caliber, as well as by a national newspaper so respected as a household superbrand, were two major reasons we were able to make so much progress. Andrew always supported the dogs, and I'll always remember when the *Mirror*'s rival, the *Sun*, wrote a fantastic article on Lucy's Law, Andrew shared it online as he believed our campaign's messaging was more important than silly tabloid rivalry: a true hero of animal welfare, I'm sure you'll all agree.

Furthermore recognition of our campaign by a national newspaper made us much harder to ignore. As well as the obvious shares, screengrabs, and tweeted pictures of Andrew's columns in actual print, we were now reaching a much wider audience beyond just animal-lovers. There was a palpable anger at the injustice to the most vulnerable, which was calling for Lucy's Law, focused on how Lucy had been mistreated, which seemed to resonate with the British public, and beyond. Andrew and the *Mirror* were being contacted by dog owners all around the world offering their support, as well as hundreds of small to mid-size animal welfare organisations, all generously offering up their logos to be included in yet another article, keen to tell the world that they were also proud supporters and fully onboard with our campaign. But as well as endorsement by a national title, it was also important to secure regular support from the dog press: one newspaper and one magazine, to be more precise. I already had history writing for *Our Dogs* newspaper, the weekly, official paper for the dog breeding and showing world; and I'd known and been a huge fan of Beverley Cuddy, editor of *Dogs Today* magazine, for years. Having friends in high places really does help sometimes, especially with campaigning, and *Our Dogs*' Adam Williams proved he was no exception. Over the years, and especially since attending the Lucy's Law launch in Westminster, Adam and I spoke almost every week. I'd give him the latest news from Parliament, he'd usually feature the story on the front page, and just like Andrew's weekly columns in the *Mirror*, they were photographed, tagged, and widely shared on social media. Of course banning third-party puppy sales and Lucy's Law was very warmly welcomed by dog breeding and showing fraternities too; after all, responsible breeders will always meet prospective puppy buyers and never choose to sell their pups through third parties. Continued acceptance by the pedigree dog world was greatly received, especially at championship dog shows like Crufts, and many breeders played their own individual parts in building the campaign's momentum.

Beverley Cuddy, as many reading this will already know, is quite simply a legend. For years she's been reporting from the coalface of canine welfare, bringing dog fans all the latest news, fads, and controversy too. She was showing her first Bearded Collie at 13 years old, which became a Champion. At 22 years old Beverley became a Championship show judge and Secretary of the Bearded Collie Club. Once a responsible breeder of Bearded Collies herself, Beverley is respected and admired by many, earning her position as Queen Bee of the dog world; and as well as editing her monthly *Dogs Today* magazine, she seems to really enjoy getting stuck into campaigns that aim to improve and protect the lives of the country's dogs. This couldn't have been truer than with Lucy's Law, for as well as attending some of our most important campaign moments, such as big Westminster meetings and handing the Lucy's Law petition into Number 10, Beverley single-handedly organised one of the cleverest projects to help brief MPs I've ever witnessed. It was a few days before the Lucy's Law debate in Westminster Hall in May 2018, and Beverley decided to have our campaign briefing document for MPs designed and printed professionally. For in every one of the 650 envelopes delivered to each individual MP, Beverley included an official bright pink Lucy's Law rosette as well. Now most MPs, if not all, receive briefings for debates as attachments on emails which they print off or read off their tablets in the chamber. But to receive an individual professionally designed document, coupled with campaign rosette, really was something else. So much so that when the debate finally arrived, some MPs were even proudly wearing their rosettes at the start of proceedings, totally against parliamentary rules; unsurprisingly they were promptly warned and made to swiftly remove them!

The power of mainstream media, whether newspapers, TV, radio, or online, can never be underestimated. At the end of the day, providing as it does an opportunity to inform, educated, and engage the wider audience, even inspire them to action, this can only be a good thing for any campaign. All this provides valuable content and influences different sectors and demographics, largely dependent on which news brand is sharing, and often which celebrities are involved. For example, one of the earliest TV appearances for raising awareness and educating the public, before we started campaigning in Westminster, was to officially launch the 'Where's Mum?' campaign on Channel 5's *Live With...* show, in which presenter Gabby Logan was joined by special guests 'for interviews with the public and interesting stories from around the UK'. As well as myself, I recommended stars of the recent reality TV show smash *The Only Way is Essex* – Debbie Douglas and her daughter Lydia Bright – to appear on the show to discuss the importance of seeing puppy interacting with mum, as well as the benefits of rescue dog adoption of which both Debbie and Lydia were already fans. This story was then picked up by the *Sunday Mirror* and featured as part of their Mother's Day 'Celebs on Sunday' feature in 2012. It was this simple matching of appropriate and relevant celebrities and media brands to the campaign which allowed us to effectively reach more people, but also to make our campaign more desirable to other celebrities and brands so they would want to become a part of it. We always tried to be approachable and inclusive, keeping our brand values clear and simple, one of the many reasons the 'Where's Mum?' campaign grew in popularity so quickly and became so well known.

Soon after the Channel 5 and *Sunday Mirror* publicity involving Debbie and Lydia, and as a direct result of that same mother and daughter theme, Meg Mathews and daughter Anais Gallagher were interviewed for *MailOnline*, the largest entertainment news website in the world. As well as Meg and Anais' close relationship and professional pictures together, Meg also described the problems she'd experienced with her Boston terrier Oscar, most likely purchased from a puppy farm via a third-party dealer, as well as Meg's involvement as patron of Pup Aid. As an extra bonus the article included some useful 'Dos and Don'ts when buying a puppy' section. We were using celebrity to educate the masses, and we'd spent no money doing it; it felt great. This type of content is crucial to campaigns with limited resources such as ours. Using pictures and links from each and every mention in the media, a powerful groundswell of campaign recognition and support was created that eventually helped suck in even more celebrities and therefore media. The more noise we made about our campaign, the more demographics and sectors we were reaching, making us eventually impossible to ignore; it was like we'd ambushed the Government: public, MPs, celebrities, press, social media, online, the majority of animal welfare organisations, and finally Number 10 itself; everywhere they looked they were being reminded of Lucy's Law.

Our campaign's numerous TV appearances over the years included the hugely popular BBC *Breakfast*, Sky News, and *This Morning*, to the more politically focused *Daily Politics*; all golden opportunities to keep spreading our campaign net even further, influence more people, and ultimately gain more supporters. On one appearance on *Daily Politics* in May 2016, filmed live outside the Houses of Parliament after a rally, I was interviewed alongside model, TV personality, and self-confessed rescue dog addict Jodie Marsh, who was holding little Lucy in her arms, wearing her 'Stop Puppy Farming' t-shirt. When quizzed about puppy farming and the campaign by *Daily Politics* reporter and respected political commentator Giles Dilnot, Jodie replied 'Puppy farming is definitely cruel in so many ways; not only are the dogs sick, unhealthy, and mistreated, kept in tiny boxes and used for breeding over and over and over again, but it's also cruel on the owner because when you go to buy a puppy from a puppy farm you'll end up spending thousands on vets bills because the dog's so sick.' In just a few comments Jodie had nailed it – talk about being totally 'on message', but she wasn't done yet. Giles then quizzed Jodie about third-party dealers, and why puppy farming was totally legal and regulated by the Government, to which Jodie replied, still clutching Lucy in her arms, 'That's why we need the Government to answer for themselves, because why is this legal? Why is this allowed to happen?' When I was then asked my question by Giles, I duly followed up with some more points about the hypocrisy of the Government's advice regarding prospective puppy buyers being told to see pup with mum but licensed legal sellers selling without mum, as well as mentioning our 'Where's Mum?' e-petition debate, lost in the Commons two years previously though unanimously supported by all attending cross-party MPs; and once again called on Government to ban third-party puppy dealers. Looking back at that interview for *Daily Politics*, just 3 minutes and 32 seconds long, it was definitely one of the most influential news pieces we were involved with, as being a political show it was watched by the decision-makers themselves, and most importantly, starred little Lucy herself.

When campaigning in the media it's important to keep your message and mission statements as simple as possible. That way it's less likely your message will be edited, diluted, or worse still misrepresented; this is why live interviews, either on television or radio, are often preferable. I always enjoyed radio interviews more than television; in a way you have to work that much harder to get your point across, and I still laugh to myself looking down noticing my waving arms helping me explain something, either over the phone or in a radio studio when no one can see me. Radio also allows you to have a list in front of you, and my rule is not to end the interview thinking to myself 'Why didn't I say that?'; so while I'm chatting I'll cross out lines and vital points as they're made, so all my information has been offloaded and I can hang up, or leave the studio without regrets, knowing I've done my best. One of the most eagerly anticipated interviews about puppy farming and Lucy's Law was in late 2018 with BBC Political Editor John Pienaar on his popular Sunday morning BBC Radio 5 Live show *Pienaar's Politics*, recorded in London, but my item was dialled in remotely from a booth below my local BBC Sussex studios in Brighton. Fans of John Pienaar will of course already be aware of his incredible knowledge of politics, and you'll also be pleased to know John's a huge dog-lover too. So when preparing for a live interview with John you make sure you do your homework. Furthermore, as per the usual format on his show, he was joined in his London studio by MPs and political commentators who all joined John in firing testing questions down the line at me. The interview went well, with all questions answered in detail, referencing any necessary evidence. On that rainy Sunday morning after being effectively grilled by MPs, experts, and political commentators, I left my little booth feeling an immense feeling of pride at just how far Lucy's Law and my knowledge of politics had come, considering I knew less than nothing when I started campaigning a decade ago.

History is full of inspiring stories of successful campaigns and awareness-raising, and it's usually one moment that's sparked or inspired each and every one of them. These campaigns, whether advertising or animal welfare, world wars or games of chess, all rely on making progress to achieve their goal. It stands to reason that certain individuals, parties, or organisations, usually with dangerous egos or vested interests (often both), will always attempt to prevent progress from being made, for a vast number of different reasons, not always obvious at the time. But one feature of any campaign that's important for making progress is strategy: some sort of path to follow, however convoluted, that eventually leads you to the finish line. This is where I think my early years, brain-training from endless games of chess came in most handy, about 30 years later. So once again, thanks Dad. As part of any strategy it's also important to assemble a group of experts and make a team, as we did, way back on that rainy day in Twickenham. Furthermore, if you're hoping to change the law, then for goodness' sake make sure your team contains someone to advise on the legal details. It may sound obvious but there's really no point getting near to achieving your goal and finding out that the law you're trying to change wasn't ever possible in the first place.

Away from Westminster my other campaigning advice would always be to think outside the box. Make sure your campaign stands out from the rest, encourage people to notice and engage, and then they'll hopefully lend their support. For the Lucy's Law campaign, imagination was key at many points along the way, even coming up with the whole original Lucy's Law concept itself. But creativity played a part long before the final push over the line, and included celebrity-judged fun dog shows, a signed guitar, movie premiere in Parliament, bright-pink rosettes, 'Crazy Puppy Party' YouTube video, an *X-Factor* finalist playing in the House of Commons, a giant Mother's Day card, Crufts Welsh Springer Spaniel flashmob, and the Scottish flag terrier breed picture too. These all helped us show off our brand's personality: cheeky, fun, different, and eye-catching – just like little Lucy herself. These publicity stunts enabled us to grab headlines in different arenas, win more PR, and become even more visible. This increased awareness would lead to more recognition, to winning awards, and ultimately to success for the dogs. Rallies and events with relevant celebrities and politicians are also very effective campaigning tools, and can be organised with minimal resources – extremely satisfying for grassroots campaigners competing with organisations with unlimited budgets and dedicated in-house PR and marketing teams.

Another one of my favourite quotes is by American cultural anthropologist Margaret Mead, who said, 'Never doubt that a small group of thoughtful, committed citizens can change the world; indeed, it's the only thing that ever has' – which couldn't be truer in the case of our Lucy's Law campaign. We proved you don't need any previous knowledge or background in law, politics, or history to make progress, raise awareness, or even change the law. Just believe in your campaign; keep it simple and relevant; develop appropriate communication skills and relationships with fellow like-minded campaigners; seek out media contacts, celebrities, politicians, journalists; say thank you a lot, and ideally work alongside a legal professional to make sure what you're trying to achieve, if it is a law change, is in fact possible. Make sure you're always aware of the dangers of campaign fatigue and burn-out too. Campaigning, especially when working a full-time job at the same time like we were all doing, can be emotionally, physically and financially exhausting too. Be prepared for likely, and sometimes unlikely, obstructions and barriers, vested interests, and of course having the patience to play the long game and never give up fighting for what's *right*.

I started off this journey as a third-generation refugee kid, feeling like I lacked any identity, and totally ill equipped to interact with other humans. Lucy began her journey with no name, totally ill equipped to be a dog. Two very unlikely law-changers, I think you'll agree. Luckily, mainly thanks to Lisa, our paths eventually crossed, and the rest, as they say, is literally history.

Lucy's Law will help ensure every dog and cat has the best start in life. Not only will puppies and kittens be protected, but their mothers will be too. Lucy truly is a little dog that changed the world; and as I write this, Northern Ireland looks like it's now in the process of bringing in Lucy's Law as well; if successful that'll be Lucy's fourth country, not to mention the influence she's having in other countries around the work, including Victoria's Law in the States.

I'm often asked, 'Why did it take so long?' Well, I hope it's now clear why. After 10 years of campaigning, over 300 visits to Westminster, two 100,000 government e-petitions, one Select Committee Inquiry, formation of APDAWG, a few Early Day Motions and rallies, as well as hundreds of interviews and thousands of social media posts, I am incredibly proud of what our little team achieved, and we remain thankful to each and every individual, human and canine, who helped make Lucy's Law happen. Little Lucy will be forever missed, but her incredible legacy will live on forever, and she will hopefully encourage changes to similar legislation to protect more animals in even more countries around the world. Perhaps our Lucy's Law campaign will inspire you to change something that's making you unhappy? Either way, I hope you'll agree from reading about Lucy, and how she changed the world, that there's *always* something you or anyone can do to protect the most vulnerable, from sharing something on social media to changing the law to stop that cruelty or injustice happening in the first place. We did it, and you can too!

Acknowledgements

As you'd expect for a campaign that's spanned over 10 years, there are many people, organisations, and brands involved, so please excuse me if I've left anyone out.

First thanks must go to my dedicated core team of fearless grassroots campaigners, my second family, always available 24/7, a tiny coalition that's worked tirelessly in our spare time to help drive the campaign forward, and eventually to victory. Campaigning sister Linda and the 'beeps' (ask her), her phenomenal colleague Sue, amazing superbrain Julia, best barrister ever Sarah, very missed Philippa, amazing Eileen (Friends of Animals Wales), Mark (Hidden Insight), Jenny (Naturewatch), Andrew Penman (Mirror), Beverley Cuddy (Dogs Today), Adam, Ali, and Vince (Our Dogs). Special thanks of course to Lucy's owner Lisa, for her friendship, lots of time spent in Lucy's company, and for giving me permission to write this book – it really couldn't have been easy reliving certain parts of Lucy's journey, but she was no doubt helped by the support of little Minnie; and Carol the fosterer for her invaluable time and input too.

My wonderful Pup Aid team of Bex, Stuart, Julia, Laura, Chloe, Emma, Charlotte, Simon, Phil, Jo, Sarah Louise, Dawn, Emily, Lloyd, Leigh Catherine, Milton, Owen and Haatchi, Trip Hazard, Pip and Buddy, Southern Golden Retriever Display Team, Halo Dogs, Rupert Street, Village Vets, all the volunteers, stallholders, Gail and her team from Primrose Hill Pets, Nick (Royal Parks), main sponsors including Barking Heads, Nutriment, Jo Delbridge (Specsavers), PetsPyjamas, Leucillin, Agria, Zoflora, Rebecca (Leivars Design), Brewdog, and Hownd. As well as master retweeters Paul (Protect All Wildlife), Rory (Animal Advocate), Barbara (Animal Watch), Ana (Foster First).

As well as my Lucy's Law team, I've been truly inspired by other campaigners who crucially all work hard to provide solutions, essential to making any progress. Some of the most incredible individuals I'm lucky to know, and in some cases have worked alongside, include Jill Robinson (Animals Asia), Grace and Steve (Finding Shelter Animal Rescue), Abodh Aras (Welfare of Stray Dogs India), Erika and Jim Abrams (Animal Aid Unlimited), Margot Homburg Park (was Soi Dog Foundation), Lola Webber (Change for Animals Foundation), Christopher Grimes and Chris Ksoll (DogByDog), Pen Farthing (Nowzad), Marian Marchese (New Leash on Life USA), Debra Tranter (Oscar's Law), and of course, the first vet I ever worked with on weekends and in my school holidays, Tony Lewis.

Acknowledgements

Closer to home, campaigners I'm a big fan of have supported Lucy's Law, and regularly attend my APDAWG group in Westminster, including Carrie Symonds, Debbie Matthews (Vets Get Scanning), Dr Dan Allen (Pet Theft Reform), PC Dave Wardell and Finn (Finn's Law), Lorraine Platt (Conservative Animal Welfare Foundation), Eduardo Goncalves (Campaign to Ban Trophy Hunting), Linzi Follett (Be Puppy Farm Aware) Michelle (Dogs on the Streets), Anne (Save Me), Lucinda (Greyhound Compassion), Trudy (Greyt Exploitations), Victoria and Pola (K9 Angels), Yonni and her phenomenal SayNoToPetShopPuppies team, Aaron and Rachel (Boycott Dogs4Us), Duncan McNair (Save The Asian Elephants), Linda Rimington and Lord Alex Stockton, Angela and Martin Humphery, and campaigners of the future Sophie and Kyra (Hedgehog Friendly Town).

Of course, once things got political I sought the best advice possible; luckily all generously given pro bono by some of the nicest, kindest, most knowledgeable individuals in the sector, including Mark, Caitlin, Andy, and Chris (Newington Comms), Johanna (Scottish Labour), Paula Sparkes (UK Centre for Animal Law), and Dan Davies (Institute of Licensing); as well as expert help greatly received in Westminster from some truly remarkable individuals including Nikki da Costa, John Randall, and Cleo Watson.

Unsurprisingly I've been fortunate to work alongside many MPs (past and present); everyone listed has helped the campaign – these include Westminster parliamentarians Rob

Flello, Paul Monaghan, Lisa Cameron, Caroline Lucas, Zac Goldsmith, Michael Gove, Neil Parish, Roger Gale, Tracey Crouch, Kerry McCarthy, Alex Chalk, Andrea Jenkyns, Ann Clwyd, Ross Thomson, Giles Watling, Sue Hayman, Martyn Day, David Rutley, David Amess, Sarah Champion, Justin Tomlinson, Sherryl Murray, Simon Hart, Chris Davies, Henry Smith, George Eustice, Cheryl Gillan, Gareth Johnson, Liz Saville-Roberts, Rupa Huq, Tommy Sheppard, Matthew Offord, Chris Evans, Margaret Ferrier, Jim Shannon, Boris Johnson, Sharon Hodgson, Maria Eagle, Angela Eagle, Tracy Brabin, Emma Lewell-Buck, Rosie Duffield, Robin Walker, Luciana Berger, Jim Fitzpatrick, Lord Gardiner; as well as Welsh Assembly Members Eluned Morgan, Andrew RT Davies, Marc Tierney, Vikki Howells. I'd also like to take this opportunity to thank all MP assistants, as well as staff of Portcullis House, Palace of Westminster, and No. 10 Downing Street, who have all been so kind and helpful. Also a special mention to the Borzois in the mural in St Stephen's Hall, off Central Lobby, the focal point for all my lobbying in the Palace of Westminster.

Since the beginning of the campaign we had the unprecedented support of numerous charities and organisations including All Dogs Matter, Mayhew, Raystede, Edinburgh Dog and Cat Home (EDCH), Oldies Club, German Shepherd Rescue Elite, National Animal Welfare Trust (NAWT), Cats Protection, Celia Hammond, Forever Hounds Trust, Birmingham Dogs' Home, Dublin Society for Prevention of

Acknowledgements

Cruelty to Animals (DSPCA), OneKind, Guernsey SPCA, Humane Society International (HIS), International Fund for Animal Welfare (IFAW), Hearing Dogs for the Deaf, Dog Breeding Reform Group (DBRG), Four Paws, and Kennel Club/Crufts especially Sara, Heidi, and Bill.

Running a campaign that's invited so many celebrities to be involved means I've been fortunate to have met, worked alongside, or received support from some incredible individuals over the years; so huge thanks to Peter Egan, Ricky Gervais, Jane Fallon, Ricky's manager Jon Parramint, Rachel Riley, Susie Dent, Ben Fogle, Gail Porter, Brian May, Paul O'Grady, Deborah Meaden, Meg Mathews, Anais Gallagher, Liam Gallagher, Pink, Paul Weller, Mick Jones, Jimmy Page, Keith Richards, Eric Clapton, Gary Moore, Roger Daltrey, David Gilmour, Michelle Collins, Eamonn Holmes, Ruth Langsford, Jon Richardson, Bob Geldof, Claire Balding, Ali Bastian, Matt Johnson, Joanna Page, Tracy-Ann Oberman, Hannah Waddingham, Jay Kay, Pete Wicks, Sue Perkins, Anna Richardson, Britt Ekland, Sarah Harding, Jodie Marsh, Penny Lancaster, Nicky Campbell, Nicole Appleton, Nicola Appleton, Sinitta, Candice Brown, Tony Robinson, Tim Vincent, Jenny Campbell, Sarah Champion, Elle Macpherson, Nicky Campbell, James Whale, David Gandy, Victoria Stilwell, Kirsty Gallagher, Kay Burley, Debbie Douglas, Lydia Bright, Lucy Watson, David Spinx, Michael Watson, Matthew Wright, Storm Huntley, Calum Best, Angie Best, Stephanie Pratt, Patsy Palmer, Mark Williams, Jasmine Harman, Chris

Ellison, Lucy Watson, Lucy Spraggan; reporters including Andrew Neil, Jo Coburn, John Pienaar, Giles Dilnot (all BBC *Daily Politics*), Danny Pike (BBC Sussex), Anna Webb and Jo Good (BBC London), Hannah Murray (Talk Radio Europe), Sam Poling (BBC Scotland), Jess Lester (The Sun).

Back in Brighton (and beyond) I'm lucky to have an amazing support network of friends who've put up with me talking about this journey for a decade. Anyone who's ever campaigned will know only too well how isolating, lonely, and depressing it can be, so really can't thank all my gang enough for always being there; including best mate Russ, Nads, Pacey, Andy, Alex W, Chris, Rebecca, Mena, Dave, Tine, Rachel, Alex H, Sara, Shakira, Louise, Emma, Luke, Matt, Sam, Armand, Abigail, Barry, as well as Emma and everyone at football. Not to mention places that have also played a big part, so thanks Waggon and Horses, Franco Manca, Raf and Harry at Marwoods, Craig and Tabby at Polpo for negronis, Esther and David at Marks & Co, Gareth at RBS, Tim at Griffith Smith LLP, and Colin at Galloways. The Harvester near Palace Pier became Lucy's Law campaigning HQ for most of 2018 when my Wi-Fi at home went down, and I would spend hours there working away, emailing MPs for hours in the evenings and on weekends. Thanks to Julie Ann Gilbert and staff at her Whitecliffs Cafe. Thanks to everyone at Saltdean Lido, Prince Regent Swimming Pool, and a special thank you to Martin and the team at Colourfast for always looking after me, usually at very short notice.

Acknowledgements

I'd also like to thank my publishers Mirror Books, especially editor Ajda for inviting me to write this book, and her patience and guidance during the writing process; I appreciate help from Mel, Julia, and Victoria too. Thanks also to my lovely agents Knight Ayton Management.

Also Lisa would like to give a huge, heartfelt thank you to every single person that followed, interacted, shared posts and loved little Lucy – without you her page wouldn't have had the phenomenal impact it did. Thank you to some amazing small businesses that gave their time and expertise to help raise awareness, including Amanda Stuart (Your Watercolour Portraits), Mel Baldwin (MelOn Design) and Sharon Trueman. Thank you to all those lovely people that took gorgeous pictures of Lucy at events, Karen Nicholson (Little Pip Photography) Teresa Keohane (The Dogvine) and Natasha Balletta (Natasha Balletta Photography). Please know that every single bit of help and support was truly appreciated, and Lisa's sure that Lucy is looking down proud of every single one of you. Lastly an enormous thank you to Lisa's family who loved Lucy beyond words, and as Lisa did, their hearts shattered when she passed away; but in true Lucy style, Lisa's young nephews (Charlie and Harry) continue to spread her message and frequently tell people all about her.

And finally to my family, I can't thank you all enough for your understanding and support during the whole campaign, and of course way before. Especially my amazing mum, inspirational grandma Judy, streetwise sister Danielle, banteriffic nephews Nathan and Jordan, Ilyce and David in Philly, and Martha and David. Last but definitely not least Dad, my role model, my hero, my mate, how I wish you could've seen the results of what you influenced. I can only hope you, Lucy, the other campaigners' deceased parents, and victims of the third party puppy trade, are all hanging out together, smiling down on us, and proud of what we've achieved. We love and miss you all X